FOR AND AGAINST THE BIBLE:
A TRANSLATION OF
SYLVAIN MARÉCHAL'S
POUR ET CONTRE LA BIBLE (1801)

Studies in Critical Research on Religion

Haymarket Books is proud to be working with Brill Academic Publishers (www.brill.nl) to republish the *Studies in Critical Research on Religion* book series in paperback editions. This peer-reviewed book series offers insights into our current reality by exploring the content and consequences of power relationships under capitalism, and by considering the spaces of opposition and resistance to these changes that have been defining our new age. Our full catalog of *SCRR* volumes can be viewed at https://www.haymarketbooks.org/series_collections/6-studies-in-critical-research-in-religion.

Series Editor
Warren S. Goldstein, Center for Critical Research on Religion (U.S.A.)

Editorial Board
Christopher Craig Brittain, University of Toronto (Canada)
Heather Eaton, Saint Paul University (Canada)
Titus Hjelm, University of Helsinki (Finland)
Darlene Juschka, University of Regina (Canada)
Lauren Langman, Loyola University Chicago (U.S.A.)
George Lundskow, Grand Valley State University (U.S.A.)
Kenneth G. MacKendrick, University of Manitoba (Canada)
Andrew M. McKinnon, University of Aberdeen (U.K.)
Sara Pike, California State University, Chico (U.S.A)
Dana Sawchuk, Wilfrid Laurier University (Canada)

Advisory Board
William Arnal, University of Regina (Canada)
Roland Boer, University of Newcastle (Australia)
Jonathan Boyarin, Cornell University (U.S.A.)
Jay Geller, Vanderbilt University (U.S.A.)
Marsha Hewitt, University of Toronto (Canada)
Michael Löwy, Centre National de la Recherche Scientifique (France)
Eduardo Mendieta, Penn State University (U.S.A.)
Rudolf J. Siebert, Western Michigan University (U.S.A.)
Rhys H. Williams, Loyola University Chicago (U.S.A.)

For and Against the Bible: A Translation of Sylvain Maréchal's *Pour et Contre la Bible* (1801)

Sheila Delany

Haymarket Books
Chicago, IL

First published in 2020 by Brill Academic Publishers, The Netherlands.
© 2020 Koninklijke Brill NV, Leiden, The Netherlands

Published in 2021 by
Haymarket Books
P.O. Box 180165
Chicago, IL 60618
773-583-7884
www.haymarketbooks.org
info@haymarketbooks.org

ISBN: 978-1-64259-426-3

Distributed to the trade in the US through Consortium Book Sales and Distribution (www.cbsd.com) and internationally through Ingram Publisher Services International (www.ingramcontent.com).

This book was published with the generous support of Lannan Foundation and Wallace Action Fund.

Special discounts are available for bulk purchases by organizations and institutions. Please call 773-583-7884 or email info@haymarketbooks.org for more information.

Cover design by Jamie Kerry and Ragina Johnson.

Printed in United States.

Library of Congress Cataloging-in-Publication data is available.

10 9 8 7 6 5 4 3 2 1

In memory of two comrades: my father, who'd have appreciated Sylvain's ornery wit, and Jim Robertson, whose lifelong dedication to revolutionary politics helped shape my work and much more

Contents

Preface XI
Acknowledgments XII
Translator's Note XIII

Introduction 1

For and Against the Bible

Epistle to Ministers of All Religions 23
    Post-script 37
    Addendum 38

PART 1
Jewish Scripture

The Old Testament 43
I   Genesis: First Book of the Pentateuch of Moses 43
II   Exodus 44
III   Leviticus 47
IV   Numbers 48
V   Deuteronomy 50
VI   Joshua, or Jesus the Liberator 53
VII   Judges 54
VIII   Ruth 55
IX   The First Book of Kingdoms, or Kings: First Book of Samuel 56
X   The Second Book of Kingdoms or Kings: Book 2 of Samuel 57
XI   Kings: Book III 59
XII   Kings, Book IV 60
XIII   Paralipomenon: Book I, Chronicles 61
XIV   Paralipomenon: Chronicles, Book II 62
XV   Ezra: First Book 64
XVI   Nehemiah: Book II of Ezra 64
XVII   Tobias 65
XVIII   Judith 67
XIX   Esther 69
XX   Job 72

XXI	The Psalms of David 74	
XXII	Proverbs, or the Wisdom of Solomon 86	
XXIII	The Parables of Solomon 87	
XXIV	Ecclesiastes, or the Preacher 91	
XXV	The Song of Songs or the Song Par Excellence of Solomon 93	
XXVI	Wisdom 95	
XXVII	The Ecclesiasticus of Jesus, Son of Sirach 97	
XXVIII	Isaiah 101	
XXIX	Jeremiah 108	
XXX	Lamentations of Jeremiah 115	
XXXI	Baruch 116	
XXXII	Ezekiel 116	
XXXIII	Daniel 120	
XXXIV	Hosea 122	
XXXV	Joel 123	
XXXVI	Amos 124	
XXXVII	Obadiah 124	
XXXVIII	Jonah 124	
XXXIX	Micah 125	
XL	Nahum 126	
XLI	Habakkuk 126	
XLII	Sophonius 127	
XLIII	Haggai 127	
XLIV	Zachary 127	
XLV	Malachi 129	
	N.B. Extract from the Catechism of Curé Meslier 129	
XLVI	Maccabees, or the Murderers: Book I 131	
XLVII	Maccabees, or the Murderers: Book II 132	
	N.B. Extract from the Catechism of Curé Meslier 133	

PART 2
Christian Scripture

The New Testament 137

I	The Holy Gospel of Jesus Christ According to Saint Matthew 137
II	Holy Gospel of Jesus Christ, According to Saint Mark 147
III	The Holy Gospel of Jesus Christ, According to Saint Luke 148
IV	Holy Gospel of Jesus Christ, According to Saint John 151

V	Acts of the Apostles 157	
VI	Epistle of Saint Paul to the Romans 159	
VII	First Epistle of Saint Paul to the Corinthians 161	
VIII	Second Epistle of Paul to the Corinthians 165	
IX	Epistle of Saint Paul to the Galatians 165	
X	Epistle of S. Paul to the Ephesians 166	
XI	Epistle of S. Paul to the Philippians 166	
XII	Epistle of Saint Paul to the Colossians 166	
XIII	First Epistle of S. Paul to the Thessalonians 167	
XIV	Second Epistle from the Same to the Same 167	
XV	First Epistle of S. Paul to Timothy 167	
XVI	Second Epistle of S. Paul to Timothy 168	
XVII	Epistle of S. Paul to Titus 168	
XVIII	Epistle of S. Paul to Philemon 169	
XIX	Epistle of S. Paul to the Hebrews 169	
XX	Epistle of S. Paul to Seneca the Philosopher 169	
XXI	The Catholic Letter of S. James the Minor and the Just 170	
XXII	The Two Catholic Epistles of Saint Peter 171	
XXIII	The Three Catholic Epistles of Saint John 172	
XXIV	Catholic Epistle of S. Jude, Called the Zealous 172	
XXV	The Apocalypse of S. John 172	
XXVI	Prayer of Manasses, King of Judah 174	
XXVII	Epistles of the Virgin Mary 174	
XXVIII	Testament of the Holy Virgin 175	
	N.B. Extract from the Catechism of the Curé Meslier 175	
XXIX	Collection of Ancient Gospels or *Monuments of the 1st Century of Christianity, Taken from Fabricius, Grabius and Other Scholars; by Father B*****, London, 1769, 284 *Pages* 175	

PART 3
Result of Reading the Bible

Result of Reading the Bible 179
Post-script 190

Bibliography 193
Index 199

Series Editor's Preface

This is a translation of Sylvain Maréchal's *Pour et Contre la Bible* (*For and Against the Bible*), originally published in 1801. Maréchal, an atheist and revolutionary, edited one of France's best-known radical journals, *Révolutions de Paris*, from 1790 to 1794. His *Almanach des Honnêtes Gens* (*Almanac of Upright People*) served as one of the bases of the revolutionary calendar. He was a friend and close collaborator of "Gracchus" Babeuf, whose failed 1796 coup—the so-called "Conspiracy of Equals"—against the Directory marked, for Maréchal, the end of the French Revolution. In *For and Against the Bible*, Maréchal engages in a critical analysis of Jewish and Christian scripture, evaluating both its negative and positive content. His rationalistic approach, in the tradition of Spinoza, Voltaire and others, anticipates nineteenth-century Bible criticism and much scholarship of our own day. Thus, the text is an important historical document for those interested in a critical approach to the study of religion.

> Warren S. Goldstein, Ph.D.
> Center for Critical Research on Religion
> www.criticaltheoryofreligion.org

Acknowledgments

This is the third and last in a set of translations of texts by Sylvain Maréchal, all of them engaging issues of sex and gender, religion and politics, in varying proportions. I'm grateful to the University of Alberta Press for taking a risk on this now obscure but once well known French revolutionary writer, in publishing the first two: *Anti-Saints* (2012), a translation of Maréchal's *Nouvelle Légende Dorée* (1790), and *The Woman Priest* (2016), a translation of his *La Femme Abbé* (1801). Subventions from Simon Fraser University and the Canadian government assisted these publications.

The foundation of all my work on Maréchal, his work and times is the generous support from Canada's Social Sciences and Humanities Research Council (SSHRC) that over a period of several years enabled me to consult original editions of work by Maréchal, his sources, and his contemporaries as well as rare secondary sources at Berkeley, Stanford, Columbia, Yale, and the New York Public Library. Later, in 2014, participation as faculty in a National Foundation for the Humanities project at Oxford provided an opportunity for further research there and at the British Library. The University of British Columbia library here in Vancouver kindly granted me extended loans for their original edition (1801) of *Pour et Contre la Bible*; special thanks to librarian Keith Bunnell for facilitating this. At Simon Fraser University, Ivana Neseteo was, as always, wonderfully helpful in turning up obscure locations and publications.

There are few Maréchal scholars worldwide. *Prima* among us is *dix-huitièmiste* Professor Erica Joy Mannucci of Milan, biographer of Sylvain for our day. Erica's encouragement and advice have meant much to me along the way: *mille grazie*! My friend Chantal Pourcelot of Nice and Naisey-les-Granges assisted with translation of several puzzling colloquial phrases; Susan Weber and Karyn Huenemann provided indispensable IT help. Yaffa Goldfinger's rapid and thoughtful initiative, on the eve of closure of the Tel Aviv Museum of Art due to the COVID pandemic, enabled my use of El Lissitzky's wonderful illustration as my cover art.

I thank Warren Goldstein, editor of the series in which this volume appears, for shepherding my proposal through his editorial board and for his meticulous editing; Tessa Schild at Brill for her patience in responding to questions about format and production; as well as the two erudite Brill readers whose suggestions made this a better translation, and whose generous appreciations were exhilarating and fortifying.

Sheila Delany
Vancouver, 2020

Translator's Note

"'What are the two major inventions of French and British culture?' 'Where France is concerned: the language of the eighteenth century, and soft cheese'". Muriel Barbery's (2008, 266) endorsement—or that of her narrator and heroine, the discerning concierge Renée—of the linguistic "invention" is well supported in the work of Sylvain Maréchal. Though not considered a premier stylist of the age, nonetheless Maréchal displays a command of rhetoric coupled with a passionate flow of ideas and language—what he might term energy or movement—allowing a glimpse into the culture at large.

But translating *Pour et Contre la Bible* differs from translating any other of Maréchal's work. This is because it is not a primary original work such as a novella, treatise or poem, but an extended commentary on another text known to Maréchal only in translation. And not only in one translation but many, for the Bible came down to Maréchal, as it comes to us, virtually a palimpsest incorporating levels and layers, translations of translations reflecting different cultures, histories, and religions. Some versions attempt to be faithful to a source, others consciously revise according to current manners or doctrines. Maréchal had several French versions of Biblical material at his disposal: individual books of scripture (e.g., Psalms), dramatic or poetic treatment of specific episodes or figures such as Susanna, Judith and Esther, as well as the entire corpus. Any of these might reflect a Catholic or a Protestant scholarship translating into French, with greater or less fidelity, the earlier French or the Latin of their source (generally St. Jerome's Vulgate). This Latin in turn, if Jerome's, translated earlier Greek material which relied on Hebrew or Aramaic sources. When working with Biblical material, then, one might replace Umberto Eco's image of "translation as negotiation" (Eco 2003) with "translation as *mise-en-abîme*".

A major difference that readers may note between their own Bible and the one commented and translated here is the order of texts and texts included. This is largely because of Apocrypha: texts whose divine inspiration has been doubted and debated down the centuries at various religious councils. They are usually considered canonical by the Roman Catholic Church and therefore included in and as scripture. Most Protestant or Jewish authorities have not agreed, so in their Bibles the Apocrypha will be excluded or attached in an appendix as useful, historical, but not of equal authority to canonized scripture. That said, there are many more texts—other gospels, other apocalypses, other letters, other mystical treatises—that have not qualified as official (see Barnstone 1984) but that can considerably enhance the reader's appreciation of religious life and belief before, during and after the life of the figure we refer to as Jesus.

The layering of Biblical translations is a situation that Maréchal himself found frustrating, as he makes clear both in his commentary and in the handwritten notes to his personal Bible, held at the International Institute for Social History in Amsterdam. Often, he is contemptuous of a translator's lack of fidelity to (Latin) Biblical language, whether because of the translator's prudishness or a general fear of offending contemporary sensibilities through a crude but striking metaphor. Elsewhere, the French interprets terse Latin rather than giving an exact or literal equivalent. In Ecclesiastes, for instance, where the Latin reads "laudavi magis mortuos quam viventes" (I have praised the dead more than the living—Trans.) the French has "I have said that it is better to be dead than to live", bringing the sentiment down to a more prosaic level.

Maréchal often gives a Latin verse with a French translation by Sacy—his primary source—the latter in square brackets. It is often the case that Sacy's French does not faithfully render his Latin source, and where both are given, the reader who knows Latin will spot these discrepancies. My effort has been to translate all the French—Maréchal's and Sacy's—as accurately as I can and to mark significant discrepancies from the Latin in my notes. Maréchal did annotate his translation. I have indicated with his initials all of his notes; where I have added something to a note of his, I have placed the addition in square brackets and specified "—Trans."; unsigned explanatory notes are mine.

In my notes, I use BCE and CE (Before the Common Era and Common Era) rather than the more traditional BC (Before Christ) and AD (*Anno Domini*: year of the Lord). Contemporary scholarship generally prefers to avoid the heavy ideological burden of the older system. The archaic spelling of Biblical names has been adjusted to modern usage, and occasionally I have modernized a phrase for the sake of fluency, while hoping to maintain as much as possible of the author's eighteenth-century French sensibility. Last but not least, I use "humanity", "humankind" or "people" for the human species rather than the original French "homme" (man) in order to avoid sexual specificity where it is clearly not intended. Some may complain, not unjustly, that this lends more universality to Maréchal's ideas than they really have, given his relegation of women to second-class citizenship (an attitude not uncommon among revolutionaries of the time). It is an infidelity I admit without a blush, not least because women would necessarily be included in Maréchal's recommendations on religion and moral virtue. I have also replaced the ubiquitous French "on" (one) with the more contemporaneous "we". As Robert Alter observes, "The practise of translation…entails an endless series of compromises, some of them happy, some painful" (*Art* 2019, ix). I hope that most of my compromises are of the happy sort for the reader.

Roman numeral headings for the Biblical books were used by Maréchal and have been preserved as conveying a sense both of the period's classicism and the commentator's erudition. My table of contents is in accord with Maréchal's headings, though *Pour et Contre* lacks a table of contents as such.

Introduction

On February 23, 2017, American Vice-President Mike Pence spoke passionately and reverentially about the Bible on which he had been sworn into office a month before, for it was the very same Bible on which, in January 1981, the 40th president of the United States, Ronald Reagan, had also been sworn in and, in Pence's words, had "actually used"; indeed, Pence claimed to have uncannily opened that Bible at the very same verse to which Reagan had opened it.[1] The book had acquired an aura. It had become what a medieval priest, or a medievalist nowadays, might think of as a relic: an object touched by a holy person and which therefore confers special healing power—or, in this case, prestige, an aspect of political power—on whoever touches it next.

This is exactly the sort of religious fetishism Sylvain Maréchal despised; he denounced it in much of his writing throughout his life, and especially in *Pour et contre la Bible*, his lengthy commentary on Jewish and Christian scriptures. The title suggests an even-handed approach to this monumentally influential text, or set of texts. But such balance is not quite the case, for although Maréchal took pains to praise the literary beauties and spiritual profundity of some scriptural writing, his real theme is "contre": to demonstrate that this book stands at the origin of age-old oppressive and destructive practises as their theological justification and practical example; that it should no longer be read, much less venerated; that, far from being "the good book", it is a harmful book. Maréchal was no mere skeptic but claimed with pride the title of atheist; he didn't merely doubt, he denied.

The title alone is provocative enough—for and against the Bible—in a society for which, on the whole, there ought to be no "against" in this case. We need to remind ourselves that there was as yet no Darwin, and the notion of the extinction of species was only just being hypothesized by Cuvier on the basis of gigantic skeletons discovered in several distant lands. For a medievalist, Maréchal's title recalls the equally provocative *Sic et non* (Yes and no) of Peter Abelard, whose work Maréchal acknowledged in his own *Dictionnaire des*

---

1 Though Pence didn't cite the source, it was 2 Chronicles 7:14; nor did he cite it quite accurately, and managed to transmute it into a preface to the American Pledge of Allegiance (as revised in 1954 to include the phrase "under God"). The speech was given at the Conservative Political Action Conference in National Harbor, Maryland. Alter (2010, 1) documents "this American biblicizing impulse … the pervasiveness of the Bible in American culture from the colonial period onward".

athées anciens et modernes (*Dictionary of ancient and modern atheists*, 1800); indeed, Abelard takes pride of place as first entry in this alphabetical collection.[2] The great twelfth-century philosopher and teacher presented contradictory opinions by Christian *auctores* on various theological questions, showing how they might be argued in dialectical logic and suggesting methods of possible resolution. Maréchal owned a copy of a French translation of the letters Abelard exchanged with his wife, the nun Héloïse; the philosophical tracts were available at the Mazarin Library, where Maréchal worked as a librarian for several years as a young man. But Sylvain had already used, or seen, this meme in the 1794 *Fable de Christ dévoilée* (A fable about Christ revealed), a fictional letter presenting an imaginary history of how certain priests invented the Bible, Judaism and Christianity, an effort for which they required "le pour et le contre" (Maréchal 1794, 44, 47) in order to appear authentic. Clearly it was a common phrase both before and after Maréchal used it,[3] albeit not about the Bible.

Living as he did as a lifelong atheist in a predominantly believing culture, Maréchal confronted some of the very issues we do now. For some of us, the Bible guides behavior—no work on Saturdays, honor your parents, avoid and denounce homosexuality, tell the truth, pay your taxes, etc. Others take it as a portrait of historical reality a few thousand years ago when dinosaurs, human beings and every other life form were made *ex nihilo*, out of nothing, in a magical moment of creation. For most scholars it is a literary anthology compiled by various hands over a period of several centuries, reflecting evolving social forms and political events. Maréchal's Bible commentary, despite its two-sided title, is not motivated by a desire to bridge such gaps; his hatred of all organized religion and of theology itself remained steady and intact throughout his life. Nonetheless it can speak to both sides of the divide: to atheists confirming their rejection of dogma, clergy and what Richard Dawkins calls "the God

---

2   This is not to say that Abelard, or indeed most of the figures populating Maréchal's *Dictionnaire des athées*, were actually atheists. Maréchal spread his net extremely wide, to include skeptics, deists, rationalists, heretics and doubters of any kind from every historical period, including his own. Some cannot have been pleased, in this oppressive environment, to find themselves included; indeed, Kors (1976, 297) writes that the inclusion of Naigeon prevented the latter's appointment to important positions. The low-set bar was, however, normal throughout the previous two centuries' discourse in theology and morality (Febvre 1982; Kors 1990). The work had a *succès de scandale* upon publication and was reprinted twice during the nineteenth century (Karmin 1911, 439).

3   A London literary journal (1733–40) was published by the Abbé Prévost under the title *Le pour et contre*, and a polemical correspondence between Diderot and the sculptor Falconet, from 1766–7, was published under the title *Le pour et le contre*, but not during Maréchal's lifetime (see Benot 1958, 37–38). Authorship of the *Fable* is uncertain.

delusion"; to believers in affirming the (intermittent) poetic value, literary skill and occasional moral sublimity of Jewish and Christian scripture.

•••

Maréchal was distinctive in his day, but neither unique nor as thoroughly radical in his views as others. Atheism had long been an issue in France and elsewhere: the great dramatist Molière was accused of it; well-known writers hypothesized about its origins or debated the possibility of a virtuous atheist. During and after the seventeenth century, the Church carried on a constant struggle against atheism—albeit broadly defined—with the paradoxical result, according to Kors, that it had to raise arguments in order to refute them, thus serving as a source or conduit for the very arguments it hoped to defeat (Kors 1990, 79). Some of Maréchal's friends and collaborators were atheists, among them the eminent astronomer Jérôme Lalande, the scholar Jacques-André Naigeon, the rebel aristocrat and utopian scholar Pierre Antoine Antonelle—Maréchal's co-member in a Parisian club during 1799 (Serna 1997, 416)—and others less well known (see Dommanget 1950, 383). Another class traitor, the revolutionary Marquis de Sade, renounced his title to become a leader in a section of the Paris Commune; his 1795 novel *Philosophy in the Bedroom* incorporates a passionate defense of atheism. King Frederick of Prussia was known to be an atheist. One acquaintance, the physiocrat Fréville, debated with priests in cafés, like a "public professor of atheism" (Mannucci 2012, 52 n. 51). Maréchal knew the work of other free-thinking contemporaries such as the scholarly atheist and best-selling author Baron d' Holbach (Darnton 1995, 194–96), whose biweekly salon has been described as an "enormous and clandestine atheism factory" (Curran 2019, 235); the Prussian-born atheist and political writer J.-B. "Anacharsis" Cloots, "millionaire et sans-culotte, baron et jacobin" (Mortier 1995, 13); British-American radical Thomas Paine, elected to the National Assembly in 1792 and author of *The Age of Reason*. He may have known some of these luminaries in person: Cloots notes in 1790 that he dined every Saturday with M. De Lalande amidst "une société choisi" (Mortier 1995, 255); the famous astronomer was one of Sylvain's closest friends and collaborators, so it is not impossible that Sylvain might have been among that chosen group. Much of this pathbreaking work was inspired by even earlier writing: the deistic philosophy of the rationalist Dutch Jewish scholar Benedict Spinoza (1632–77), the work of Encyclopedist Denis Diderot, and the posthumously discovered "Testament" of the atheist priest Jean Meslier, the latter two earlier in the eighteenth century.

Most of these figures, admired by Maréchal, appear in his *Dictionnaire des athées* and other of his writings.[4] Many of these men (and some women) met regularly to discuss their ideas on the arts, religion, science and politics, frequently with distinguished guests from England or Italy. As a young man, Maréchal participated in similar if less exalted groups, whether artistic salon or masonic lodge, as Mannucci shows in her magisterial cultural biography. Besides other factors cited above, the study of classical authors would disseminate materialist and skeptical views from the much-admired ancient world; Maréchal styled himself "le Lucrèce français" in an early work, after the Roman materialist poet Lucretius. There was, in short, a thriving intellectual milieu—what Mortier dubs "the anti-Christian front" ("le front antichrétien": Mortier 1990, 361)—of rationalistic skepticism, doubt, and (at its extreme) atheism which nurtured Sylvain's development. Much of this material, to be sure, was illegal or simply displeasing to one or another authority, hence printed outside of Paris or abroad, under false authorial or publishers' names, or false, even fictitious, place names (see Brunet 1866). Sometimes a book of offensively unorthodox character might be condemned by Parlement to be publicly torn and burnt, as was the fate, in 1788, of Maréchal's own *Almanach des honnêtes gens* (Almanac of upright people). Yet as Maréchal testified in the journal he edited—the well known *Révolutions de Paris* (#212)—this only increased the prestige and price of the work, corroborating Diderot's observation that the more severe the proscription, the higher the price of the book and the more it is bought and read; the sentencing of a book causes joy among print-workers and booksellers (Darnton 1991, 13).

In a similar vein, there existed a broad current of critical Biblical scholarship from the late seventeenth century onward, produced by Catholics, Protestants, and Jews, clergy and lay, in several European countries. Some of this material was generated by "the Jewish question" regarding legal rights and enfranchisement for Jews, some by the desire and need of Christian theologians to understand their own origins and guiding texts. Again it is Spinoza whose writing on the Bible generated much of this stream of scholarship, both pro and con; in France, Richard Simon (1638–1712) initiated rationalistic Bible scholarship. Voltaire wrote extensively on the Bible in many formats—essay, letter, pamphlet, treatise, book—with a lifelong interest that has been called "compulsive" (Schwarzbach 1971, 7) and "obsessive" (Hertzberg 1970, 285). So did Diderot, Holbach and numerous others. In short, demystification of the sacred text was well under way by the time Maréchal took up the subject. As a well-educated

---

4 Antonelle, Sade and Paine are not in the *Dictionnaire*, though Paine appears in the *Calendrier des républicains* for September 27.

Parisian—in fact a law student—and as a librarian at the prestigious Bibliothèque Mazarine for several years, he would have access to much of this material and to a field already well established.

But beside books, there was reality. The Revolution was never on the whole atheistic, despite its enemies' propagandistic efforts to portray it so; its aim was to reform, not to abolish, the extremely corrupt Catholic Church. As Vovelle observes, "If the Assembly refused on 13 April 1790 ... the demand ... that Catholicism should be declared the national religion, it did so on the grounds that 'the devotion of the National Assembly to the Catholic, Apostolic and Roman cult was never in question'" (Vovelle 1991, 13). (Similarly, it did not begin as anti-royalist; the aim was to create a constitutional monarchy along British lines until treasonous acts by Louis XVI and Marie Antoinette ended this possibility and led to their execution in 1793.) A rich and longstanding tradition of anti-clerical writing by clergy and layfolk, some of it extending back to the Middle Ages, at last bore fruit in a series of decrees from the National Assembly—many of whose deputies, we need to remember, were clergy: this was the old "first estate". The new laws of 1790–93—exhaustively detailed by Latreille—included appropriation and sale of Church properties, and a requirement for clergy to swear loyalty to the new Constitution rather than to the Vatican. Many did—perhaps half (Tackett 1986, 40–43)—indeed, some renounced their ecclesiastical positions and went on to marry. Those who refused—the "refractories"—went into hiding or into exile in England or North America. Anti-clericalism deepened into the short-lived "de-Christianization" campaign of 1793, during which the cult of Reason was introduced as a substitute for revealed religion, bells and other metal objects were taken to be melted down for the war effort, and Notre-Dame cathedral was transformed into the Temple of Reason, as were other churches across the country.

What a shock it must have been, then, when in May, 1794, after several years of anti-clerical legislation and anti-religious demonstrations across the country, Maximilien Robespierre, de facto leader of the revolutionary government, declared atheism an immoral aristocratic offense, punishable by imprisonment. Suddenly, admiration for the goddess Reason was replaced by reverence for a "Supreme Being". Motivated by political calculation—to avoid offending France's few allies, and to control a population portions of which were demanding ever more radical reforms—Robespierre ordered massive new festivals and new holidays enshrining a new religion.

The Catholic Church, immensely wealthy and corrupt, once profoundly critiqued and punished for its sins in the early days of the French Revolution, made its comeback only a few years later. Already during the post-Robespierre Thermidorean reaction of 1794–95, churches began to reopen and royalist priests began to return from exile in England. Working peoples' insurrections were brutally put down; the hall of government itself became, in the dramatic words of the great historian Albert Mathiez (1965, 5), "a place of trafficking ... an open sewer". Laws were passed against women's activity, against popular sovereignty and political transparency. During these years, the aim of reversing the revolution was explicit among those who governed, and, as Luzzato (2001, 338) writes, the police acted not only against the guilty but against anyone who, because of their past, their convictions or their experience, could, if need be, be guilty. In the words of a popular song of the day: "Mais l'homme sage/ dans son ménage/ verse des pleurs/ sur toutes tes horreurs" [But the good person in his household pours out tears at all your horrors—Trans.] (Woloch 1970, 360 n 24). One can imagine Sylvain doing exactly this. And worse was coming.

Napoleon Bonaparte, commander of the French army abroad, returned from his Egyptian campaign in October, 1799; the following month, he established himself as consul in a coup. Mass repatriation of émigré clergy and nobility continued, with restoration of their expropriated property and works of Catholic propaganda were published and widely read. There was press censorship, government control of the arts, reversal of revolutionary laws on freedom of divorce and other family matters, preventive detention for those suspected of anti-government sentiments, police spies everywhere. The revolutionary title "Citizen" was banned (Schom 1997, 195, 291–92). There was a climate of fear for many, decadence for others. In 1801, Napoleon concluded an agreement or concordat with the once reviled Vatican, and when he crowned himself emperor in late 1804, Pope Pius VII himself was invited to officiate.

Maréchal, who died in 1803, did not live to see this horror, but it culminated a process that he determined to intervene in as best he could, to remind French society of what it had accomplished only a decade before, and what remained to be done. *Pour et contre* was that intervention, recognized as such by both friends and enemies. It was not the only one, for others produced anti-religious or anti-Biblical satires (see Mannucci 2012, 270 ff.), while Maréchal expressed his views in other genres such as the *Dictionnaire des athées* mentioned above, a charming but incisive epistolary novella, *La femme abbé* (1801), and a history of Russia (1802) which enabled him to attack tyrants and their enablers. Yet here he expressed the depth of his bitterness and disillusion, his dismay that the new century must begin with such a defeat for liberty and equality. Nearly a decade earlier, Sade had inserted into his 1795 novel *Philosophy in the Bedroom* a passionate exhortation to his countrymen to continue the revolution, to press rationality to its logical atheistic conclusion, to abolish capital punishment, liberate women, socialize family duties and childcare: "Yet another effort, Frenchmen, if you would be republicans" is its title. In those days, Maréchal too hoped and worked for that further effort to create what he called "that finer, grander, revolution" that would create an egalitarian society. But by 1801 he knew that this was not going to happen, for the Revolution, as Napoleon had already proclaimed, was over; its best potential leader, Maréchal's friend Babeuf, had been executed in 1797, his arrest having evoked Sylvain's most powerfully heartfelt piece of writing, "L'avis d'un homme" (One man's/a man's opinion). Writing against priests and saints had not stanched the religious flood; now he must turn to the source of it all, the basis of everything wrong with the culture—its irrationality, its corruption, its authoritarianism—in a last gesture of despair and defiance.

∴

"How odd a thing is the Bible!" observes Sylvain in his mock legendary, after a sardonic one-sentence comment on the story of Judith. How, then, does Sylvain read the Bible in a commentary on that originary text, the basis of the religion in which he and everyone he knew were raised? And what Bible did he read? His main French source, as acknowledged in the chapter on Genesis, was that of Isaac-Louis Le Maistre de Sacy (1613–84), a priest and scholar associated with the Augustinian reform movement centered at the abbey of Port-Royal in Paris. Though not the only French translation (see Legoupil 2011), this became the standard Bible of Catholic France once its Old Testament books came out between 1672 and 1695; to this was joined a New Testament by another writer of similar doctrinal persuasion. It was often reprinted in whole or in part, with 34 editions in the course of the eighteenth century (Desroussilles 1986, 81); Maréchal owned a 1717 edition.[5] Yet although Sauvy (1986, 33) observes that Sacy's translation was renowned for the clarity and beauty of its language, Maréchal is less enthusiastic than many of his compatriots, remarking that while "fort estimable ... elle laisse beaucoup à désirer" [quite good ... it leaves a lot to be desired—Trans.], and throughout his commentary Maréchal doesn't spare Sacy the criticism and correction of someone who would prefer a more literal rendering. This was not an uncommon scholarly criticism of Sacy's work, even though the Port-Royal project was deliberately not literal—this the scholars viewed as "servile"; rather their idea was to render spiritual meaning for the edification of the broad population. Indeed, one of their major points of difference with orthodox Roman Catholicism was their idea that scripture ought to be read by all. But it isn't only because of translation that Maréchal would have

---

5 The catalogue of Maréchal's personal library sold after his death appears in several places, among them Aubert (1975, 156–74).

taken issue with Sacy's version, for the scholars of Port-Royal considered scripture to be authored by the Holy Spirit, to be read and revered "non comme les livres des hommes" [not like books of human beings—Trans.] but as those of God himself, "preuves incontestables de la verité de notre Religion" [incontestable proofs of the truth of our religion—Trans.] (Sacy, Avertissement).[6] This is, of course, exactly the point of view Maréchal targets with such vigor.

Besides Sacy, many other sources were available to Maréchal, most of them acknowledged in his text or notes: other Bibles, in Latin or French (he owned a 1664 Vulgate); translations of individual books, especially Psalms, of which he owned several versions; commentaries; poems and plays about specific incidents or characters.

Some of Maréchal's reading is filtered, as might be expected, through the lens of revolutionary patriotism and the experience of a well-known writer on political affairs. Thus, he admires the Maccabees because of the early days of the Revolution, when the new French government, like the band of priestly brothers, had to defend itself against foreign invaders. In a similar vein, his hypothetical speech for Jesus echoes fears of revolutionary France being overwhelmed by European powers, fashioning a portrait of the ideal popular leader that Jesus could have been. As with other of Maréchal's themes, this was not unique, for the Bible was used in France, as elsewhere, to prove many points on all sides. As Menozzi points out, the 1790s saw a series of biographies of Jesus, presenting him as "prototype of republican virtues ... come not only to announce liberation from the slavery of sin, but also liberation from political slavery" [Trans.] (Menozzi 1986, 692–93).

In a negative key, the dissolute King David is portrayed as "the Louis XIV of the Jews" (Kings II), and the prophet Jeremiah is denounced as a traitor to his people, preaching submission to Babylonian exile rather than resistance or flight. (Historically, of course, the many Jews who opted to stay in Persia rather than return to Israel to rebuild the temple, did very well there, founding famous academies and eventually producing the Babylonian Talmud.) The role of and respect for kings and priests, as well as those prophets who support them, is a major Biblical offense for Maréchal—not surprising for a proud egalitarian and revolutionary who, during the 1790s, worked closely with one of the

---

6   This "Avertissement" or preface would most likely have been added after Sacy's death. The 1701 edition in which it appears was the first printed in Paris. Modern opinion on Sacy's style seems to have swung toward Maréchal's view: Henri LeMaître writes that it is "très étudié" and "cherche de dépouiller le texte sacré de ses grandeurs et de ses beautés profanes, sans reculer devant une certaine infidelité" [very elaborate ... aims to strip the sacred text of its grandeur and its profane beauties, without worrying about some infidelity—Trans.] (LeMaître s. v. Le Maistre de Saci [sic]).

most radical figures in France, the proto-communist journalist François-Noel ("Gracchus") Babeuf. Maréchal's hatred of priestly authority and corruption comes through everywhere in his commentary, most explicitly in its vitriolic prefatory "Epistle" to "priests of all religions". Though it may seem bizarre that this preface urges priests to leave their posts, return to civil life and get jobs, this is just what had happened in sixteenth-century England during the Henrician Reformation, when Catholic monasteries and convents were closed and their inhabitants returned to civil life; on a much smaller scale it had also happened in the early days of the French Revolution.

Other politically-grounded evaluations surface throughout. Not all of them, however, are what one might expect. Paradoxically and perhaps disappointingly, the revolutionary Maréchal does not sympathize with the Jews' grumbling and rebellion against the authoritarian Moses and Aaron (throughout Exodus and Numbers). On the contrary, he blames the populace, who become victims of brutal suppression, arguing that the Jews were not worthy of their leader but required brutalization because inadequate to Moses's grand vision and genius. Surely this is the tyrant's classic argument: the people require suppression for their own good—indeed, in Deuteronomy Sylvain compares Moses to Czar Peter I! Is this a latent anti-semitism, setting the worthless people against their inspired leader? Is it the consequence of Maréchal's own patriarchalist political ideal? An argument can be made for either of these interpretations, though the trope is not original: Machiavelli, for instance (who appears in the *Dictionnaire des athées*), had justified Moses's violent suppression of his rebellious followers on the grounds that innovators must use force of arms in order to prevail (*The Prince*, Chapter 6). Holbach, on the other hand, floated the possibility that Moses was "un menteur impudent, un fourbe ambitieux", even a "fanatique" [shameless liar, ambitious fraud ... fanatic—Trans.] (Holbach 2008, 20), along with many other unflattering remarks, so the option was certainly available in contemporary intellectual life.

In other places Maréchal's literary sophistication, that of a man well read in classical and contemporary literature, evokes enthusiastic praise of some Biblical books and passages, especially in the major prophets. Sublimity is a key critical term of praise in his lexicon (as it was for eighteenth-century art criticism in general), along with "unction" (smooth flow, sweetness, feeling), energy, movement, and simplicity. Vivid imagery, intensity of imagination, and force of expression are all praised, even though these are often exemplified in sexual or scatological terms that Maréchal knows will offend the artificial "good taste" of prudish middle-class readers. Yet in Maréchal's view, imaginative intensity must not go too far; metaphor and imagery are all very well, but must not be overly dramatic, farfetched, or unlikely (e.g., Ps 97, "the rivers applaud"). In commenting on John's Gospel he reveals a deep distrust of figurative language generally because of its abuse by religious writers, and views its excess in the Apocalypse as the effusion of a fevered brain.

Also disadvantageous is what Maréchal considers the crudity of much Biblical thought and writing as compared with the Greek classics. Not all the Biblical authors suffer from this comparison: Jeremiah, for example, is considered by Maréchal to be the equal of classical poets and orators, and Ezekiel XXXVII is described as more sublime than anything in Homer or Greek myth. But for the most part, scripture comes off second best. This is a venerable contrast—Athens vs. Jerusalem—going back to several Church fathers, most memorably to Augustine's *De Doctrina Christiana*, justifying, indeed glorifying, scriptural simplicity as against classical sophistication and elitism. Voltaire and other eighteenth-century Biblical commentators made similar observations. The trope continued to flourish in the earlier twentieth century in the work of philosophers and culture critics such as Leo Strauss, Lev Shestov, and the Franco-Roumanian Benjamin Fondane; it resurfaced in Erich Auerbach's famous essay "Odysseus's scar", and—as a Google search readily shows—in our own day at various levels of sophistication and from differing religious perspectives. It has had particular traction in Europe and among francophones because the long exclusion of Jews from citizenship created a sense of rivalry or conflict between Judaism and normative civil society (see Delany 2012).[7]

Thanks to his own inclinations and an already thriving stream of critical scholarship, Maréchal gets a lot right about the Bible, much of it not generally accepted in his day by any but academic specialists or elite intellectuals, certainly not by the average clergy or the population at large. Like most serious Bible scholars of his day, he knows that scripture is an anthology by various hands, often reflecting a priestly point of view. He knows that it is therefore not only permissible but necessary to read these documents as one reads any literary production, with a critical eye. He knows that there were many gospels, though only four of them were selected for inclusion in the Catholic canon. He knows about the Essene sect, to which some scholars thought Jesus may have belonged, and he knows that Jesus may not have existed. In his "Result" conclusion, he writes of "l'ère commune" (the common era), as modern scholars now do, rather than A.D. (*anno domini,* year of the lord). He uses new-fashioned terms like "ideology" (in, e.g., Psalms 6 and Job) and "civil society" (Psalms 36)

---

[7] The conflict wasn't as developed in the United States where Jews were not excluded to the same extent as in Europe. Partly this was due to the different constitutions of various colonies and states, several of which granted Jews the vote even before the French (see Chyet 1958).

as well as the newly invented "tachigraph" (speedometer, in Nehemiah). Many of his literary and moral judgments are irrefutable.

Nonetheless, I haven't found this text to represent Maréchal at his best or most attractive. Everyone who knew the man praises his character, noting a gentle, modest nature, erudition, delightful conversation, generosity to all and loyalty to friends, and a loving marriage with a younger woman of Catholic devotion. But in *Pour et contre* and in the handwritten marginal notes in his personal Bible (*La sainte Bible* 1712), we find a fuller picture, a more multi-faceted self-revelation than what appears in most of his other works that are not specifically religious in theme. Here and in the manuscript marginalia Sylvain releases a darker, more sardonic impulse: one glimpsed a decade earlier in his mock satirical legendary—*La nouvelle légende dorée*, 1790, a collection of lives of women saints—that was meant to win its audience, especially women, away from Catholic devotion. In the Bible marginalia one gets a continuous, spontaneous dialogue with the text, full of sarcasm, scorn, quasi-obscene insults, scatological asides, wise-cracks and cheap shots, skeptical or hostile comments about theology, demonstrations of logical or narrative flaws, cynical interpretations of behavior, and mocking interjections. There are hundreds of these, so a complete survey is impossible here; a few examples will have to suffice. A partial list of insulting words for Moses, priests, prophets, patriarchs or Jahweh includes: *charlatan, fripon, brigand, menteur, diable incarné, pillard, scelerat, execrable scelerat, imbécile, villain, fou, gaillard,* [faker, fraud, bandit, liar, devil incarnate, thief, scoundrel, cursed scoundrel, imbecile, villain, crazy, big guy: perhaps with overtones of homosexuality—Trans.] The Jews may be *gueux, cannibals, horrible, vilaines gens* [vagabonds, cannibals, horrible, awful people—Trans.] Exodus is a *recueil de bêtises* [collection of stupidities—Trans.]. Crowds or the disciples are often *ânes, benets, sots, imbéciles, gueux* or *canaille* [asses, donkeys, fools, imbeciles, beggars, low-class mob—Trans.]. Various statements of Jesus or other speakers are annotated as *verbiage, galimathias, fanatisme, menterie, conte d'enfans* [mere words, a confused mess, fanaticism, lies, fairytales—Trans.]; much of Matthew's gospel as *mauvaise logique, mauvais raisonnement, mauvais conseil* [bad logic, bad reasoning, bad advice—Trans.]. Snide or sarcastic comments are everywhere. Abraham's self-circumcision and that of his son Isaac calls forth many sneers, among them: *Et que diable cela nous fait-il?* [What the devil has it to do with us?—Trans.] and *Puisque ce bon dieu n'aimait pas les prepuces pour quoi les avait-il faits?* [Since this good god didn't like foreskins, why did he make them?—Trans.]. In Hosea 6:10, where Jahweh says that he will spread his anger like water, Sylvain ripostes, "so they'll have to take umbrellas". There are occasional vulgarities and near-obscenities: when Pharoah tells Abraham *t'en va* [go—Trans.], Sylvain adds *te faire* ... but omits the last word, *foutre* from the well-known phrase *Va te faire foutre* [Go fuck yourself—Trans.]. When Judith claims that Holofernes didn't rape her, the note reads *Vous mentez, putain!* [You lie, whore!—Trans.]. There is also no shortage of piss and shit in various notes, especially those annotating an incident of fear. And so on.

The unfiltered response of handwritten notes in a personal Bible is not, of course, what could go into a more or less scholarly commentary for public consumption, although most of the theological objections briefly noted in the marginalia are expanded into arguments in *Pour et contre*. In the commentary, though, Maréchal expresses some of the prejudices that don't emerge in other texts or in personal relations. Jews and women, specifically female sexuality, are the two main areas where this can be seen. Both of these specially-oppressed groups were much in the public eye during the Revolution (and long after), as subjects of debate in the National Assembly and other public venues.

Although there were significant Jewish communities—some quite prosperous—in France at the start of the revolutionary period, and had been for centuries, Jews were not legally full citizens until autumn, 1791. Their enfranchisement was hotly debated in the National Assembly and elsewhere, and enacted at that time, but this did not ensure social integration or put an end to negative stereotypes; rather, the dominant motivation was to "reform" the Jews as a whole by making them citizens. Nonetheless, the study of Hebrew and of ancient Israel, the reception of work by famous Jewish scholars, and the social presence of intellectually gifted Jews—such as the Polish-born scholar Zalkind Hourwitz, an associate of Cloots (Mortier 1995, 127)—as well as bankers, merchants and articulate community leaders, did create a certain respectful awareness among some intellectuals. Some took Jewish pen names, as did Richard Simon writing as Rabbin Shimeon bar Joachim. Holbach is said to have done the same, and his mansion was referred to by its frequenters as "the synagogue"—indeed by one correspondent as "the Great Synagogue of the rue Royale" (Kors 1976, 16). When the revolutionary organizer Théroigne de Méricourt addressed the radical Club des Cordeliers, she was heckled as "la reine de Saba qui vient voir le Salomon du district" [It's the Queen of Sheba come to see the local King Solomon—Trans.]. She responded: "On vous l'a dit, les Français ressemblent aux Juifs, peuple porté à l'idolatrie, le plus vulgaire se prend par les sens, il lui faut des signes extérieurs auxquels s'attache son culte" [You've heard that the French are like the Jews, a people attracted to idolatry; the most vulgar are trapped by the senses, they need external signs to anchor their religion—Trans.] (Bouvier 1931, 65). This last, while scarcely flattering for either party, does show an easy colloquial use of Hebrew Biblical referentiality.

But Maréchal does not participate in any current of appreciation. Rather he tends to exhibit disdain for Jews as a whole, referring to them occasionally as a race or species ("gent"), a tribe ("peuplade") of brutal sensibilities, or a "nation": a term easily turned to the uses of anti-semitic exclusion because it implied loyalty to a foreign nation, Israel, rather than to France. In Luke, he buys into the old association of Jews with money (n. 4) and characterizes them as nearly as despicable ("vil") as the Chinese. The same well-worn trope appears when, in manually annotating the golden calf incident, he has Aaron say, "et moi, j'aime l'or" [As for me, I love money/gold]. In this vein, in his journalism Sylvain blamed Jews for helping to cause France's financial emergency by taking advantage of their newfound citizenship to engage in disreputable or illegal practises, thus showing ingratitude for the privilege bestowed on them (Mannucci 2012, 168–69). In the "Results" section of *Pour et contre*, Jesus's fellow Jews are referred to as "ses compatriots dégénerés" [his degenerate compatriots—Trans.], and a disgusting anti-Semitic anecdote about the Hebrews' origin in bestiality and incest, erroneously said to be by Plutarch, is recounted (n. 19, "Result").

For Maréchal, the Biblical Jews were an "Oriental", Asiatic people and therefore prone to the traits of "Orientals" that are seen in much of their Biblical writing: emotional excess, sensuality, lack of restraint. "Who doesn't know", he asks in Malachi, "that the oriental poets are more inflated than sublime, have more emphasis than eloquence, and are not always troubled to put justice, truth and nature into their frequent extended metaphors?" Job, Judith and the Song of Songs are especially "oriental" despite the admiration he has for these texts; Kings II (Samuel II) shows "oriental servitude". In this way, Maréchal's Bible commentary participates in an Orientalist discourse stimulated by, though long antedating, Napoleon's 1797 Egyptian adventure. One finds it in medieval literature (the "Saracen", the Turk) and in ancient literature (attitudes toward the populations of Asia Minor) as well as in several French and English projects contemporaneous with Maréchal (Said 1978, 76–87).

Women, like Jews, were also disfranchised. The Revolution did not rectify this exclusion despite the importance of women in rural and urban labor, the existence of women's periodicals and political clubs, the militancy of working women in the revolutionary army as well as in specific uprisings, and despite frequent appeals to the National Assembly by both men and women to grant them the vote and full political participation. Maréchal opposed this proposed reform, as he wrote in the well-known journal, *Révolutions de Paris,* that he edited for several years, from about 1790 to its demise in early 1794. His reasoning, like that of many of his colleagues, was the essentialist argument that Nature intended women for domestic and maternal duties, not the rough-and-tumble of political life. This reasoning stands behind what is surely his most obnoxious treatise, the 1800 *Projêt* listing 138 reasons why women should not learn to read. Some in his day and our own have viewed this pamphlet as a (bad) joke, making a *reductio ad absurdum* out of the government's failure to educate women properly, as they needed to be in order to educate their offspring into good citizenship (Perrot 2007, 95). Others have considered it a genuine extension of his real beliefs, consistent with views expressed elsewhere.

The attitude toward female agency and sexuality that emerges in *Pour et contre* partly reflects revolutionary legislation, partly not. Although revolutionary legislation had required proper treatment of children born outside of marriage (as many were in a period of frequent commonlaw unions), and had legalized divorce in 1792, female adultery (not male) remained a crime. Maréchal makes both illegitimacy and adultery special targets of disdain. Hosea memorably allegorized the Jews' attraction to other religions as an adulterous wife bearing bastards. This imagery Maréchal refuses even to translate. Later he describes it as "worthy of the bordello"; even as an allegory the imagery is unacceptable. The scandalous "bastardy" of Jesus, owing to the married Mary's "adultery" with the Holy Spirit, is the cornerstone of his critique of Christian theology. Elsewhere a rather narrowminded prudery emerges, quite at odds with the hot love-poetry he addressed to his wife (see Dommanget 1950, 382). Clearly, marital sex is the only acceptable norm, and indeed always had been for Sylvain, even in his earlier pastoral poetry (ibid., 97). Socially, of course, commonlaw cohabitation was quite normal among working people, especially in cities, but social reality is not always Sylvain's strong point. The explicitly erotic *Song of Songs* evidently caused some embarrassment: the most obviously sexual line (5:4) he declines to translate, then avoids any actual textual analysis, confining his commentary to moral and literary-historical generalities. There is a contradiction to this prudery, of course, since elsewhere Maréchal criticizes his main French source, Sacy, for bowdlerizing the Latin to accommodate eighteenth-century middle-class standards of polite discourse by eliminating sexual or defecatory imagery, yet not daring himself to comment on the "Song" beyond a few condescending remarks.[8]

Even apart from attitudes toward female sexuality, though, Maréchal sometimes disappoints. In response to the truly awful story of the incestuous rape of Tamar by her brother, engineered by a cousin and covered up by another brother, Sylvain can only muster a shallow cynical remark about Tamar's naiveté.

---

8 A similarly squeamish or evasive attitude toward sexual matters can be seen in Maréchal's commentary to the 1780 *Antiquités d'Herculanum*, where illustrations plainly depicting a homoerotic or bestial dalliance are ignored in the text.

Elsewhere, he responds to St. Jerome's suggestion that Judith herself might have composed the book bearing her name by saying that he prefers a needle or spindle in a woman's hand rather than a pen or a sword. This despite a close friendship with two well-known women writers, one of whom, the novelist Mme. Gacon-Dufour, sat at his deathbed, wrote a memoir of his last days, and edited one of his works posthumously!

Some readers will observe, correctly, that these were normative or majority attitudes of the day regarding both Jews and women. Yet there were enough contemporaries of Sylvain—lay and cleric, men and women—who rejected them, often very publicly, in writing and in political debate, that this is not really an adequate justification. Moreover, even among earlier Catholic scholars an anti-Jewish attitude was not always necessary. For Claude Fleury (1640–1723), cleric and famous ecclesiastical historian, the Israelites offered an "excellent modèle de la vie humaine la plus conforme à la nature" [an excellent model of human life in conformity with nature—Trans.] (Fleury 1682, 1) and a simple, sensible, spiritual life far superior to the corrupt and idolatrous cultures of Egypt, Greece or Rome. Although his view was idealized, and he did at the end of his opus have to blame the Jews for their mistreatment of Jesus, Fleury did nonetheless take a historicist perspective, inviting the reader to look at the Israelites "dans les circonstances des temps et des lieux où ils vivoient ... et entrer ainsi dans leur esprit" [in the circumstances of the times and places where they lived...and thus to enter into their spirit—Trans.] (ibid., 5).

These retrograde attitudes of Sylvain are at odds with his professed egalitarianism. As contradictions both personal and social—common in the surrounding culture—they are not, I think, to be resolved but constitute instances, on both levels, of what today we might call combined and uneven development.

• • •

What about us?

According to polls, 20% of Americans consider themselves non-religious, though not necessarily atheists (Townsend 2012). There are specialized online groups such as Black Atheists or Black Atheist Alliance as well as groups such as Black Nonbelievers, among a minority whose majority do believe and attend church regularly (Brennan 2011, ST1). There are online networks, the Clergy Project and Recovering from Religion among others, for clergy who no longer believe in God, along with the Freedom from Religion Foundation (Worth 2012). Former conservative Republican President Reagan's son Ron publicizes a national atheist organization, the Freedom from Religion Foundation, which advertises itself on television: "Not afraid of burning in hell" is the closing line. Several military bases host a chapter of the Military Atheists and Secular Humanists, a movement that began at Fort Bragg, North Carolina. Numerous books are published by reputable presses defending atheism, recounting its history, or attacking various religions; some of them employ rhetoric reminiscent of Maréchal's: for instance, a characterization of "the Pauline contamination" as "ravings of a hysteric" inflicted on the rest of the world (Onfray 2007, 131). Many campuses have a secular student union or an atheist or humanist club. The University of Miami in 2016 received a large endowment for a chair in "the study of atheism, humanism and secular ethics"; Pitzer College in California has a Department of Secular Studies; Trinity College has an Institute for the Study of Secularism; scholars have formed an international "Nonreligion and secularity research network" with a journal, *Secularism and nonreligion* (*New York Times*, May 22, 2016). Groups for atheists and secular humanists meet regularly worldwide. Even *Vogue* has joined the fray with a first-person contribution by a Catholic woman who has lost her faith in response to clerical abuse of children (Keane 2019, 16–18). And, in stark contrast to the Mike Pence incident with which I began, the Socialist prime minister of Spain was sworn in without a Bible, while the new Georgia county commissioner took her oath on *The Autobiography of Malcolm X* (both in June, 2018).

Abroad, organized religion appears to be less popular than ever. The famous incarnation of Harry Potter, the British actor Daniel Radcliffe, declared himself an atheist, as has novelist Ian McEwen along with other writers (see Bradley and Tate 2010). In 2004, the BBC (British Broadcasting Corporation) broadcast a three-part TV series called "Atheism: A rough history of disbelief"; it aired in the U.S. in 2007 on PBS. Atheism is the official position in Cuba, China, and North Korea (although many in these populations do believe and practise various faiths or rituals). Pew Research indicates 60 million atheist or agnostic Latino/as (with varying percentages per country, the highest in Uruguay at over one-third. Mexico has an atheist association with annual congress, as do Chile and Argentina; the Argentinians won a suit against a Jesuit university for anti-atheistic rules, and others in other countries have proceeded against school systems for discriminating against atheists. Even in Switzerland, cradle of Calvinism, the proportion of non-religious is now virtually equal to the proportion of Protestants, about 25% each (swissinfo.ch 2018). Also in Switzerland, in November 2018, six parliamentary women resigned from the Catholic Church to protest its "patriarchal power apparatus" and Pope Francis's denunciation of abortion.

As for France, Sarah Fainberg describes the situation in 2013 as "a steady decrease, even a crash, of Catholic faith and religious practise", observing that

35% of the general population and 64% of those between ages 18 and 24 "define themselves as completely without religion" (Fainberg 2014, 87). Admittedly, figures can't be exact: often people who define themselves as non-believers, non-observant or agnostic are reluctant to use the term "atheist"; while some secularists oppose the Church less for theological reasons than because of its corruption, sexual abuse of children, anti-abortion or homophobic positions. Nonetheless, the trend is clear and obvious.[9]

Nor, of course is it limited to Christians. Muslims who have left the faith are not limited to the famous names—Salman Rushdie, Ayaan Hirsi Ali—but include many internationally. The Council of Ex-Muslims, started in Britain in 2007, is now a worldwide organization; there is the group Ex-Muslims of North America, and an online movement called #ExMuslimBecause (for samples of messages sent to it, see Rizvi 2016, 72–75). As for Jews in America, over half do not believe in God, including those active in a synagogue or temple, and doubtless quite a few rabbis, and at least 75% rarely attend services (Putnam and Temple 2010, 23, 138 Fig. 5.1).

All this is not to claim that religion is dead (despite the claim some make that God is dead). Far from it: religion thrives in many places, often in regrettably extreme versions whether Catholic, Jewish, Muslim or Hindu, and is likely to continue to thrive whether for psychological or political reasons. For some, it is useful: as Napoleon is said to have observed, "Religion is excellent stuff for keeping common people quiet. Religion is what keeps the poor from murdering the rich". For others, comforting: "Religion is the expression of real distress and the protest against real distress. Religion is the sigh of the oppressed creature, the heart of a heartless world, just as it is the spirit of a spiritless situation. It is the opium of the people" (Marx 1964, 42).

Some of Maréchal's comments seem peculiarly appropriate today. For example, his remarks about David in the Psalms section seem appropriate now, as the Israeli government protests its morality and purity while committing massacres against Palestinians whom it has driven out of their homes and off their land, and practises internal government corruption that has landed more than one official before the courts or in prison. The declaration by Israel's finance minister, Yair Lapid, that "There will be no separation of church and state here [in Israel]" (Yehoshua 2014, 173) would perfectly illustrate the reason for Maréchal's hatred of priesthood in Hebrew scripture and in any organized religion. Moreover, the veracity or historicity of the Jewish Bible is once again contentious because of its use to justify political claims, despite evidence

---

9 For a survey of polls worldwide, with graphs and discussion, see Zuckerman 2007.

brought to light by a post-zionist generation of historians and archaeologists showing the limits of an earlier politicized archaeology.

If the restoration of the ancient Bourbon monarchy in 1814, in the person of Louis XVIII—a brother of the deposed and executed Louis XVI—would have been Maréchal's worst nightmare, yet some developments in our own day as cited above—the existence of atheist organizations, clubs and academic departments, the general acceptance of atheism, the widespread belief that it is possible to be virtuous without religion—might have restored some of his faith in humankind. He was, after all, always oriented toward the future. This is especially prominent in his *Ad majorem gloriam virtutis: Fragmens d'un poeme moral sur Dieu* (To the greater glory of Virtue: Fragments of a moral poem on God), published when he was only thirty-one. Fragment IX, voicing "l'homme de bien" (the comfortable/ content man) offers this scenario:

> Un jour j'aurai pour moi tous les coeurs vertueux:...
> Le pere à ses enfans transmettra mes écrits
> Long-tems après ma mort, utile à mon pays,
> On viendra sur ma tombe épandre quelques larmes.
> Pour moi, quel avenir peut avoir plus de charmes!
> One day all virtuous hearts will be mine: ...
> Fathers will pass on my writing to their children
> Long after my death, useful to my country;
> People will come to drop tears on my tomb.
> For me, what future could hold more charm! [Trans.]
> And the last lines of Fragment XII read:
> Eh bien! Par nos écrits & surtout par nos moeurs,
> Dans le chemin du vrai soyons ses précurseurs.
> Very well! By our writing and above all by our behavior,
> In truth's road let us be its precursors.

Some years later, Sylvain put it this way in a song he wrote for the working people of France when part of a group trying to bring about a genuinely democratic revolution:

> Je m'attends bien que la prison
> Sera la prix de ma chanson,
> C'est ce qui me désole:
> Le people la saura par coeur,

> Peut-être il bénira l'auteur,
> C'est ce qui me console.
> MARÉCHAL 1796, 28–29[10]

> I expect that prison
> Will be the price of my song,
> That's what dismays me:
> The people will know it by heart,
> Perhaps they will bless the author,
> That's what consoles me.

As it turned out, prison was not to be Maréchal's fate, although it well could have been in the spy-ridden political life of his day; indeed he had already spent several months in prison as a younger man, punishment for an iconoclastic earlier work.[11] He finished out his days in the countryside on the outskirts of Paris, in quiet retreat from political activism but continuing to read and write, see friends and family, and attract denunciation for his publications. He died of natural causes, surrounded by friends and family and had a Catholic burial in a Catholic graveyard. Although he had composed epitaphs for himself during his lifetime, it's doubtful any of them was used, and the grave itself no longer exists. Nonetheless we may end with one of them here, the same with which Maréchal ended his *Fragmens*:

---

10   Maréchal's song, several stanzas long, was based on a popular air about a young widow alternately grieved and relieved. He wrote numerous songs which, like his leaflets on behalf of the group of revolutionaries around F.-N. ("Gracchus") Babeuf, were posted in Paris and other cities, and widely known. It would have been composed between 1795 and early 1797 (when Babeuf was tried and executed). Maréchal managed to escape identification by a police informer; as Serna observes, Maréchal "n'existe même pas pour la police" [doesn't even exist for the police—Trans.] (Serna 1997, 316 n.3). The reason for this is likely, as Dommanget argues on the basis of police reports and other accounts, that the informer did not recognize Maréchal at the meeting he had infiltrated, and that documents using Maréchal's name were scarce and well hidden (Dommanget 1970, Ch. 10).

11   This was his 1788 *Almanach des honnêtes gens* (Almanach of upright people), a form of calendar popular at the time, but substituting political people, scientists, writers, artists and non-Christian as well as Christian religious figures from various countries for the usual saints. The book was condemned in Parlement to be publicly torn and burnt as scandalous, monstrous, blasphemous, sacrilegious, etc.; the author spent several months in prison, released through a friend's influence. It was republished a few years later and again in 1836 (Karmin 1911, 265–66).

Cy repose un paisible Athée:
Il marcha toujours droit sans regarder les Cieux.
Que sa tombe soit respectée:
L'ami de la vertu fut l'ennemi des Dieux.

Here rests a peace-loving atheist:
He walked upright without watching the skies.
May his tomb be respected:
The friend of Virtue was the enemy of gods.

For and Against the Bible
*By Sylvain M****

∴

The book of holy Scripture must be closed to the people... *The venerable* BEDE.

AT JERUSALEM,
THE YEAR OF THE CHRISTIAN ERA,
M.DCCCI.

N.B. The Bible, having always been outside the list of other books, has never been submitted to an impartial critique. Whether prejudiced for or against, readers have almost always brought dubious judgment to it. Theologians have palliated its faults and exaggerated its beauties; those who are not theologians have too often taken the contrary position. It is time to bring the Bible back into the class of ordinary books; and, leaving aside all extraneous considerations, to make it undergo the examination of reason.

Frankness and impartiality!.... Such a work was needed.

This *Treatise for and against the Bible* is placed under the protection of the liberty of thought. The liberty to think and write what one thinks is a sacred thing.

Epistle to Ministers of All Religions

THIS Treatise *for and against the Bible* will teach you nothing new; more than anyone, you know the strength and weakness of your books, and the chinks in the armor of your gods; let others cast an impartial eye into the depths of the sanctuary where, for long enough, imposture has enjoyed the right of asylum. Suffer if need be...

Or rather, blush for the role that you have transmitted from hand to hand for four thousand years. Having outgrown its early childhood, the human race is old enough to move from the rule of nannies to that of reason.

It would doubtless insult you to believe you to be dupes—the first ones—of the fables in which you traffic. Not at all! you are not dupes; stop acting like it. Dare to aspire to liberal ideas. It is still possible for you to take your place among respect-worthy beings. We will willingly consent to forget what you have been, if you sincerely promise us to work to become again what you ought never to have ceased to be. The task you have taken on (we would like to think) is not necessarily permanent.

Already, several among you[1] have thrown off the mask and the distinctive clothing; follow this example, or be in as good faith as some of your predecessors during the second century of Christianity. In the vault of their church, the Montanist[2] priests suspended an air-filled balloon and danced beneath it, chanting the hymn of the Holy Spirit, of which this air-filled balloon was the symbol.

In the name of reason, to which it is never too late to return; in the name of morality, which has suffered for so long and groaned over its alliance with religion; in the name of the pitiless posterity that is preparing to condemn you, if you obstinately continue to drag the people in your old ruts: respect yourselves, respect your fellow human beings, enough to put an end to the degradation of the human race. Shouldn't you be satisfied? Don't four thousand years of lies suffice? Put down the sceptre of opinion, which you have allowed to be sullied in your hands. Reflect that eighteen centuries have already passed since the second epoch or the renewal of your gross, ridiculous and criminal rites: does the 19th century have to be infected with them? You can see that every day

---

1 several among you: During the early phase of the revolution, some priests and highly placed clergy abdicated their office either voluntarily or under threat. The most famous was Archbishop Gobel of Paris, who resigned his clerical function in November 1793.
2 Montanists: A second-century Christian ecstatic and ascetic sect, located in what is now central Turkey, practising direct inspiration by the Holy Spirit.

nearly all knowledge takes a step toward the light; will only you remain stationary in the shadows?

How will you be able to escape universal ridicule, if some obnoxious chemist decides, in the middle of a class, to put the blood of your God into an alembic and his body into a crucible, and then repeats his analysis at every streetcorner?

So hurry to abjure a profession that you can no longer practise without evoking laughter, and without laughing at it yourselves behind your altars. Seize the only means remaining to you to deserve a pardon, in doing justice to your own fabrications. What are you waiting for? One day the role you insist on filling will become nothing more than a historical problem. The future Saumaises[3] will have trouble, with all their erudition, in making your real present existence believable. No one will want to believe them; no one will want to believe that there was a time during which, under the eyes of philosophy, men without shame[4] offered for the adoration of the entire world a God turned into bread[5] between their blessed fingers: at least, fear the future. A little while longer and this plebeian population who kneel before your altar to consume a God you've made, will perhaps want to avenge itself with violence, with intensity, for having been your plaything for many long years. Fear the awakening of those whom you have kept, for so many centuries, in a stupor. Realize that you owe your domination only to an ancient habit. Had religions not degenerated into mere routine, there would have been no religions for a long time; but everything deteriorates and disappears.

"But" (you will say) "we force no one. All are free to come or not to come, any day of the week, to prostrate themselves before our holy mountebank stages. The plebeians apparently enjoy being fooled,[6] and perhaps it's good that they be fooled... Better us than more dangerous charlatans. In a despotic state, it isn't the despot you have to reprimand but the multitude that endures him". These are things to which one ought not respond; they are revolting or self-refuting. We will continue to say to you:

---

3 Saumaise: Claude Saumaise (1588–1653), Protestant anti-papist scholar of classics and religion.
4 SM's note: Honorable readers, forgive the expression; only this old-fashioned word could render the thought.
5 SM's note: It's a major question to know whether God is in the bread or around the bread, on or under the bread. Consult the History of *Consubstantiators*. ["Bread" refers to the Catholic rite of taking communion with a wafer said to be God's body (consubstantiation), placed by the priest into the communicant's mouth.—Trans.].
6 SM's note: *Mundus vult decipi, ergo decipiatur.* [People want to be deceived, hence they are deceived.—Trans.].

Ministers of all religions! Understand that you are not liked and indeed that you are not likeable. Your mythologies are sad, your ceremonies[7] monotonous and ridiculous, your harangues boring, your books heavy and ill-tempered. Don't resist the torrent of history, which carries with it empires and religions. Do better. If the zeal of the Lord's mansion still devours you, all right, abandon the profane and impious to their destinies; go repopulate the holy land, that first theatre of the Bible and the Gospel; take your God back there, and your books and three-legged stools; we don't want them any more. You are proud of the poetic beauties of your Bible[8] and of some grand features scattered through your Gospels; but the literary merit of these two religious productions cannot preserve them from the fate which, sooner or later, puts into its place every book filled with indecent fables.

Let us add that the books of every religion resemble one another. That is why we address ourselves to the ministers of all religions. If we pause especially at Catholicism, it's because we have its spectacle before our eyes, and because this Treatise is only about the Bible and the Gospel; for religions differ among themselves only in their decoration.

Christian priests, you insist:

> For some time, many known literary people have expressed admiration in these words: *beautiful as the Bible*. At least (you add) one can't refuse to keep in one's hands the most beautiful of existing books. No one has made a better one: the Orientals, the Egyptians, Greece and Rome have produced nothing that might eclipse the Bible. This book holds the first rank in literature as in religion.

---

7   SM's note: Little novels, prettily written (*Atala*, for example, by Auguste Chateaubriand), will never save the mass and the scapulary from ridicule. It is deplorable to see in the 19th century a still-young man waste his talent in trying to render likeable the mass and the scapulary, priests and Jesuits. [Chateaubriand, a libertine aristocrat, recently returned from exile in England, was a major propagandist for the Catholic revival under Napoleon. His books were much in vogue.—Trans.].

8   SM's note: The authors of *Atala* and of *The Knight of the White Swan* promise their fans respectively a *Poetic dictionary of the Bible for the use of artists* in two large octavo volumes, and three large octavos on the *Poetics of Christianity*. [Mme. de Genlis authored the immensely popular *Les chevaliers du cygne*, set in the time of Charlemagne, as an antidote to the Robespierreian phase of the Revolution; she became a staunch proponent of Napoleon, whom she saw as a new Charlemagne.—Trans.].

Ministers of religion! But people also say, with all sorts of motives, *as beautiful as Homer*; people have even said *as beautiful as Telemachus*.⁹ This proves, evidently, that there are in the Bible, as in Homer and in the small number of original books, beauties of the first order; but the genius of Homer occasionally drowses: *Aliquando dormitat Homerus*¹⁰ . The authors of the Old and the New Testament not only slept as did the author of the *Iliad* and the *Odyssey*, but they did something worse; they scandalized and revolted their readers with obscene pictures, horrible scenes, and faulty structure. Whence it follows that the Bible, written by the hand of God or inspired by his holy Spirit, is full of beauties, like other books composed by men of genius, but is not a more perfect book than those—even though it should be, according to the high claims of its eternal supporters.

There is more: the Bible is worse than some profane books. Really! I would blush to have published certain passages, quite numerous, from the Old and the New Testament. Jean Lafontaine¹¹ disavowed his tales. I would consider myself even more criminal if I were the author of the Bible and the Gospel. I would have shown genius in some places; but at the same time, I would have created a very poor opinion both of my judgment and my morals.

In a word, if you asked an educated and unprejudiced man which of all the famous books he'd most like to be the author of, such a man, if he respected himself, doubtless would not want to answer, *of the Bible*.

Ministers of every religion! you place yourselves under the shelter of this epigram by Montesquieu,¹² which many echoes repeat today: "Religion is the best possible guarantee of men and of the stability of states" (*Grandeur and decadence of Rome*, x.) Priests! you haven't known how to preserve the throne of your very-Christian kings; your gods and your books have not been able to shelter the people and its leaders from a political revolution. Your cults and your books are thus poor guarantors.

In vain, too, do you glorify the long and elaborate praise of Jesus by the most eloquent but not the wisest author of the 18th century; J.J. Rousseau's "Apologia for the Gospel" and Newton's "Commentary on the Apocalypse" ¹³

---

9   Telemachus: the son of Odysseus (hero of Homer's *Odyssey*), subject of operas by Scarlatti (1718) and Gluck (1765) and a play (1699) by the theologian François Fénelon.
10 Sometimes Homer sleeps.
11 Lafontaine (1621–95), author of the fabliau-like, risqué, and irreverent *Contes* and, later, of the well-known and more conventional animal *Fables*.
12 Montesquieu: Charles-Louis, Baron de Montesquieu (1689–1755), lawyer, philosopher, political theorist.
13 Rousseau, Newton: Jean-Jacques Rousseau (1712–1778), prolific author and philosopher, in other respects one of SM's intellectual heroes; Isaac Newton (1642–1727), English mathematician and physicist credited with formulating the theory of gravity.

prove only that men of genius have weaknesses of judgment, just like other men.

Let's proceed. People still speak about you; you are dreaded even more today. You still frighten small children and old women. There are even politicians who opine that you are a necessary evil, that you must be used like a scarecrow to frighten and control the rabble, that religion is a supplement to the police.[14] Far too many publicists persist in saying that vast estates, populous cities, cannot do without priests and executioners. These considerations give you pride and confidence; but would that little remaining honor suffice for you to boast, to take advantage of such an existence? Is it anything to be proud of? Don't forget that you owe your credit among weak spirits only to an ancient political error about their fate. A little more time, and people will dispense with these vain arrangements. A little more time, and even the shoemaker will think himself dishonored by touching a priest's hand.

So do not be unaware of the disdain and disgust that you necessarily inspire in every honest and reasonable person who sees you in the street. Clever as you are, don't rest imprudently on the impunity you enjoy in your functions, which corrupt good morals. You are allowed to do almost anything. Don't think that therefore you have acquired the right to continue your holy scandals. Adultery, deified[15] for the last eighteen centuries in your temples, has not therefore become a virtue. There is no expiry date for vice.

We would like to consent to wipe a sponge over the past to erase it, but on condition that you respect the present and the future, that you embrace a useful and honest profession, that you leave sons with their parents and young virgins with their mothers, that you no longer incite workers of both sexes to waste their time and their inexperienced reason with your frequent representations. Stop tormenting the best age of life in obliging young girls to engrave in their tender brain[16] the most ridiculously absurd passages of your sainted books. Soon enough many of them may well imitate the scandals of the virgin Mary.

---

14   SM's note: Certain people say, "I'd like a police without spies, a religion without priests". These nice people demand the impossible. A God without priests can no more exist than priests without God.

15   Adultery deified: For Maréchal (and numerous other scholars both Christian and Jewish), the story of the virgin birth conceals a probable adultery by Mary; and even if it does not, strict morality would claim that as a married woman she was not entitled to conceive by anyone or anything other than her husband, Joseph.

16   SM's note: Doubtless it is a lesser evil to catechise young girls than to cut their throats, as was done by the ancients. (Cf. the sacrifices of Jephtha and Iphigeneia.) However, one may lead to the other. [Jephtha sacrificed his daughter (Judges 11: 29–39), and Iphigeneia was sacrificed by her father, Agamemnon, in plays by Euripides, Aeschylus, Jean Racine, and Goethe as well as an opera by Gluck, all of which Maréchal could have seen.—Trans.].

If at least the holy literature that you profess could lead to some great profitable or interesting results! Higher mathematics or transcendent geometry, little necessary in themselves, have given rise to major discoveries in the mechanical arts. What fruits can be drawn from the Bible and the Gospel? And what good are those who consecrate themselves wholly to the study of these two volumes? Pilgrimages to Mecca and to Calvary lead only to tombs or to nothingness.

Ministers! your religions are costly: you require rich ornaments, brilliant costumes, wax, incense, perfumes, golden cups, carpets and tapestries, vast and sumptuous buildings. This luxury, in order to be respected, is not a good example. At the present time, when heads of households have to know how to keep accounts, it would be an excellent economy to suppress both religion and the priesthood; much better that a father of a family should fulfill those functions at no cost and surrounded by his children:[17]

> An upright old man, instructed by his years,
> Guiding the destinies of his numerous offspring:
> Can he not teach virtue better than a priest?
> Is he not clothed with a saintly character?
> S.M.

You will tell us: "But the wise and devout Egypt made its priests the gift of a third of its treasury, so grateful did it feel toward us". This is because Egypt was devout but not wise.

Ministers of every religion! Even glory itself no longer makes us feel enthusiasm. Don't flatter yourselves with lighting the torches of religious fanaticism.[18] Henceforth we will have no more crusades than civil wars; we will fight for priests no more than for masters. We have won at least that, and that is something.

Ministers of every religion! your good times are over; don't deceive yourselves, because you ought to have expected it: it couldn't have lasted forever. We did too much for you and you did too little in exchange, for really what equivalent did you give for all the goods and honors lavished on you? From time immemorial you held first place among the ranks of the state. The good

---

17 SM's note: See *Project for a law concerning regulation of a religion without priests*, octavo, Paris, 1790. [The quatrain that follows is the epigraph to this pamphlet, both authored by Maréchal. See Dommanget 1950, 454.—Trans.].

18 SM's note: "Religion can no longer be fanatical" (*Nouveau Mercure de France*) says a journalist who must never have written anything but verse; but it doesn't follow, as this fine fellow claims, that philosophy should become religious.

people of Egypt exempted you from all debt. You had separate jurisdiction;[19] your persons, your goods, your books, were sacred; even the fines levied against those who dared to doubt aloud the holiness of your character and the purity of your morals were turned over to you. You were the censors of kings.[20] For ages you were the only magistrates, the only judges. On the banks of the Nile and elsewhere, you took over the education of children and the instruction of the people. In Ethiopia it was otherwise; the monarch of that country was chosen by priests and consequently was always a priest. The magi, or sages (thus the Persian priests modestly named themselves), were teachers of kings and their counsellors; and monarchs had engraved on their tombs—as in France—that they had the honor of becoming priests before they died. Julius Caesar boasted of having controlled the high priesthood.[21] In several countries, you wore on your forehead the diadem of sovereigns. In Albania, in the Orient, the first person after the monarch was the pontiff. In India, the Brahmans, who styled themselves philosophers but who were only priests, obeyed neither the king nor the law. The Druids combined, in their sacerdotal hands, temporal and sacred powers; they judged the nation's princes and made kings. Among the Germanic people they put in chains whomever they wished without giving a reason. In Greece, the grand pontiff several times declared to the chief magistrates that he didn't depend on them but only on God. Denis Halicarnassus[22] tells us that in Rome, the priests were accountable neither to the people nor to the Senate. The priests at that time gave the signal for battles and for retreat. Always and everywhere, people have built you the finest buildings. The first-opened flowers, the earliest of the best fruits, the master-pieces of every art, have been heaped up on your altars. Mothers have confided their daughters to you, husbands even their wives.

Ministers of every religion! how have you responded to so many anticipations of your desires? In exchange for so many benefits, what services have you given back to the world? In the minor persecutions that you have brought upon yourselves through your conduct, you have inspired the tenderest concern from your flocks of both sexes. Women have pampered you; what have they received from you in return? Prayers, sermons, rituals, panicked terror, servile fear, talismans, rosaries; books filled with maxims that are insolent,

---

19   jurisdiction: The Church had its own courts, separate from civil courts, in which clerics accused of a crime were tried by other clerics.
20   SM's note: Even today, the king of Portugal does not go hunting without the permission of his confessor. Cf. *Voyage du D. Duchatelet en Portugal*, p. 91, vol. 1 octavo, 1801.
21   priesthood: Julius Caesar, like other Roman emperors, was elected "pontifex maximus" or high priest of the state religion. The term was later used of the Roman Catholic Pope.
22   Halicarnassus: First-century BCE rhetorician and historian, born in Asia Minor.

immoral, or upsetting, etc. We are tired of putting out so much and getting so little back. There is no compensation; the entire advantage of this trade is on your side. Holy wars, crusades, inquisitions, fasts, the boredom of your rituals and your speeches, festivals so rarely cheerful, howling hymns, old ceremonies that no longer have either motive or aim: priests! admit that all these practises are poor recompense for the people. And the people are beginning to notice that you cost them too much.

Please do admit the justice of the following observation:

> If religion, whose ministers you are, were not already founded, tell us! Would you dare today to use the same means to establish it, the same instruments, that were used back then? Wouldn't you shrug off the propositions that would be made to you? If there were no religions now, it wouldn't be easy to establish one, judging from the trouble you experience in maintaining the religions that hardly enable you to live.

It is painful to remind you of, and to publish, all these hard truths; but you force us. A religious *reaction*,[23] quite noticeable, characterizes this first year of the 19th century. Quick to seize any circumstance, you abuse it with a shamelessness that alarms the friends of reason. But let them be reassured! and be well warned for once that reason will never lose its rights; that its hearth-fire, tended by a small number of pure hands, will not be extinguished; that its torch may suffer occasional prolonged eclipse without ever lacking the fuel to rekindle itself all the more brightly; that it has seen all religions pass in turn; that not only does it not change but survives in all centuries. Know, too, that—despite your small success, your ephemeral triumphs, your musk-scented apologists of both sexes—most of those who haunt your religious clubs shrink from embarrassment when leaving and are surprised that you allow so many anarchic and revolutionary maxims[24] to be uttered in your divine rites. Know that your altars have undergone a shake-up from which they will always feel

---

23   SM's note: This word is particularly appropriate here since people of both sexes who currently display the holiest zeal for the house of the Lord, were previously distinguished by completely profane conduct.

24   SM's note: In the Old Testament, which is (as everyone knows) the prefiguration of the New, Jewish history breathes on almost every page the most pronounced *sans-culottism*. It's the same with the Gospel. [Maréchal refers here, ironically, to the Catholic theory of figuralism, which interpreted phrases and incidents in Jewish scripture as advance representations of those in Gospel or in Christian theology. The "sans-culottes" were the radical urban working population during the Revolution, so called because they didn't wear the elegant trousers of more prosperous classes.—Trans.].

the aftershock, and they will never recover that early stability of which you have been so vain. Know that, without women,[25] your galleries would be deserted. Know that peasants, on whom you counted the most, are finally persuaded that it isn't you or your lustrations or your psalmodies but their own arms and the sun that fertilize the earth and fill their barns and cellars. Labor is their only tutelary god; they can do without your *triune God* and prefer to give their alms to genuine indigents rather than to you, who are nourished by food that has never been watered with the honorable sweat of useful work.

So abandon a bad cause, thrown out by common sense. You have had nothing more to do in this world, starting from the moment when people realized that what people in organized society require is not a religion but a code drawn up by reason and according to the counsel of experience. In a word, no one needs you any more.

Show us a single phase of human life that requires your presence. Once born, we have a mother's breast. In youth, a father is present to train us. A little further along, another woman comes in to complete our education and make us an adult. As spouse, our companion fulfills our wishes. Parents in our turn, the lessons we have received from ours we pass on to our children. As citizens, the nation claims our participation in the shared work of the beehive. Born sensitive, we find a friend to add the finishing touch to our happiness. We ask you: is there a single circumstance in human life, a single moment where a priest might be involved? Is there a place for the priest in the paternal or marital home? We can quite well, without you, be born, live, and die; we have no need of a priest to love and to repay our debt to nature. Will a priest teach the newborn to find its mother's breast and the path to her heart? Does a young virgin need a priest's lessons to please others and be adored? Does the young wife need to go consult a priest to preserve her husband's esteem and keep the reign of order and harmony in her household?

Ministers of every religion! your profession is absolutely precarious. Your orders are a heavy and harmful superfluity. You are the parasite druidic mistletoe, which grows on the oak at its expense.

"But the salvation of souls!" you will say.

---

25   SM's note: Christianity also has its *knitters*. Those who have followed the French Revolution will recall this word and its meaning. [The word "knitter" ("tricoteuse") referred to urban working women who knitted while attending meetings of radical women's political clubs, or while observing street incidents and perhaps reporting them to the authorities, or witnessing executions at the guillotine. One of the items they often knitted was the red cap, symbol of loyalty to the Revolution.—Trans.].

Does one need a priest in order to pray? Isn't a paternal benediction worth as much as the laying on of priestly hands? And also, can't the great issue of salvation be treated otherwise than by a middleman?

"Look through history and geography" (you'll add). "In every time and place, from Siberia to Otaiti island, from the Ganges to the Amazon River, you find a God and priests to serve it. Priests are thus as necessary as God itself. Why not add: we are even more necessary than God, for, after all, God can't be seen and we are here to represent him, to remind distracted mankind of him?"

Ministers of every religion! Always and everywhere people have believed in sorcerers; is that to say we can't do without them? Simply because there have been priests, it is not sound logic to conclude that they are still needed. To the contrary, it's because we've had them that they are no longer needed. The lengthy testing that has been made of them has caused permanent disgust, and the people themselves are disenchanted in this respect. If everyone wanted to have his own oven and bake his own bread, the profession of bakers would cease. By the same token, let everyone serve God in his or her own way, and take communion from his or her own hand in his or her own house—then there would be no more talk of temples and services, as the axiom says: Do not multiply entities without necessity.[26] This very axiom condemns the Bible and the Gospel. A father's good example is the best book for a child.

Priests! reflect on how little your condition is secured by. Once, a multitude worked for you; you took the trouble to think and to pray for them. The time has come when every one of us would like to exercise both our intellectual and physical faculties. Thereafter there will be nothing more for you to do. So agree with us that there is nothing more useless in the world than you; even poets are less useless. The laborer adds something to nature. The artisan modifies, the courier exchanges and distributes products of the earth. The magistrate preserves social order. What real services can one derive from you? Panic and terror, imaginary hopes, etc.

Moreover, if we weigh the authority and privileges remaining to you, the decadence of your empire is no longer in doubt. Passionless women, party hacks, journalists whom Bayle[27] wouldn't want even as a transcriber, a few opportunistic hypocrites, greedy professors who play the market, and finally the unthinking ordinary folk: such are your resources.

Ministers of all religions! We know you don't like one another much; that's inevitable: each one of you preaches for his own flag. All right then: to

---

26   axiom: Known as Ockham's razor, after the fourteenth-century English nominalist William of Ockham (*Pluralitas numquam ponenda sine necessitate*).

27   Bayle: Pierre Bayle (1607–1706), rationalist Protestant scholar.

re-establish proper thinking, carry no more banners or uniforms. Even better: own no more books. This expiatory sacrifice to good sense will cost you, we are sure; but a fine and generous *auto-da-fé*[28] of holy writings from every land has become necessary, even indispensable to peace everywhere. Theology[29] , at once so sterile and so fecund, has invaded two-thirds of our libraries; it seems that good books are acquired there only reluctantly and few of them at that. Reason and truth take up little space in our libraries.

If you can't immediately resolve to sacrifice your already printed books, at least don't reprint them, and above all don't publish new ones; we have enough of them. We are repelled to the point of nausea by theology. Recall that Jesus was no maker of books; far from being obsessed with them, like you, it is claimed he didn't even know how to read. In certain countries there still are priests who imitate him in that, and they are not the worst.

But there is another important and more general measure in which we exhort you to cooperate. To put an end to those interminable disputes which have led us to the confusion of things and the degradation of humanity, priests! agree to forbid yourselves, as we have done, to ever speak of religion, whether as a good or as an evil. We all ought to be tired of repeating the same ideas without being able to attach a meaning to them. This simple measure, once proposed in Switzerland, was quite successful during the time when its execution was supervised. Now that we are a few steps closer to the truth, such a rule ought to be far less unfeasible. So take what is perhaps the only wise decision remaining given the present state of mind. Let us burn, without regrets and with not a single exception, books in every language treating of holy things: the *Bible* and the *Gospel*, the *Koran* and the *Zend-Avesta* before all others. Let us even rip out the pages mentioning them in other volumes. Let us promise each other to no longer occupy ourselves with all that. Let us no longer argue topics whose stench has so often asphyxiated people's brains; but principally let's avoid these superficial, useless labels such as materialists, spiritualists, Catholics, Protestants, Muslims, Jews. Let us attack anything that could recall or keep alive these old ideas, which fortunately we no longer have anything to do with. Let us return to that grand, ancient distinction among men: good ones and wicked ones. Let us simplify as much as possible, in order to understand one another better. Misunderstandings, especially about religion, have caused almost all the ills of the world.

---

28   *auto-da-fé*: literally, "act of faith", most often used during the Spanish Inquisition for the burning alive of a heretic or other offender.

29   SM's note: We read in the old French Encyclopedia: "No science demands more subtlety of mind than theology". Article *Bible*. This is why it has given birth to so many volumes.

Priests of all religions! how honorable it would be for you not only to adhere with hearts and minds to this fine, peaceful measure, but indeed to mount your apostolic thrones to preach this sublime devotion with your own mouths. How worthy you would be of respect if, following the example of curé Meslier[30] and others both before and after that good man, you were heard to speak straightforwardly the following homily!

We confess, with truth and repentance, that up to now we have not walked upright before reason. Alas, we have unworthily compromised the dignity of the free and thinking human being through our servile, lying, absurd and evil-doing institutions. Then a sudden flash of light struck our eyes; yes, we willingly consent to never again pronounce the name of our God. God has no further need of priests to serve him, any more than candles to light his way. Human worship can never affect him; he is too high for them. So let us leave him to enjoy himself, completely comfortable in his celestial beatitude and for all eternity; we needn't disturb his majestic leisure or pester him with indiscreet promises or perfectly useless prayers. God doesn't feed on our incense any more than we do on his flesh at our holy altars. The moment has come to make honorable amends for the fact that, over so many centuries, we have vilified God and deceived humanity, by insisting that by our voice and by our request the divine majesty forsook the heavens to suddenly descend into our little chalices and to obligingly place himself on our lips. We make this confession in all humility, and in confusion: such a religion was the peak of ridiculousness, idiocy and impertinence. Never, one has to admit, never has sacerdotal empyrism been taken to such a reversal of natural ideas.[31] In a word, this worship diminished God without enhancing humanity. To expiate such a monstrous scandal, we agree to break these false links with our own hands, this magical chain which connected earth to heaven. Let every being stay in its place: God in the empyrean, humanity on earth! Henceforth we will never meddle in his affairs if he won't involve himself in ours. We have nothing to sort out with him, any more than with the fixed stars. Virtues belong and suffice to those who practise them. So, for the world's peace of mind, let there be no question of God; let's speak no more of it.

---

30   curé Meslier: A curé is a parish priest. Jean Meslier's (1664–1729) posthumously discovered atheistic "Testament" influenced Maréchal as well as earlier writers such as Voltaire and Diderot. In 1790, Maréchal published his "Catéchisme du curé Meslier", an anti-religious parody of Catholic catechism.

31   SM's note: The overturning of natural ideas, which has been produced by religions, is at least as significant as the overturning of different parts of the earth occasioned by volcanic eruptions. [By "empyrisme", Maréchal means ideas associated with the classical idea of the empyrean, or that part of the sky inhabited by the gods.—Trans.].

People in government, for their part, are beginning to notice that it's completely useless for them to bring in the Highest to affairs down here. It would be insulting the highest magistrats of an empire to suspect that they require priests in order to govern with wisdom or to watch out for materialists and miscreants. This pusillanimity belonged to an outdated politics whose emptiness and inadequacy is felt today. A government strong enough to be just, similar to the supreme ruler of worlds, remains neutral and indifferent to all religious opinions: it knows neither priests nor atheists; it sees only human beings born free and endowed with reason.

We therefore, priests of all religions, who have imprudently propagated so many errors fatal to public and individual tranquillity, we are firmly resolved to remedy all the evil we have been able to do; we renounce our functions and our books. We return with pleasure and docility to civil status, there to fulfill honest and useful professions.

"We also promise, on our conscience, never to utter any of those sacramental words, the basis of all religious sects, inexhaustible sources of animosities and crimes. Committing to recognize only two classes of people—good and wicked—we will do our best to merit as soon as possible a place among the good".

What a wonderful day that sees this solemn and simultaneous declaration by ministers of all religions! This would really be peace, true peace, universal and lasting peace; the perpetual peace of the good Abbé de Saint-Pierre,[32] which is not only the dream of a good man; perhaps it is connected only to this single measure.

"But" (you will doubtless object) "wouldn't such an extreme measure be a bit inopportune or premature? Let's wait a bit; let's not rush anything".

Ministers of all religions! We understand you. In your hands, religion is a Pandora's box at the bottom of which you always see hope; but know that, sooner or later, this salutary revolution must have its full and complete effect. Every day brings it closer. Without looking back, hasten its fulfillment. Support the efforts of our day. Help us to make a clean break with every religious system. Instead of replastering the old idol, which served for a moment as a rallying point for our first ancestors, let it fall of its own weight. Don't you perceive that it's worm-eaten? Don't you see that its bases are clay and sand? Help us to strip your books of this divine symbol, the deceptive varnish that impresses simple folk. Have the merit to collaborate in this great work. You must have observed how many religious opinions have lost their influence along with their celebrity; they will soon end by being completely ignored. The labors of

---

32 Abbé Charles Castel (1658–1743) proposed a universal peace project.

reason will necessarily help it win out over the divine service, since its foundation and support is the eternal rights and daily needs of humanity.

Know, moreover, that we are not much in the mood to leave in your hands and at your disposition much longer the ideal power to which you have given the most pompous names: this power grows weaker every day.

Take away your scaffolds; the edifice is built.

You have certainly felt that divine worship is only an hors d'oeuvre: in order to render yourselves necessary, you affect to preach a religious morality; but know further that:

"Morality ends where religion begins". S.

Don't touch on morality and education if your holy scriptures are going to serve as elementary and classic books. Sorrow to the people whose primary instruction is entrusted to priests! Sorrow to a nation whose priests take over the duty of fathers! Sorrow to the fathers who need the help of a priest to inspire virtue in their children! Sorrow to a city whose priests can be legislators!

People make books. The Bible was published by priests who, for sure, were no angels; but in their turn, do not books also make people? This question is not difficult to resolve when one has read the Bible and the Gospel, and when one has observed the Jewish nation and the Christian peoples.

Ministers of religion! It is true that people still frequent your solemnities, but without believing in them; religion is no more than political business; and you are tolerated only to be used against others who are feared more than you. For several years, people who still attend divine services disdain your preaching; single women and old men sit there to take their siesta. Less than ever do serious sinners come to your judgment courts and to your holy altars. Religion is not being passed on; the scepter, falling out of your hands, becomes a spindle and things are no worse for that.

Since the government, keeping an absolute silence about God, gives no example of any religion, is it less obeyed when it commands only in the name of law? Does it need you, ministers of religion, to sanction its public acts?

Since the French armies speak no more of God, either for good or for ill, has the French soldier become less courageous, less patient, less devoted to discipline? Ministers of religion! does he need you to sing the mass before a battle in order to bring home a victory?

So stop regarding yourselves as necessary and important citizens. It's a huge step toward human perfection to have come to think that we can do without priests and even without their God; that not everything is in the Bible or in the Gospel. Our poets aren't worth the prophets; but our books of mathematics and physics have seriously damaged holy literature. For us, the marvels of nature have replaced miracles. Ministers of every religion! the scientists will kill you off, or at least will cut off your means of survival. Instead of vegetating in your chairs or running the risk of dying of hunger at the holy altar of your Lord, believe us; abandon a trade which can neither feed nor honor its master. Once more we say to you: take up the love of labor; embrace a useful and honest profession; stop being priests; refashion yourselves as men, and we will see in you nothing other than our fellow beings and our brothers.

Post-script

Ministers of all religions! In reading this *Epistle*, you will no doubt exclaim: "Haven't we suffered enough in our goods, our opinions, our persons? Must we still see ourselves the butt of reproach, recrimination, sarcasm? What can anyone fear from us now? We hardly have a refuge to house our God and place our altars. How can anyone have the heart to attack people whom it would be better to pity?"

Ministers! to lie every day to one's conscience, fool the people, live only by charlatanism—all this is, to be sure, a disagreeable and painful existence; but who forces you to it? Who obliges you, who condemns you to the profession you practise? Why want to reknit threads[33] woven by fakery, but worn out by time? Who gave you the job, who ordered you to preach Gospel rather than morality? Show us the authority for your mission. Lastly, why do you remain priests? And, since you persist in this occupation, allow the spectators to whistle, jeer, despise and even to brand men who prostitute themselves to serve a sacred or profane mountebank's bench. You have no right to pity yourselves for the treatment you've endured; indeed, to use a turn of phrase common in your books: those who sow a lie must reap dishonor—that is your salary, *cuique suum*.[34]

But (you'll say once again), don't we have to live?

Why would that be necessary? we might reply, following a former statesman (d'Argenson to the abbé Desfontaines).[35] We'll be pleased to offer you the

---

33   SM's note: *Religio à religando.* [The word "religion" comes from the Latin word for binding or tying.—Trans.].

34   *cuique suum:* to each his own, or, more broadly, everyone gets what's coming to him.

35   D'Argenson, Desfontaines. Pierre Desfontaines, a Jesuit scholar, critic and translator, carried on a lengthy quarrel with Voltaire, a friend of the noble-born d'Argenson brothers, both of them statesmen. When the abbé justified one of his tracts with the necessity to

example of one of your own who, in Paris, from *porte-Dieu* became *porteur d'eau*.[36]

Addendum

We read in antiquarian books: "There were some Greek cities, such as Argos, where women exercised priestly functions". In the second century of the Church, women were not forbidden either priesthood or episcopacy.

Ministers of every religion! believe us and turn over your powers to the hands of women; they know enough about them to exercise them as well as you do: moody and hypocritical, credulous and fearing nothing, enamored of marvels and holidays, their vocation is not at all uncertain. We'll all gain from this: besides, if religion were banished from the world, it would shelter in women's heads.[37] The Church has had deaconesses, abbesses, canonesses; why not priestesses! At least they would be of better faith than you: more indulgent, they would make more lovable the gentle morality that they would preach to us. Pass the censer over to them; it suits their hands much better than yours: good manners will be better observed. You groan to see your temples abandoned and deserted: let the divine office be celebrated there by young virgins! For the greater glory of the faith, leave the sanctuary and have yourselves replaced by women; all men will be at the foot of the altars and confessionals when there are only women confessors and priestesses.

---

make a living (or, in French, to live), the younger brother, count Marc-Pierre (1696–1764), gave more or less the quoted reply.

36   *porte-Dieu, porteur d'eau*: an aural pun; literally, the instrument of God became a water-carrier (the priest became a useful worker).

37   SM's note: Ancient mythographers used the elephant as a religious symbol. Modern iconographers are more correct in their imaginations; they represent religion in the image of a veiled woman, or with her eyes blindfolded, carrying under her left arm the Old and New Testament, and on the index finger of her right hand, a fine white dove. A smoking censer is at her feet. She stands on a foundation stone (or a stumbling block).

Nature is a Book Superior to the Bible. S.M.

PART 1

Jewish Scripture

∴

The Old Testament

I   Genesis: First Book of the Pentateuch of Moses

This first book of the Bible is also its finest. We recognize in it the traces of the highest antiquity. Sublimity and simplicity are its principle qualities, though too often altered by crude minor details. The famous *fiat lux* [let there be light!] would give the Bible pre-eminence above all other known books sacred and profane, if Brahmah's *Shastah*[1] did not exist. The Englishman Holwell[2] has brought us fragments of it that equal Genesis; its account of creation is equally sublime and better motivated. One may judge by this single passage: "These beings (angels) did not yet exist. The eternal being desired it, and they existed".[3]

The juxtaposition of these two lines of Genesis produces the finest effect: *Uterque nudus Adam et uxor ejus, et non erubescebant;* [Adam and his wife were both naked and did not blush] and in the following chapter: *Timui, eo quod nudus essem,* [I was afraid, because I was naked] says the guilty Adam. In Chapter IV, what God says to Cain is truly divine: *Vox sanguinis fratris tui clamat ad me de terra.* [The voice of your brother's blood cries to me from the earth.] The story of the flood[4] has not the same dignity.

The embarrassment of Noah's two sons on seeing their father naked, drunk, and asleep, is cleverly ingenious; but the details about Sodom, like those about the cohabitation of Lot and his daughters, contrast all too well with preceding chapters. The sacrifice of Abraham is of great beauty. The *ecce ignis et ligna, ubi est victima?* [Here, says Isaac, are fire and wood; where is the victim for the sacrifice?], in the mouth of the young Isaac, pierces the soul.

The marriage of Isaac and Rebecca is a charming idyll. I don't much care for Jacob's deception of his father and brother, although there is a pleasing good

---

1 Brahmah is one of the three major Hindu gods, or the creative spirit; shastra (not shasta/h) is a verse or prose Sanskrit treatise on Hindu ethics, morality, obligations, etc.
2 John Z. Holwell (1711–98), an amateur scholar and a colonial administrator in India, published a three-volume work on the history and Hindu religion of India.
3 SM's note: God pronounced the word KOUN, *let it be done!* and the human race was created... Gel Aleddin. Moses recounted the creation of light less, apparently, because he imagined it than because he learned or copied it from ancient works. *Esprit des Religions*, by N.B. in-8, page 42, first part. [This is a 1792 work by the radical writer and editor Nicolas de Bonneville (1760–1828), an associate of Maréchal. Gelaleddin: name or title of several medieval Middle Eastern scholars and sultans.—Trans.].
4 SM's note: Problem to resolve: why did God need forty days to drown the world he had created in six days? In 1643, one Hugues de Picou published a tragedy on the deluge and dedicated it to Cardinal Mazarin.

humor to it. Jacob's ladder is impressive, but this patriarch wrestling with an angel does not present as good an image. The adventures of Joseph[5] are perfect and too justly famous to repeat their beauties here; Chapter XXXVIII, which is added on, spoils them.

The Latin translation *vulgatae editionis*[6] is not in very elegant prose; but perhaps it is all the more exact and loses less of the original. The French translation of Lemaistre de Sacy, which we are using, is quite respectable, but it leaves much to be desired. It is the pale copy of a vigorous painting.

The book of the Gospel does the Bible wrong; it is much more widely read. But this is a mistake. The New Testament is not worth the Old in every respect. Allow me a reflection.

The Bible is not the book or code for all mankind; the story of earthly Paradise and the consequences of original sin is not the allegorical history of the entire human race; it concerns only a small corner of the earth. Moses, leader of a lazy tribe, in a country too infertile to inspire a taste for labor in this tribe, or to make it patiently endure the trouble of working, thought he had to condemn the Hebrews to labor on behalf of God himself. This is why the creator says to Adam: *You will eat your bread in the sweat of your brow;* and to Eve: *You will give birth in pain.* But this judgment coming from a divine mouth, is not without appeal for everyone. If the Hebrews submitted to its execution in all its rigor and extent, various other nations were not condemned to it. For example, South Sea islanders live without paying so much for their existence. Nature left them almost nothing else to do than to enjoy themselves, and I like to think that others would have nothing to envy them for, if we understood one another better.

II   Exodus

This second book of the Bible, less interesting than the first, is more curious. Moses appears on the scene; he is the hero of the Old Testament. Everything is done and said by him. Disdaining to take on a specific personality, he offers whichever one he wants to those around him. The touching circumstances of

---

5 SM's note: The poem about Joseph, by Bitaubé, is only an amplification that one ought not to permit oneself; the ancient literary monuments are sacred, not to be touched. I would say as much about the *Death of Abel*, by Gessner. [The texts are Paul J. Bitaubé's 1767 poem on Joseph in nine cantos, and Solomon Gessner's 1760 poem on Abel in five cantos.—Trans.].

6 *vulgatae:* the Vulgate translation by St. Jerome (about 347–420), so called because it translated the various Biblical books from Hebrew, Aramaic, Greek or earlier Latin into contemporary Latin, the common language of the Roman Empire; from *vulgus*, the people.

his birth already dispose us in his favor; and, from Chapter III onward, an experienced mind foresees everything he is capable of doing afterward; I have in mind the *burning bush*.⁷ Only a man of genius could, if not imagine, then at least describe the fine scene where God appears and says: "I am the one who is. Here is what you will say to the children of Israel: He who is has sent me to you". *Sum qui sum. Dices filiis Israël: Qui est misit me ad vos.* It will be observed that the *sum qui sum*⁸ is no newer than the *fiat lux*. Moses drew all that from his reading.

The plagues of Egypt are not equally sublime, far from it; only necessity and foresight could determine him to advise *Aegypti spoliationem*:⁹ nonetheless I would rather believe it to honor him. The song of thanks after the passage through the Red Sea is a superb lyric piece. The detail of hands raised skyward, which procure the victory of the Jews over the Amalekhites, has something in it original and grand.

Moses did not, perhaps, show his usual sagacity in having his chapters about Mount Sinai immediately preceded by Chapter XVIII, where he admits having received very good advice from his father-in-law, Jethro, who suggests that he establish a religion, etc. Did not Moses let a sort of contradiction slip by him, in having himself ordered by God to do what his father-in-law had already told him? This fault doubtless comes from those who edited his history. Among all the little details in which God has the goodness to descend on behalf of his people, there are some extremely useful and some very beautiful; others are trivial and quite severe, to say no more. The legislator is sometimes sublime; sometimes he is obliged to distance himself from a people *durae cervicis* [a hard-headed people].¹⁰

Gospel is not the only book that has recommended that people should do good, even to one's enemies, and to pray for them. Exodus offers a fine example:

---

7   SM's note: This *burning bush* was perhaps only the *aurora borealis*. A man such as Moses knew how to derive a benefit from everything; and he played with a people who knew nothing.

8   SM's note: The Egyptians' Isis had temples with this inscription. Plato calls God *what is, what exists*, giving us to understand that only God truly *exists* and merits the name of supreme *being*. The Greek expression *To on* resembles that of the Bible, *ego sum qui sum*. In the Alcoran this definition is found, which is as good as the *sum qui sum*: God is God. The Jews designated *God* by saying *He who is*. The Turks expressed themselves with even more sublimity; a single word sufficed for them to define God; they said, *He*, HOUA, (*ille*). The author of *The Spirit of Religions* filled paragraph 9 of the first part, entitled *God*, with three lines of dots. All these writers have given no proof of this good spirit. [*Sum qui sum* is literally, "I am who I am".—Trans.].

9   The destruction of the Egyptians.

10 But literally: "stiff-necked", i.e., refusing to bow the head.

[If you encounter your enemy's cow or ass that has wandered away, you shall lead it back to him.] *Si occurretis bovi inimici tui, aut asino erranti, reduc ad eum,* etc. Further on there are superb passages, this one among others: [You shall do no wrong to the widow or the orphan. If you offend them in something, they will cry out to me, and I will listen to their cries; and my anger will burst out against you, I will make you die by the sword, and your wives will become widows and your children orphans. 22, 23, 24. XXII.] *Viduae et pupillo non nocebitis; si laeseritis eos, ego audiam clamorem eorum, percutiam vos, et erunt uxores vestrae viduae, et filii vestri pupilli.* What a fine book the Bible would be, if everything in it were like that! Moses had taught his masters the Egyptians to know the human heart; he knew that it's necessary to dilute the good to make people adopt it; that you have to speak first to their senses in order to arrive at their understanding; in a word, to fool them in order to educate them. Could there be a politics in which one could speak the whole truth, without passing it through the mouth of a lie? Until when will it be necessary to frighten people with thunder, astonish them with columns of fire and with clouds, forbid them upon pain of death to approach a mountain[11] so that they might with more docility receive the law-code that a man of genius would bring back after having meditated there for forty days?

Nonetheless the Decalogue, Chapter XX, which for so many centuries people have tried to represent as the distillation of all morality, has none of the sublimity that ought to characterize commandments spoken by the mouth and written by the finger of God himself. Imperfect as was the *Law of the Twelve Tables*[12] it was superior to the Decalogue, which is far from embracing the principal duties of man and society; it does no honor at all to the genius of Moses, which here remains unequal to its subject. The Decalogue does not deserve to be rhymed as flat-footedly as it often is in Catholic catechisms; nonetheless those are the first lessons to be impressed upon the tender brain of children. One can only judge their education by what forms its base! Fortunately, it is only custom and habitual usage that give a sort of existence to this barbaric monument.

---

11 SM's note: People addressed their first sacrifices and their prayers to the gods on mountain tops. Our ancestors had the simplicity to believe that in standing closer to the sky and in shouting loud cries, they approached closer to God and made themselves better understood. They judged their divinities according to themselves: often they had only too many reasons to suspect that their gods were deaf. Epicurus preferred to suppose them careless. [Epicurus (341–270 BCE): Greek philosopher who emphasized freedom of will.—Trans.].
12 Twelve Tables: traditional basis of Roman law, going back to the fifth century BCE.

About the claimed shining horns[13] of the Hebrew lawgiver, XXXIV: 30 allows us to make a comparison: Like Moses, *Hoang-tan-che*, a very ancient king of China, had (says an old chronicle from that country) a very large head, and two rays of light that rendered it resplendent.... He was terrible when provoked, adds the same chronicle. See the *Chinese Memories*,[14] volume XIII, in-4.

III Leviticus

This book is a sequel to the preceding one, but its principle object is the cult and condition of priests or Levites:[15] the legislator brings particular attention to this, and it is especially here that we observe his plan. Religion seems to be the unique foundation on which he raises his political edifice. It is always God who speaks through the mouth of Moses. [The Lord called Moses and said to him: You will speak to the children of Israel and you will say. 1 and 2.1.] *Locutus est Dominus ad Moysem dicens: Loquere filiis Israël*, etc. This phrase has become something like a consecrated formula.[16] Moses further imagined a refrain which gives much weight to his laws: [Keep my sabbath days. I am the Lord.] *Sabbata mea custodite. EGO DOMINUS.* Sometimes he adds: *Deus vester, qui eduxi vos de terra A Egypti.* [I am the Lord your God, who rescued you from the land of Egypt.] It makes good sense to remind the Jews of such a circumstance.

Chapter XIX is among the finest, and no doubt Jesus Christ knew it: [Love your friend as yourself.] *Dilige amicum tuum, sicut te ipsum.* He only extended this passage by changing one word to *proximum* [your neighbor]. It appears, too, that Moses knew whom he was dealing with, and it isn't accidental that he multiplies and recommends to the limit the minutest practises[17] of religion, doubtless to multiply the connections to the people he was preparing for the docility of slavery. In Chapter X, he releases a show of force, which he thought necessary to constrain the multitude and to command veneration toward

---

13 horns: The notion that Moses had horns is based on St. Jerome's mistranslation of the Hebrew phrase for "shining rays" (of his face) as "shining horns"; this error was perpetuated in many representations of Moses in medieval and Renaissance art.
14 There are several eighteenth-century works with this or a similar title, by French missionaries, explorers, colonial administrators, etc.
15 priests, Levites: Priests were *kohanim*; Levites were keepers of the shrine.
16 SM's note: This was also the formula of the priestesses of Delphi; their oracles always began with these words: *This is what Jupiter says!*
17 SM's note: As Gregory the Great said, visual scenes are the books of the ignorant. This is why, one might add, the Roman Church, in the eyes of its faithful, is always theatrical.

priests. There are also many precepts on health and propriety, which don't give a very exalted idea of the people to whom one is obliged to recommend such things. Chapter XVIII contains other details which also constitute no praise of Israelite behavior. What corruption!

We complete this section with a word about the *bouc émissaire*.[18] XVI. This ritual has, from one point of view, something sublime to it. We seem to hear the Hebrews' legislator telling them symbolically: "Friends! all of you have committed wrongs against one another; get rid of them on the head of this goat, and forget them: let him go shroud them in the desert sand!" This Feast of the Pardon honors the Hebrew nation and would deserve to be nationalized by other peoples. The Jews had many holidays, most of them religious. They dressed up for the shearing of their herds and for harvests. They had a feast of sheaves.

But in reality, the Jews had only one true festival, which was much more political than sacred; that is to celebrate their deliverance from the Egyptian yoke. In no nation, no matter what may be said, has more importance been placed on public liberty than with the Jews.

IV Numbers

One notices that by Chapter XVI of this book, we are no longer in the golden age of the Bible, the happy centuries of the patriarchs: here are murderous attacks, for no good reason, ordered by God.

The Book of Numbers is one of the least interesting of the collection. We find in it many enumerations, many rules concerning priests. It's true that all these details entered Moses's plans, for he wanted to submit the Jewish people to a strict theocracy. [19] He believed, to this end, that there could never be too many sacred places, so necessary to subjugate and train to the yoke a turbulent and undisciplined nation. However, he had to understand the temperament of those whom he addressed, to propose most of his laws, and above all the one called *lex zelotypiae*,[20] Chap. V. But the greatest of the miracles that sanctioned his ordinances, is that Israel was sufficiently credulous to obey

---

18 *bouc émissaire*: literally, (male) goat that has been sent away. The community would symbolically lay its sins on the head of this goat and send it out into the desert where it, and the sins it carried, would die; hence our term "scapegoat".

19 SM's note. Government whose head is God; a religious monarchy. Before the Athenians—who, in order to no longer have a king, chose no other monarch than Jupiter—the Jews wanted to depend only on God. Ambitious people, men of genius, deceived them, as everywhere else.

20 The law on jealousy, Num. 5: 29–31.

them. Occasionally people grumbled when hunger or boredom pressed, but a magic trick delivered Moses from all these set-backs: Chaps. XII and XVII. XVIII could not be indifferent to the clergy, those great tax-collectors; it is there and in many other passages on the same subject, that priests see the finger of God and divine right. The minor reproach which is made to Moses by God, Chap. XX, is quite clever. As for the bronze serpent of the next chapter, I don't see in it anywhere near the same finesse.

The tale of Balaam and his ass is amusing: peoples characterize themselves in their mythology.[21] One of the finest moments in the Bible is found in the prediction of this same Balaam; some of his expressions are courageous and reveal an inspired man: [when he lies down he sleeps like a lion and like a lioness which no one dares awaken.] *Accubans, dormivit ut leo, et quasi leaena, quam suscitare nullus audebit.* In any other mouth than that of a God, these words of Chapter XXXI would appear atrocious and worthy of a cannibal: *Cunctos interficite, quidquid est generis masculini etiam in parvulis; et mulieres quae noverunt viros in coïtu jugulate: puellas autem et omnes feminas virgines reservate vobis.* [Destroy all the males, including even children, and kill women whom men have touched; but reserve for yourselves all the young girls and all the others who are virgins.][22] The same holds for expressions that conclude Chapter XXXIII: [If you don't want to kill all the inhabitants of the country... I will visit on yourselves all the evil that I had resolved to do them. 55.]

What a horrible book the Bible is!

The intervention of divinity has wonderfully served tyrants. Good souls extend their necks to the sword or their hands to chains, saying: *God wishes it so.* They see in a despot's brutality only the chastisement of a father toward his children. A tyrant is respected by his victims as a sacred instrument that GOD[23] uses. This pious resignation has been carefully sustained by priests, almost always the provocateurs of despotism when they can't be its principal agents. That is why Moses instituted theocracy and priesthood.

---

21 SM's note. The Jews have been reproached for their idolatry of an ass's head. If apes made a God for themselves, it would be an ape. [A mistake about Judaism by a few obscure Greco-Roman authors. Maréchal almost certainly knows it was wrong, but it permits him to make a nasty ironic dig at the Jews.—Trans.].

22 The Latin is more vivid than Sacy's translation allows; it specifies the manner of killing the women (cutting their throats) and that this is for women who have had sexual relations (*coitus*) with men.

23 SM's note. The ferocious Attila styled himself *the scourge of God, the rod, the hammer of the Lord.*

V   Deuteronomy

This book could also be called the Jewish code, or the political testament of Moses. In effect, here this great character reviews for his people all that he has done for them. Firmness and nobility characterize his style. At times, though, one notices some harshness; but, even through his threats and absolute orders, a few traces of feeling emerge; for example, this passage, Chap. 1.31: *Et in solitudine (ipse vidisti) portavit te Dominus Deus tuus, ut solet homo gestare parvulum suum filium, in oni via per quam abulasti*. [And you have seen for yourselves, in this desert, that the Lord your God carried you along the road you have traveled, like a man who carries his little boy in his arms.] Moses doesn't forget to remind the Jews of their captivity and their leaving Egypt, the best ornament in his crown, as well as the promised land where he cannot enter.

It also appears that his people were fearful and that they had to be led more by threats than by fine promises; for Moses paints God only in irascible colors: [Because the Lord your God is a devouring fire, and a jealous God. IV. 24.] *Dominus Deus tuus ignus consumens est, Deus aemulator*. [God will make the iniquity of fathers fall upon the head of their children, unto the third and fourth generation.] *Reddens iniquitatem patrum super filios in tertiam et quartam generationem*. Doubtless the theologians find in this verse an irrefragable argument in favor of original sin, by which all the children of Adam are responsible for what their father did.

Nihil addens amplius: [Without adding anything further. 22.V. You will add nothing to nor remove anything from the words I speak to you. 2. IV.] This repeated reference to the Decalogue has something imposing to it, suitable to earning the confidence of a people whom it was necessary to treat with some harshness in order to make laws. The end of Chapter VI is satisfying: *Cumque interrogaverit te filius tuus cras dicense, etc.... Dices ei: Servi eramus....* Verses 20 and 21. [When your children later ask you: What do these commandments mean?...You will say to them: We were Pharaoh's slaves.]

Amidst a heap of repetitions and precepts about apparently puerile ceremonies, but which aim to unite twelve tribes under the same banner, one is pleased to encounter such laws as these: *Et vos amate peregrinos, quia et ipsi fuistis advenae in terra AEgypti*. Chap. x. [Befriend the traveler because you yourselves were strangers in Egypt. 19.[24]]

Moses was jealous of his work and apparently believed it to be the highest point of perfection; or rather, as a wise legislator, he foresaw and wanted to

---

24   SM's note. This law seems to be directed against the Egyptians, an inhospitable nation because of their prudence, as are the Chinese, from time immemorial.

avoid any innovation, often repeating: [Honor the Lord only as I have ordered you to, without adding or taking away anything. 32.] *Quod praecipio tibi, hoc tantum facito Domino; nec addas quidquam, nec minuas.* XII.

In the following Chapter, XIV, have not the laws of humanity and of nature been constrained only to cement social peace, when the laws order the people to sacrifice brother or wife, and to throw the first stone at them, if they propose a new religion or foreign gods? In this case, the remedy is worse than the disease. There is much reason and less fanaticism, in Chapter XVII. Chapter XX is remarkable because of a passage of the finest eloquence: *Quis est homo,* etc... *vadat*...etc.[25] 6 and 7.

There are many details in the following chapters, among others those in Chapter XXII: *De signis virginitatis* [on the signs of virginity]. These claimed faults were perhaps valid at the time, or were necessary among a people who had to be spoon-fed (if we may be permitted this expression!) and told everything, even the superfluous, to make them grasp the essentials. Chapter XXIV is more satisfying and contains a finer morality. The *maledictus* and the *amen* of Chap. XXVII seem to me of a sublime simplicity. There is also much energy and poetry in the benedictions and maledictions of the long chapter that follows. In XXIX, the canticle is very beautiful and completely imagistic. What could be more poetic and bold than this expression, among others: *Inebriabo sagittas meas sanguine, et gladius meus devorabit carne!* [I will make my arrows drunk with blood, and my sword will devour flesh. 42]

Chap. XXXII. Moses could hardly end his career more gloriously. It's unfortunate that he did not have a less abased people to deal with, one with whom he could have deployed the full extent of his genius. Through what he did for the Jews, we sense what he would be capable of doing for a more uplifted nation. His morals and his politics, his code and his religion, would not have been tainted by so many ridiculous or atrocious precepts, such as were necessary under the circumstances; at least it is certain that only a great man could conceive the plan that he conceived and executed, and whose traces remain even today; one couldn't have an ordinary mind and say:

> My nation crawls and stagnates under the yoke; let us pull it up from slavery, make it a free people, raise it in its own eyes that it may believe itself God's chosen people, heaven's eldest son. In following my laws let my nation be seen to obey only laws written with God's finger; let it believe itself the only privileged nation on earth, the only one for whom all the others were made and to whom the others must give in; this is the only

---

25 Is there anyone who ... Let him go....

way to save my nation again from servitude. Let it have no other sovereign than God himself; this is how I will succeed in giving it greatness and a position that will make its neighbors respect it; and that my work, traversing the long centuries unmixed and undegraded, may attest to distant posterity all the resources of my genius and all the profundity of my views.

This was a fine project, we must agree, and Moses had everything needed for its accomplishment; but Moses chose his world badly. It isn't the legislator who failed his people, but the people who were incapable of responding to its legislator's creative voice. One might find some analogy between Czar Peter I and Moses.

As for the golden calf, which we have said nothing about, see *Free Thoughts about Priests* (Rome, year VI, page 84).[26] "O Richardson! (exclaimed Diderot at the front of an edition of *Clarissa*) if necessity constrains me, I will sell my books, but you will stay with me, with Moses and Homer, and I will read all of you by turns".[27]

Hobbes and Spinoza deny Moses the glory of having written the Pentateuch. Deuteronomy was lost for a long time. It was found buried and nearly erased, says Saint Chrysostom.[28] Origen speaks of a lost book of *The Assumption of Moses*.[29] As for the *Book of Enoch*,[30] there is still much to discover, and this is too bad. This patriarch seriously treated the carnal cohabitation of heaven's angels with daughters of earth. What a shame as well that we lack the *Apocalypse of Adam*! But let us console ourselves that perhaps it never existed.[31]

---

26   *Pensées Libres sur les Prêtres* (1798) by Maréchal. His date uses that of the declaration of the Republic in 1792 as Year 1. The book was not really published in Rome: many books of the period gave false places of publication, whether for protection or provocation.
27   Samuel Richardson (1689–1761), English novelist; Denis Diderot (1713–84), French rationalist philosopher, novelist, playwright and editor of the great mid-century intellectual project the *Encyclopédie*.
28   Chrysostom (c. 347–407), Greek preacher and scholar.
29   Origen (c. 185-c.254), ascetic theologian. The "Assumption of Moses" was a sixth century Jewish text, a version of which was discovered and published later in the nineteenth century. "Assumption" means the taking of someone up into heaven; one hears more typically of the assumption of the Virgin Mary.
30   Enoch is mentioned in Genesis (5:18–24) as one of the long-lived patriarchs who walked with God. Later Jewish literature, from about 200 BCE to about 100 CE, produced imaginative and religious works voiced by him, some of which exist in several ancient languages.
31   There is in fact an "Apocalypse of Adam" from the first or second century CE, discovered with the rest of the Nag Hammadi codices in 1945.

There are in the Pentateuch, as in the rest of the Bible, some very false opinions; for example, that the moon is a luminary equal to the sun. Or that the sun stopped. Or that the heavens are solid, etc. Theologians do us the grace of agreeing, but at the same time they have their response at the ready. They borrow from Saint Augustine: "The spirit of God, which spoke through the sacred authors, did not want to instruct human beings in these things, because they were useless to human salvation". (*Exposition on Genesis* l. 11.)[32] If the bishop of Hippo had been a braggart, he would have responded no differently.

The Pentateuch of Moses is scattered with a profuse number of miracles, such as the passage through the Red Sea, the column of fire in the desert, etc. We invite the French Institute in Cairo[33] to take the trouble to verify them. A struggle between scholars and theologians can only be very profitable, whichever side wins.

VI   Joshua, or Jesus the Liberator

Joshua succeeded Moses, that is, the warrior succeeded the legislator;[34] and, in effect, he became the conqueror of thirty-one kings and the possessor of that famous promised land. It is irritating to see that this great occasion had as its first cause a woman of ill repute, who betrayed her compatriots on behalf of foreigners. The miracle of crossing the Jordan with dry feet isn't much more striking; it is only a second representation, a diminished one, of the celebrated crossing of the Red Sea.

The miracle of the sun and the moon stopped in the middle of their courses, and the one about the destruction of the walls[35] of Jericho, are newer, more original, but still do no honor to a general who requires miracles and prostitutes to help him conquer. His cruelty and the top-to-bottom demolition of cities, when he takes them, also is no praise to his prudence or humaneness.

---

32   Augustine (354–430), theologian and prolific writer, bishop of Hippo in Algeria.
33   When Napoleon set out in 1798 on his ultimately failed invasion of Egypt and Syria, he brought over 160 scholars in many fields; they founded the French Institute in Cairo which, among other things, discovered the Rosetta Stone and introduced the printing press.
34   SM's note. The early days of Rome show the contrary. There, the legislator followed the warrior: Numa came after Romulus, and that is perhaps the better way.
35   SM's note. Wouldn't this be the inverse of the wonderful tale of the walls of Thebes raised by the sound of Cadmus's lyre? The history of various peoples offers only variants.

He too terminated his role, less noble than the previous one, by a sort of testament, in imitation of Moses; but this testament is not as important as that of his predecessor.

This book is one of the least fine of the Bible. Its style is quite ordinary with nothing striking about it. One is only too aware that the genius of Moses no longer holds the paintbrush.

VII Judges

The annals of the Jewish people, the nation chosen and guided by God himself, rather resemble the calendrical lists and chronicles of other peoples; it is a collection of atrocious acts. The book contains more than one type; it suffices to point to the holy anecdote of Ehud. Here it's not the way liberators of their country behaved among the Greeks, the Romans, and the Swiss. In those cases, only the blood of oppressors flowed; the citizens suffered almost nothing. Liberty did not require a mattress of cadavers to rest on!

Nonetheless, there is a great deal of poetry in the song of Deborah and Barak. [The mountains melted at the sight of the Lord.] *Montes fluxerunt in facie Domini* is quite beautiful. The last strophes are superb in the images they present. Their cruel irony produces a great effect, which leads us to conjecture that there is more than one case of plagiarism in the books of the Bible. The Jews, who were not extremely scrupulous in this matter as in others, made their literature a veritable thievery, and spoiled all they touched: witness their story of Jephtha's sacrifice, which is merely a reminiscence of Iphigeneia.[36]

There are some great characteristics in their Samson, a copy of Hercules; but the author of this book, whatever he might be, wasn't able to benefit from the charming allegory of honey found in the lion's mouth. Chapter XIX offers disgusting details, but with which the Bible is only too familiar. Chapter XXI reminded me of the abduction of the Sabine women.[37]

N.B. In 1665, one M. de Coras dedicated to a queen of France a sacred poem in five cantos, entitled *Samson.* Here is a specimen of the style:

---

36   SM's note. In 1768, Baer, an almoner, dedicated to Ulrica, queen of the Goths and Vandals, a scholarly dissertation demonstrating that it is unlikely that Jephtha sacrificed his daughter. [Iphigeneia, the daughter of Clytemnestra and Achilles, was sacrificed by her father to ensure a fair wind for his navy en route to Troy; see Aeschylus, *Iphigeneia in Aulis.* An almoner is an ecclesiastic or chaplain tasked with the dispersal of alms.—Trans.].

37   An episode from Roman mythical history.

In the chamber where the idolatrous assembly dined,
A wicked theatre is prepared for Samson... Ch. v.

In 1730, in Paris, Italian actors presented with some success, at their theatre in the Burgundy Hotel, a *Samson, in French Verse* by Romagnesi, an actor in the troupe. The author didn't attach his name to this dramatic piece, which is completely forgotten today and worthy of that fate. One would have to be Racine,[38] to get extended applause for Jewish dramas. The visual arts have been more fortunate in reproducing for us this episode in Hebrew mythology.

As for Chapter XIX, J.J. Rousseau attempted to accommodate this chapter to our ways. Nor was one of our modern poets afraid to produce it for the French stage. But *The Levite of Ephraim*,[39] even from the same pen as *La Nouvelle Héloïse* and *Émile*, did not have a brilliant success, even less so on the stage.

VIII Ruth

What a precious monument the Bible would be, if it always offered scenes like the book of Boaz and Ruth! But this pastoral tale must be read with the eyes of a shepherd. One has to strip away all our trivial modern ideas and transport oneself to the happy time when such habits flourished; without this precaution, one would not feel all the merit of the book, and would be only too tempted to make malign allusions.

Is there anything more touching, more candid, than this passage spoken by Ruth: *Quocumque perrexeris, pergam; et ubi morata fueris, et ego pariter morabor; populus tuus, populus meus; et Deus tuus, Deus meus: quae te terra morientem susceperit, in ea moriar, ibique locum accipiam sepulturae....* [Wherever you go, I will go with you, and anywhere you dwell, I will dwell there too: your people will be my people and your God will be my God. The land where you die will see me die, and I will be buried where you will be buried. 1st chap., 16 and 17.]

The most delicate courtesies are observed amid simplicity and innocence, which excuse and justify everything. Theocritus and Gessner[40] have nothing more gentle or amiable. This idyll could serve as a model for the genre, and the

---

38 Jean Racine (1639–99), the most famous tragic playwright of the period, often wrote on Biblical or classical themes.
39 A long poem based on Judges 19–21.
40 Theocritus: Greek pastoral poet, writing about 270 BCE. Salomon Gessner (1730–88): Swiss bucolic painter and poet.

genius of Thomson,[41] in the autumn song of his beautiful poem about the *Seasons*, could not surpass it even while imitating it. Lavinia[42] is less interesting than Ruth.

Favart and the chevalier de Florian[43] attempted a few pleasant paraphrases, one at the theatre, the other at the academy; but they frenchified rather than translated: for the naive grace of the original they substituted in their imitations flashes of wit. There is only one way to express simple and natural things.

N.B. Boaz could have been seventy when he married Ruth; but then people lived a long time and one grew old later than today.

IX The First Book of Kingdoms, or Kings: First Book of Samuel

The hymn of Anne, Chapter II, is fine, like nearly all the Biblical hymns. Chapter VIII is remarkable; there Samuel predicts to the Jews, who have asked him for a king, the consequences of their indiscreet demand: "You want a king, blind people! Very well, learn what a king is! He will rob you of your sons to serve him as beasts of burden, your daughters to destine them for his pleasures. Your king will be a tyrant whose slaves you will be, and even the slaves of his eunuchs". It must be admitted that one occasionally finds in the Bible some valid truth. This portrait of a monarch does not at all disgust the Jews, and the reign of Saul begins to confirm what Samuel has said.[44] This moody prince is reproved by God for having felt mercy for a moment. Samuel makes good his mistake by cutting king Agag into pieces.

Biblical expressions correspond to what is happening; and if the Jews behave like cannibals, they speak like man-eaters, Chap. XV, liv. 1: *Oblatus est ei Agag PINGUISSIMUS et tremens.* [They offered Agag to him, very fat and trembling. 32.] Without the episode of Jonathan's friendship, which is somewhat

---

41 James Thomson (1700–48), Scottish poet.
42 Aeneas's wife, in Virgil's *Aeneid.*
43 Charles Favart (1710–92); J.-P. de Florian (1755–94), poet and author of romances and pastoral novels, including an eclogue entitled "Ruth", which was awarded a prize by the French Academy.
44 SM's note. A modern psalmist went even further than Samuel; he dared to say, in 1784: "7. Learn that people can do without even good kings. 8. And that kings will never do enough good for their fellow men to make them forget that they are all equal. 9. Know that royalty is an evil that people have believed to be necessary". *Psalm* IX, p. 4 of the *Book Escaped from the Flood.* [The *Livre Échappé au Déluge* is by Maréchal himself. A parody of Biblical material, its publication resulted in the loss of Maréchal's job at the prestigious Mazarin Library. (He regained it a few years later thanks to his support of the Revolution.)—Trans.].

comforting, this book would be only a tissue of ferocious or indecent anecdotes. If the story of David and Goliath is somewhat amusing, the little intrigue of the same David with Abigail is not at all edifying.

This book is curious only in its depiction of people's dress and the customs of the time. What customs! Unhappy the people who know the Bible by heart! And that's what Saint Jerome[45] calls "the holy Bible".

x   The Second Book of Kingdoms or Kings: Book 2 of Samuel

In Chapter I, David's sorrow over the crime of Saul and Jonathan is fine and well expressed. At the end of Chapter IV, the writer is careful to justify David in connection with the death of Abner. Would he have given some reason to be suspected of this murder?

It's nearly the same in connection with Isboseth, another son of Saul, Chap. VI. The death of Uzza, for having straightened up the ark of God when it leaned to one side, is a piece of advice for the religiously observant. The end of this chapter is no less strange. There we see poor Michal made sterile for having mocked her husband David because: *Discooperiens se ante ancillas servorum suorum nudatus est, quali unus de scurris.* [What glory the king of Israel has had today in in displaying himself before his subjects' servants, and appearing naked as a fool would do! 20.] It's only in the Bible and in the *Portier des Chartreux*[46] that such details are found.

In the next chapter, God gives David predictions which still haven't come true. He tells him, speaking of the temple that he wants—we don't know why—that Solomon will build it for him rather than David. He tells him: *Stabiliam tronum ejus usque in sempiternum.* [I will affirm your rule forever.] The condition of the Jews, for many centuries, still does not correspond to these fine promises: but that will no doubt happen one day. The long prayer of David, by way of thanks, is merely verbose.

In Chapter IX, where David behaves like a just man in protecting the rest of Saul's family, a certain Mephibosheth, son of Jonathan, responds to these moral acts with expressions which well depict the innate spirit of servitude among Orientals: *Quis ego sum servus tuus, quoniam respexisti super canem mortuum similem mei?* [Who am I, your servant, to have deserved that you look at a dead dog such as I am?]

---

45   Saint Jerome (c. 347–420), scriptural scholar and translator of various books of the Bible from Greek, Hebrew or Aramaic into the current Latin of his day.

46   An anonymous obscene work (1741).

And so Samuel's prediction continues to be fulfilled. While the brave Joab combats enemies in the name of the prince, the prince gives himself over to criminal pleasures, and, in bed with Bathsheba, has her honest husband, the faithful Uri, killed. There are the kings whom the people asked for![47] All the details of this Chapter XI are odd for the history of the period, but revolting: David reveals himself as a cowardly and lecherous tyrant.

It is in Chapter XII that we find the sublime apologue of Nathan[48] to the sinner David: *Duo viri erant...* [There were two men ... etc. 1.] This is one of the best passages in the Bible. Chapter XIII is full of details and atrocious behavior, among which nonetheless one can't help smiling at the naivetés uttered by the beautiful Tamar. The parable of the Tekoite woman in Chap. XIV appears to be a copy of Nathan's and is not as good as the original.

The curse of Shimei against David, in Chapter XVI, is a very good lesson for usurpers and murderers. This chapter confirms the vehement suspicions which the murder of Abner, in Chapter IV, had generated against the legitimacy of the shepherd David's right to the throne of Saul. One might call David the Louis XIV of the Jews, and Louis XIV the French David. There is more than one connection between them. Both loved luxury, women, and conquest. Both were weak and debased at the end of their days and of their reign, etc.

The seven family members of Saul, whom David asked the Gibeonites to crucify and whom he gives them in Chapter XXI, is a rather cruel political portrait, but, in that, quite worthy of this monarch. If he spares Mephiboseth, it's because the latter was lame and couldn't give him any trouble. Chapter XXII is a superb hymn, full of beautiful movements and the highest poesy.

We find in the *Iliad* catalogues and portraits of heroes fairly similar to those of Chapter XXIII; but we don't find there episodes more interesting than that of David, who makes a crime out of drinking water that three warriors have risked their lives to bring him. In Chapter XXIV, gracious God sends David the

---

47 SM's note. We can't resist the temptation to cite this passage from a too little-known book: "Who does the sin must do the penance: princes don't seem to be included in this rule; they often do the sin, and the people the penance". CCXXI. *Pensées Diverses et Proverbes Choisis.* Paris, 1712, with approval and privilege of the king, in-12. [The collection, *Various Thoughts and Selected Proverbs,* is by J.-C. Bruleé de Montpleinchamp. Permissions from the royal censor were required for all legally printed books; the in-12 is the measurement of the book.—Trans.].

48 SM's note. The German drama entitled *Nathan the Wise* shares with the Biblical character only a name and a personality. The narrative of the play is completely different. [The play (1779), by Gottfried Lessing, has a complicated romantic plot involving Christians, Jews and Muslims during the Crusades, and is meant to demonstrate the value of all three Abrahamic religions (although the Christian characters come off worst).—Trans.].

choice among three torments to punish him for wanting to review his troops as a wise and vigilant king should; but the priests have an answer for all that.

XI   Kings: Book III

In the first chapter, the Bible seems to pay tribute to David, a burnt-out, cold king, for having left intact the young Sunamite Abishag, whom the king's complaisant companions had placed in his bed, and next to whom he spent the nights asleep. Nonetheless Nathan the prophet, and Bathsheba, by various little courtly ruses, hinted that David should crown his son Solomon.

David dies, in Chapter II, as he has lived. He advises his son and successor to be a man—*Vir esto*—and, to that end, turns over to him the accomplishment of his vengeance. Solomon acquits himself in this only too well. Without any trial, he first has his competitor killed—his brother—and refuses the first favor that his mother, to whom he owes the throne, asks on behalf of that unfortunate. These are the models that religion offers to royal politics! After this fine beginning, wise Solomon doesn't stop there; and—up to Shimei, to whom he granted life on condition that he must not be judged to have broken the law—everyone will die the victim of a cowardly and illegal vengeance. If this conduct praises his political sense and his head, it doesn't do so for his justice and his heart.

Chapter III is fine and edifying; it is a very moral parable, which to some extent makes up for the first two chapters. Chapter VI. Wise Solomon builds the Lord's temple in seven years, as formerly the creator had built the world in seven days. Chapter VII. Wise Solomon puts thirteen years into constructing his palace. There is unction[49] in the long consecration of the newly built temple.

In Chapter VIII, apparently the new monarch wanted to give the people a change, and make them forget the blood with which he had recently consolidated his throne, by amusing them with the pomp of the new temple. But his nature soon took the upper hand and, faithful to his origin, wise Solomon died among seventy spouses and three hundred concubines, leaving his empire divided between two factions.

There should be read, every morning when a king inclined to tyranny awakens, the beginning of Chapter XII.

---

49   unction: a favorite term of critical approval for Maréchal, indicating smooth rhetoric and emotional appeal.

In the following chapter there is the beautiful apostrophe of the prophet at Jeroboam's altar; but the adventure of the two prophets has no morality. The end of Chapter XVII is touching, despite being completely unrealistic. One could put no more art and skill into a narrative than in Chapter XVIII.

There are great features in what follows. There are also unequivocal promises placed in the mouth of the prophet Elijah coming to sacrifice eight hundred and fifty priests, *zelo zelatus Domini* .[50] And the call of Elisha to follow Elijah is surely the original of Matthew's vocation for Jesus Christ.

Chapter XXI is justly famous; it contains the adventure of Naboth.[51] What a fine role the prophets of that time played, going about under a god's name to reproach crowned heads, right in their palaces, for their faults and crimes! It was a fine role as long as these men of God didn't abuse it! Kings doubtless tired of these importunate admonishers, and the censure was eventually obliged to disguise itself in Momus's[52] rattles, or the mask of fiction, in order to maintain its liberties at court. This is how madmen succeeded the prophets and seers near the throne, and had even more success than they, because they knew how to temporize with self-respect. But this fashion for having fools at court passed like other fashions, and that is when religion reclaimed its ancient rights. Royal preachers, who are only shadows of the prophets, ought to remember their forerunners and justify their position while using it as a passport to reason and virtue. But very few among these sacred orators resemble the missionary Bridoine who, preaching unrehearsed before the great monarch Louis XIV, opened with these words:

> "Sire! After the example of those who have preceded me in this chair, I will make you no compliments, because I have not found any for you in the Gospel". The king had sufficient presence of mind to take in good spirit this sally or this sublime naiveté.

XII   Kings, Book IV

The fear of wolves and bears, which even today we instill into small children—wouldn't it come from the second chapter of this book, where the good Elisha,

---

50   Through zeal for God. The priests, or prophets, serve Baal, Asherah, or other non-Jewish deities.
51   SM's note. Naboth's vine! This would be the subject for a wonderful drama by P. Corneille, Diderot, or Shakespeare!
52   Greek demi-god who personified the spirit of satire.

in the name of the Lord, has two bears devour forty-two children who had called him "baldhead"? What puerilities in the Bible! I laughed at the rainless water of Chap. III.

Chapter IV makes us suspect that the miracles of Elisha could be the originals of those of Jesus. The son of Nahum's widow, the multiplication of bread, etc., all these prodigies of the New Testament: why do they resemble copies of the Old, which Gospel came to invalidate? But all the preceding miracles are nothing in comparison with that of Chapter V. I'm not speaking of the cure of leprous Naaman; I have in mind here only the disinterestedness of Elisha, so noble and so rare in a prophet.

The little marvel of the axe-head that resurfaces amused me quite a bit in Chapter VI but the famine scene horrified me. Chapter IX is odd. Where would we be if it didn't take more to make a king than it did Jehu? The same follows in the next chapter. He was made king with no examination, no ceremony; he does justice without due process of law and commits himself to a vengeance as base as it is disgusting; but there's nothing to say, for this is the express commandment of God and of his prophet Elisha. Chapter XI supplied Racine with the subject of his finest tragedy, *Athalie,* at least for style. Chapter XIII. Elisha dies, but he plays his part to the end. Good God! how far it all is from our ways!

Chapter XVIII. The speech of Sennacherib's envoy to the people of Hezekiah is full of the finest movements of eloquence. Here the style of the Bible is raised again a little, especially in Chapter XIX. Nothing more energetic than the prayer of Hezekiah and the new curses of Sennacherib, and the threats of the Lord.

XIII   Paralipomenon: Book I, Chronicles

The first nine chapters include nothing but a rather dry genealogy since Adam. There would be too much to say and too little to believe if it were necessary to verify this chronological nomenclature. The following chapters, up to XVI, contain nothing more than variants of what has already been said in the books of Kings.

Chapter XVI relates a type of hymn sung before the ark of Torah, a hymn found further along in the psalms of David: it is rather fine, although wordy. Why did Sacy, in his French translation of the Bible, not accurately render *funiculum hereditatis vestrae, tibi dabo terram Canaam?* He is content to translate: [I will give you the land of Canaan as your heritage. 18.] [53] In this hymn,

---

53   Sacy omits "funiculum", or extent of an allotted heritage.

David praises the Lord: *Quia HORRIBILIS super omnes deos.* Sacy softens the word: [He is *without comparison* more fearful than all the gods. 25.]

Chapter XXII has conserved interesting details for us that are not in the books of Kings; among others, the discourse that David addresses to Solomon. This discourse has some connection with the one that Louis XIV gave on his deathbed to his successor, Louis XV, who was still a child.[54] We know how well Solomon and Louis XV benefited from those speeches.

Chapter XXIX, the last, also offers fine words from David. One observes, especially here, that the redactors of the Bible are priests who hoped that their princes would build them superbly rich quarters. In this variant, David's life is more edifying than in the Books of Kings.

XIV Paralipomenon: Chronicles, Book II

This only repeats the third Book of Kings. Solomon's beautiful prayer to God, at the consecration of the temple, Chapter VI, is the same as the one in Chapter VIII in the third Book of Kings except for a few expressions. At the very beginning of this Chapter VI, is a passage that can be taken both literally and figuratively. Solomon cries out: *Dominus pollicitus est ut habitaret in caligine.* Sacy is content to translate: [The Lord had promised that he would live in a storm-cloud.][55] This divine promise was only too well fulfilled; and, in fact, could there be anything more obscure than the dogmas of religion and the church? It is also true to say that God and the priests have won, since the people have been brought to believe and to fear whatever they don't understand and whatever they don't see clearly. I like to reread, in this same Chapter VI, the naive response of the good God to Solomon's invocation; it has a sort of unction, a lovely simplicity, a precious camaraderie.

The following chapters, up to XV, are still only variants of the already cited Book of Kings. In Chapter XV, Asa, king according to God's desire, ousts his mother's sovereignty because she sacrificed to idols, which was forbidden by the prophet Azariah. Our modern queens no longer fear prophets so much. Chapter XVII teaches us that it's nothing modern when cowardly kings pass shameful treaties and punish those with the courage to reprimand them.

---

54   Louis XIV died in 1715. SM's following remark is, of course, sarcastic, since both Solomon and Louis XV were, in SM's view, tyrants.

55   The word that Sacy translated as "storm-cloud" might be rendered as "mist" or even "obscurity".

I can't sufficiently admire those prophets, or seers, who went into the courts to reproach princes for their faults, with a truly philosophical liberty. I can't sufficiently regret that these political missionaries are out of style. But it must be said at the same time that, for one truth-teller there were thousands of lying prophets, as we see in Chapter XVIII.

King Jehosaphat makes himself beloved, in Chapter XIX, through the care he takes to appoint judges for his people, and by the exhortations he himself makes to these judges, Chapter XX. There is a sort of grandeur of spirit in the confidence that Jehosaphat and his people have in their God at the moment of peril.

Chapter XXIV. The *videat Dominus, et requirat* of Zachary, son of Jehoiada, put to death by Joash, is excellent; Sacy extended it into two or three lines of French words: [God sees the treatment you give me and he will avenge my death. 22.]⁵⁶ Chapter XXV. The comparison of the thistle and the cedar is definitely in the Oriental style.

XXVI is famous. It is to this passage of the Bible that clergy send kings who want to meddle in their affairs. This chapter, during the age of ignorance, served as pretext for many of the privileges that the church gave itself, and which it wouldn't obtain in our days. Uzziah, struck with leprosy for having dared to lay hands on the censer, once frightened more than one religious sovereign. In our day, we smiled with pity when Cardinal Bathiani, primate of Hungary, revealed the weakness of his cause by recalling this example to Emperor Joseph II.⁵⁷ Today, church and state are no longer two distinct rival bodies. The censer has been obliged to give way to the scepter or to the fasces,⁵⁸ and we have seen them even astonished to find themselves together in the same hand, as in the earliest times. Alas! when will a good law-code, in which the rights and duties of humanity will be in perfect equilibrium, put an end to all these still-ridiculous and too-often deadly pretensions? When will the earth have as gods and masters only law, that is, written rationality? But rationality will be the last thing that humanity will want to write. How many laws will be made before thinking of that!

This Chronicle, also called "the word of days" is not in agreement with other history books of the Jewish nation. The annals of this people, though considered sacred, are neither more orderly nor better written than others.

---

56 More literally: May the Lord see and requite.
57 In 1781, the Cardinal sent the Emperor a long letter demanding that the Emperor leave matters of clerical organization and administration to the Church.
58 fasces: the bundle of bound rods carried by Roman officials as symbol of state force, whence the modern term "fascist".

XV   Ezra: First Book

This book contains the re-establishment of the temple by Cyrus. Ezra narrates the history in his own name, but always from a Jewish perspective. Despite the lofty idea that he attempts to give of the prophets and of God, he utters a noteworthy vow, Chap. VIII. *Praedicavi* (says he) *jejunium ut peteremus a Domino nostro viam rectam nobis.... Erubui enim petere a rege* (Cyrus) *auxilium... quia dixeramus regi: Munus Dei nostri est super omnes qui quaerunt eum.* [I preached a fast to ask the Lord our God to lead us straight in our path; for I was ashamed to ask the king for an escort of horsemen ... because we had said to the king: God's favorable hand is on all who seek him. 21 and 22.]

The prayer of Ezra, Chapter IX, is rather noble. *Et sedi moerens ... et ego sedebam tristis*[59] ... etc. is fine, and of a truly touching simplicity. It is astonishing that the Jews were never able to become a great people, a people of consequence. It seems one could expect this from a nation who, believing itself the only legitimate children of God, had the courage to repudiate women taken from foreigners. A people that jealous of the purity of its blood, should have done great things. Lycurgus founded only a military school at Sparta; Moses, before him, made of Judea a congregation of slaves.

XVI   Nehemiah: Book II of Ezra

In the first seven chapters, it is Nehemiah himself who speaks with a simplicity full of unction: he praises himself with much nobility and with a kind of candor. There is a fine passage in Chapter V: *Excussi sinum meum et dixi: Sic excutiat Deus omnem virum qui non ... etc. sic excutiatur at vacuus fiat ... etc.* [I shook my clothing and said: May every person who doesn't fulfill what I have said be shaken thus and rejected by God, far from his house! may he be thus shaken and rejected, and reduced to indigence! 13.]

The long prayer of the Levites,[60] Chap. IX, is rather fine. Sacy, translator of the Bible, did not properly render the only somewhat energetic place in it: *Et projecerunt legem tuam post terga sua.* (Word for word: They made of your law a rag, a ....[61]) Sacy's "They rejected your law with contempt" is vague and

---

59   I sat mourning ... I was sitting desolate. IX: 3–4.
60   Levites: assistants to priests at the shrine of Jahweh.
61   SM's supposedly word-for-word translation is far from it, for the line (9:26) says: They threw your law behind them. He apparently interprets this (perhaps not inaccurately) to mean that they (the irreverent Jews) turned Torah into toilet paper. He does not give the second word in full, only "t..c", which could stand for "truc" (thing, trick, device), but this

without poetry. This alliance or contract the Jews make with God in the hands of priests, and that they sign, is worthy of notice. No other people on earth has had such a pact, that I know of; it's a stroke of genius on the part of Moses, who can be regarded as its first inventor. If a contract of this type has produced nothing great, we must infer from that, that all these supernatural[62] means, which people have tried to use effectively to control the human heart, are insufficient, and are not equivalent to good legislation founded on a perfect harmony between our purely temporal rights and our obligations.

Without Ezra, there would have been no faith in Israel; there would be no Bible. This supreme pontiff, true, was inspired by God; that's at least what had to be said in order to inspire the trust of his compatriots and posterity in his *Canon*. This is the title of the collection of books owed to his efforts, which he transcribed from memory; for the originals were misplaced or lost. Also he is called *scriba velox*, which could be rendered by our new word *tachigraph*[63], all the better since apparently Ezra consulted old men and wrote down the traditions they told him about, as rapidly as they left the narrator's mouth.

One could, one ought to entitle all the other books of the Old Testament "Ezra" since we are obliged to this priest for them. This last circumstance smooths out many difficulties. Indeed! the Bible is the work of a priest or edited by one; this is obvious on almost every page.

XVII   Tobias

This book doesn't appear to have been written by the same pen as the preceding ones. Its style is more constrained; there is less crudity and harshness.

The prayer of Sara, daughter of Raguel, Chapter III, is remarkable for the reticence used in speaking of things on which the Bible, everywhere else, discusses with more freedom. The advice that Tobias gives his son, in the next chapter, is admirable: how sensible are these three lines! ... *Panem tuum et vinum super sepulturam justi constitue, et noli ex eo manducare et bibere cum*

---

doesn't seem to be scandalous enough to warrant ellipses. Alter translates: "They ... flung Your teaching behind their back".

62 SM's note: It is completely futile that modern legislators have tried to give more weight to their constitutions by placing at the beginning this formula: "Under the auspices of the Supreme Being". On this topic, see an excellent work by Neigon, member of the Institute of France. [Although the text has Neigon, it's likely that this is a misspelling of (J.-A.) Naigeon (1738–1810), an atheist friend of Maréchal, classicist and author of a text on religion.—Trans.].

63 tachigraph: machine for measuring speed: a speedometer. "Scriba velox": speedy writer.

peccatoribus. [18. Put your bread and wine on the tomb of the just man, and do not eat or drink with sinners.] Sacy did not give the *constitue*, translating it by *put*.[64]

Chapter V is full of the most touching details. There we find all the goodness of the patriarchs. Chapter VI is the same type as III. Chapter VII: Bad luck to whoever doesn't feel all the charm in the naïveté of the narrative in this chapter!

Malicious jokers will doubtless not fail to smile at this passage from Chapter VIII: [The angel Raphael seized the demon and, after having bound his limbs, left him bound[65] in the deserts of upper Egypt (the Thebaid). 3.] *Raphaël angelus apprehendit daemonium, et religavit illud in deserto superioris A Egypti.* This verse will seem to such jokers to be the original of the popular slang French phrase "nouer l'aiguilette",[66] a malicious trick that Egyptian crones played on newlyweds and that vagabonds still do in the countryside. Fine; but as for me, I wouldn't complain too much about the precious simplicity of manners that infuses the book of Tobias. Even the precaution of the father-in-law Raguel, who needlessly digs a grave in case Tobias has died, impressed me, much like other incidents in this narrative, which seemed so delicate to edit and which is written with such truth and openness.

Chapter X. Could anyone better portray, in four or five lines, a mother's worry about the fate of her absent only son: 10. *Lumen oculorum nostrorum, baculum senectutis nostrae...* [Light of our eyes, the staff of our old age...] ? This last expression has become proverbial. How well all the niceties are observed, and above all this vow of Raguel is touching for the informed reader: *Angelus sanctus sit in itinere vestro!* [May a holy angel be present along your way!] We must admit that this mythology of the guardian angel is very consoling; it is clearly born from the *genie* or *daimon* of the ancients, or rather it was common to all peoples under different names. It is pleasant for one's self-image to believe that an invisible beneficent being should watch continuously at our side. *Ne forte*

---

64 Maréchal doesn't provide an alternative, but the *New English Bible*, which includes this book as "Tobit" in the Apocrypha section, has "Pour out your wine and offer your bread on the tombs of the righteous, but give nothing to sinners" (4:17, in a long note as not universally attested), while the Catholic Family Edition of the Bible, which does include Tobias as part of the Old Testament, gives: "Lay out thy bread and thy wine upon the burial of a just man, and do not eat and drink thereof with the wicked". The book is not included in Tanakh (the Jewish canon). Maréchal's complaint about Sacy's translation of "constitue" doesn't seem justified.

65 The Latin has "religavit" (bound) whereas the French of Sacy gives this as "relégua" (relegated, left); I have included both in my English translation.

66 "nouer..." literally: knot the cord, slang for a spell or curse creating male impotence.

offendas ad lapidem pedem tuum.[67] It is pleasant for the isolated person, whose friends have been taken away by misfortune, to believe that there is still one who preserves him from greater evils, and who cares for his frail existence which has become a matter of indifference to his fellows. If the sage refuses the fiction of a guardian angel, he has his conscience in its place, which is no chimera.

Everything speaks to the soul in the book of Tobias. The smallest details have their effect. The dog[68] that runs ahead of Tobias; the father who, despite his age and blindness, runs to meet his son; the actions of grace that he renders to God for having made him recover his sight: *Et ecce video Tobiam fiium meum,* Chap. XI. [17. And now I see my son Tobias.]

Chapter XII is like the moral of this narrative or this romance if you will. This moral is worthy of the rest. I noted in it a verse spoken by the angel, which struck me as unusual: *Etenim sacramentum regis abscondere bonum est; opera autem Dei revelare et confiteri honorificum est.* [7. For it is good to conceal a king's secrets; but it is honorable to reveal and spread the works of God.] If kings and magistrates always conducted themselves with wisdom, they would have no need of secrets or confidences; they would even manage to show themselves in broad daylight. Evidence would have to be the basis of their legislation; it's only the highway robber who hides in order to commit a bad deed. A good father of a family brings his children into his confidence, and decides nothing without consulting them. Shame on a people in whose country there are cabinet secrets! Cabinet secrets inevitably lead to *coups d'état.*

Father Tobias, who lived to age one hundred and two, was blind for four.

There appeared in Paris, in 1773, a book entitled *Tobias, Poem in Four Cantos, Dedicated to N.S.P. Pope Clement XIV, by LeClerc.* This literary production, in prose, does not let us dispense with reading the original, of which it is only a feeble copy. The subject of this Biblical book has supplied three tragedies at the old Théatre Français. It is every bit as dramatic as the Greek *Oedipus at Colonus.*

XVIII   Judith

Oriental pomp and Asiatic despotism are well depicted in the first two chapters: *Gloriabatur* (Arphaxad) *quasi potens in potenia exercitus sui, et in gloria*

---

67   Lest you hurt your foot on a stone: Ps. 91:12.
68   SM's note: Tobias's dog in the Bible recalls Eumaeus's dog in Homer's *Odyssey.* [Odysseus's dog, cared for by the shepherd Eumaeus in its master's absence, recognizes the returning hero before any person does. In *Tobias,* though, the text says that the dog follows Tobias and his angelic companion.—Trans.].

quadrigarum suarum. [4. He gloried in his power, as invincible through the strength of his army and the multitude of his chariots. *Quadriges*, says the text.]⁶⁹ And these orders from Nebuchadezzar to Holofernes: *Egredere adversus omne regnum Occidentis ... non parcet oculus tuus ulli regno, omnemque urbem munitam subjugabis mihi.* [Go attack every kingdom of the west ... your eye will spare no kingdom and you will subject every fortified city to me. II. 5 and 6.] The general obeys instantly: *Omnes resistentes sibi occidit in ore gladii... et cecidit timor illius super omnes inhabitantes terram.* What pomposity! [II.16 and 18. He made everyone who resisted feel the sword's edge ... and the terror of his weaponry spread among all the inhabitants of the earth.] *In ore gladii* does not mean "the sword's edge". *Cecedit* says more than "spread"; rather, "fell" should have been written. Sacy had more piety than genius.

Chapter III is no less expressive, nor less well done, in painting the abasement of the cowardly people who surrendered to the devastator. *Melius est ut viventes serviamus quam... Nos et filii nostri servi tui sumus. Utere servitio nostro sicut placuerit tibi.* [Better for us to live as servants... We will be your slaves, we and our children. Demand from us any service that may please you. 2,5,6.] But the last brushstroke is from a master's hand in completing the portrait of Asiatic ways: *Praecerat Nabuchodonosor ut omnes deos terrae exterminaret videlicet ut ipse solus diceretur Deus...*[III.13. The king commanded that all gods of the earth be exterminated, so that he alone should be called God.]

The abridged history of the Jews, which Achior makes for Holofernes, Chap. V, is clever and rapid. Judith's sermon to the priests, Chapter VIII, is a bit long, but the beginning is fine and full of movement. This woman presents herself well, and effectively prepares the great event she has in mind.

Judith's prayer, Chapter IX, is superb and full of energy. What fitting expression to convey a girl's dishonoring! *Denudaverunt femur virginis in confusionem.* [2. Foreigners, moved by an impure passion, violated a girl and covered her with confusion by doing her an outrage.] What a bland, cowardly translation! ⁷⁰ And this other phrase, speaking of Holofernes, whom she aims to deceive: *Percuties eum in labiis charitatis meae.* [13. Strike him with the charm of the words that will leave my mouth.] What a miserable translator is Isaac de Sacy!⁷¹

---

69   Quadriges: the team of four horses that draws a chariot, rather than the chariot itself.
70   Bland, cowardly, because the Latin reads: "They stripped bare a virgin's thighs"; *confusionem* could be read as disorder, or uniting/mingling, i.e., the act of rape.
71   More literally: the graces of my lips, where "graces" could refer to words or to the lips themselves; most translations prefer the former option.

If every detail of this adventure is recounted with energy, what are we to think of the structure? A widow who gets an army general drunk on wine and love, then cuts off his head in betrayal! It's for this that we may use the expression of holy scripture: "The ways of God are extraordinary". He doesn't disdain the vilest ruse to achieve his ends; he who, they say, created the world with a breath, he requires, in order to rescue his people, the arm and all the coquetterie of a widow. This doesn't give a grand idea of his complete power and his majesty. The hymn is quite beautiful. However, abstracting this from any religious idea, one can't blame the Jews for the method they use against Holofernes. Any ruse is permitted against a bandit stronger than oneself, and it's then that treachery becomes magnanimity and justice.

Protestant theologians protest against the historical truth of Judith; they want to see in this biblical book only an allegorical, nationalistic novel, a parable; they could add, and a hyperbole.[72] Judith was forty-five years old when she got general Holofernes drunk with love and wine; she lived a hundred and five.

Dramatic authors have not failed to seize Judith; the famous actress Chammeslé played this role seventeen times running; the author of the play was Boyer, already father of a *Jephtha*. Another poet, Bouvot, published, in 1649, a tragedy about Judith, entitled *Love of One's Country*. Saint Jerome insinuates that Judith wrote her story herself: why not? The two sexes doubtless have an equal right to divine inspiration. However, we prefer to see a needle or a bobbin in a woman's hand, rather than a pen and a cutlass.

XIX Esther

The first chapter is quite extraordinary. Because Queen Vashti will not appear before her drunken husband and his entire court, the tyrant not only repudiates her but orders all the women of his hundred and twenty-seven provinces to submit to and blindly obey their husbands. Such a law, in France, would cause cruel satire of the impolitic legislator who might risk it.

The second chapter is no less unusual; there we see an uncle produce his niece at court and keep for himself the task of spying. As for the rest, everything is within Jewish mores. What is astonishing is to see the stoolpigeon Mordecai be difficult and refuse to greet Prince Haman, who had ordered him to

---

72 In French the words "parabole" (parable) and "hyperbole" (exaggeration) rhyme, forming a type of wordplay that marks rhetorical sophistication. The book is Biblical for Catholics, not for Protestants or Jews, who consider it apocryphal.

pay homage. Was Mordecai perhaps an ambitious little man who took umbrage at seeing Haman as the king's favorite, a position which in good conscience should necessarily be filled by the favorite wife's uncle? However, the spirit of a courtier, exaggerated in his favor, is well grasped in the character of Haman, who considers his great good luck nothing as long as the only man who refuses to kneel before him exists in front of him.

Chapter VI is the masterpiece of this political novella composed in honor of the Jewish nation; nothing more adroit and better done than the events of this chapter. The narrator of this little mini-history handles everything artfully. Haman begs the queen, Chapter VII, to save his life; the king enters and takes the suppliant's humble attitude for that of an impudent man who wants to attack the honor of the princess. Nothing was less realistic; that was not, for Haman, the moment for a successful affair. This passage considerably weakened my faith in the rest of this thousand-and-one-nights tale, otherwise so well spun.

Chapter IX is disgusting in its cold, cruel details. The Jews show themselves truly the people of a "God of vengeance"; but was it up to the people of God to offer the example of such a slaughter? They cut the throats of Haman's ten unfortunate children; they create carnage of seventy-five thousand men, "returning evil for evil" as the Bible says, appearing to approve and to praise the Jews. The king himself asks the queen when she will be satisfied with all the blood she has caused to be spilt. The sweet, modest Esther continues to the very end, doubtless inspired by her dear uncle, and pardons no-one. The author of this chapter (whether Mordecai or someone else) even permits a barbaric pleasure to burst out, twice repeating the same things; but does he think to palliate this cannibalistic conduct by affecting to say, twice, that the Jews never looted the innocents whom they immolated for Mordecai's resentment and in memory of Haman?

What emphasis in the beginning of Chapter X! *Rex omnem terram et cunctas maris insulas fecit tributarias.* [The king made tributaries of all the earth and all the isles of the sea.] Doubtless to imply that this glory was the work of Mordecai, his prime minister. The translator Sacy weakened this passage from Chapter XII: *Datis ei* [Mordecai] *pro delatione muneribus.* [Mordecai received the reward for his denunciation.] He renders *delatione* as "opinion". As for the rest, all these last chapters are apocryphal. The letter-patent of Haman, through Ahasuerus, intended or not, is curious: in those days it was similar to the present.

Mordecai's prayer, in the same Chapter XIII, is quite fine and clever. How he represents the refusal to greet his rival! The niece's prayer is even more unctuous, except for this passage in bad taste, though energetic: *Tu scis... quod abominer signum superbiae et gloriae meae quod est super caput meum, et detester illud quasi pannum menstruatae.* [XIV.16. You know that I consider as an abomination the proud mark of my glory that I wear on my head, and that I detest it like dirty underwear...] But in Hebrew culture, this image would have intense power, given the extreme care that women were obliged by law to take in order to purify themselves.[73]

We could do without Chapter XV; it lets us know all the little affectations that Esther uses in order to please her lord and master. It's a tableau worthy of Albani.[74] The king's letter, Chapter XVI, which invalidates his letters-patent, is fine, a model of political tact. When Esther becomes the nominal mistress of King Ahasuerus, she could have been about twenty or twenty-five. The editing of this book is attributed to Esther herself, assisted by her uncle Mordecai. They were both actors and recorders of this courtly drama. We know that Racine made a tragedy on this subject. Shakespeare would have been less elegant but more faithful. It's been forgotten that Desmarets[75] composed on the same topic a poem in seven cantos, ending in these three lines:

Esther, in the sweetness of holy revenge,
Blessing the Lord with heart content,
Feels her beauty's perfect triumph.

N.B. If one undertook a historical list of all the lost and fallen women who play a role in the Bible, it would be a fairly large volume: Esther, Bathsheba, Lot's daughters... Bilhah, Delilah, Zilpah, Hara, Tamar, Potiphar, etc. etc. etc. Abigail, Abishag, Aiah, Bala, the three head-cutting women (Herodias, Jael and Judith), Nicaulis queen of Sheba, the sinner Magdalene, Respha, both Salomés, the Samaritan. The Bible is truly a book of bad scenes—rape and concubinage, adultery and incest—which contaminate nearly every chapter of holy scripture. "The majesty of the divine books" (to use one of the expressions of Saint Jerome) is often compromised by the turpitudes with which they swarm.

---

73 The Latin passage specifies a menstrual pad, though Sacy omits the specific reference. Maréchal relies on his reader knowing some Latin in order to get the point of his comment about Jewish law, which requires a purifying bath after menstruation, as well as a period of abstention from sex and other measures.
74 Francesco Albani (1578–1660), Bolognese artist who painted elaborate and rather sentimental religious works of important moments in Catholic doctrine.
75 Jean Desmarets (1595–1676).

XX   Job

The first chapter opens this book perfectly and already makes Job interesting. The refrain *Et ego solus ut nuntiarem tibi...*[15, 16,17, 19. And I alone have escaped to come tell you the news] is of the utmost pathos. True melancholy characterizes Chapter III. The consolations that Eliphaz offers Job in Chapters IV and V are no less energetic. The same energy and profundity, the same philosophy and poetry are in the following Chapters, VI and VII, Job's response.

Chapters XIII and XIV are especially remarkable and could furnish arguments for and against the moralist or theologian, concerning the existence of physical and moral evil under the rule of a good and all-powerful God. Chapter XV is full of fine movement and a masculine eloquence. At line 35 of the text, "stomach" signifies "heart". The next two, XVI and XVII, are dismaying. Bildad's remonstrances, Chapter XVIII, are philosophical and more consoling. In Chapter XIX, Job continues to complain; he repeats himself; but sorrow gives him imagination and causes him to find new images to portray the same things. I noticed, in line 26, the synonym "see God in the flesh" for "see God with my eyes".

The portrait of the wicked man that Zophar gives in Chap. XX is powerful. The wicked man would not recognize himself in it, and perhaps it is tactless of Zophar to show this portrait to a just man afflicted with evils which he claims should afflict only the guilty. Job feels this in Chap. XXI and opposes to his friends' vain consolation an only too true picture of the wellbeing of wicked men. The reply of Eliphaz, Chapter XXII, is harsh but beautiful, especially the first part of the chapter.

Chapter XXVIII, on wisdom, is in the best Oriental style. The following one touches and moves. What abundance, what a wealth of imagery! How they touch our soul! *Oculus fui caeco, et pes claudo ...* etc. [I was the blind man's eye, the lame man's foot.] And how beautiful is the last Chapter (XXXI) of Job's justification! Who wouldn't be enchanted with the delicacy of phrase in the first verse: *Pepigi foedus cum oculis meis, ut ne cogitarem quidem de virgine*? [I made an agreement with my eyes to not contemplate any young woman.] This plea for and against misfortune is a precious monument of style, but the moralist could conclude nothing from it.

From Chapter XXXII to XXXVIII, Elihu says very good things amid the flow of words that he launches. In verse 22 of Chapter XXXVI, he exclaims: Who is a doctor like God?

Chapters XXXVIII and XXXIX are perhaps the most sublime of the Bible. There God is made to speak as God. Is there anything in Homer or

Ossian[76] comparable to the portrait of the horse: *Procul odoratur bellum* [He scents from afar the troops' approach]? And this verse, among others, from Chap. XXXVIII: *Numquid mittes fulgura, et ibunt? Et revertentia, dicent tibti: Adsumus* ... 35. etc. etc. [Will you command the thunders and will they depart instantly? And then coming back will they say, "Here we are?"] This sublime apologue has a fine morality worthy of the rest.

There is much philosophy, and above all, high poesy, in this Oriental tale, which French versifiers have dared to translate into our language. To us they look like pygmies trying to raise the knotty club of Hercules. No one recognizes Job after he has passed through the prosaic filter of poor Isaac Sacy—even less when he has suffered the rhymes of the high-minded Isaac Benserade of the French Academy. Was it to create a contrast that this bad poet dedicated his paraphrase of Job to Cardinal Richelieu?[77] There might be more than one analogy between Job and Timon the misanthrope,[78] but the latter is far inferior to the other! Another miserable versifier, M. Rouget, a squire, published in Amsterdam in 1759, a pitiful travesty entitled *The Spirit of Job*. Here are its first three rhymed lines:

Cursed be the mass obscure
Whence the master of nature
Detached the hours of day!...

The author of the book of Job was certainly a great poet. That is what caused Saint Jerome to say: "God dictated lines to Moses, to David, to the prophets, and even to the unfortunate Job".

---

76   Homer, Ossian: Homer is the ancient Greek poet who was thought to have composed both the *Iliad* and the *Odyssey*; Ossian was a legendary Gaelic bard whose name was attached to several works actually by a Scottish administrator, James Macpherson (1736–96), who claimed to have translated them. Although their authenticity was challenged during his, and Maréchal's, lifetime, Maréchal apparently preferred to believe them genuine.

77   Isaac Benserade (1613–91); Cardinal Richelieu was his patron and, as chief minister to King Louis XIII, founder of the French Academy in 1635.

78   Timon: possibly a real Athenian of the fifth century BCE, who figured as a reference in the work of several early Greek authors and about whom Shakespeare wrote his *Timon of Athens*. In his novella *La femme abbé* (published the same year, 1801, as *Pour et contre*), Maréchal borrows the name for a misanthropic character who utters many of Maréchal's own opinions.

XXI   The Psalms of David[79]

1. The five first lines are rapid and full of poesy. What bravery in this passage: *Et iter impiorum peribit.* [And the path of the impious will perish.]
2. What movement and warmth in this one! How fine the images, albeit exaggerated! This line of Virgil: *Discite justitiam moniti et non temnere divos*[80] has a strong connection with this verse: *Et nunc, reges, intelligite; erudimini, qui judicatis terram.* [10. And now you, o kings! Open your heart to understanding, receive instructions, you who judge the earth.]
3. This psalm has only this unusual expression as something remarkable: *Dentes peccatorum contrivisti.* [You have broken the teeth of sinners.]
4. Here one notes only a few words full of unction: *Sacrificate sacrificium justitiae.* [Offer to God a sacrifice of justice.]
5. This isn't much.
6. The sixth line merits a brief pause: *Quoniam in morte non est qui memor sit tui...* [For there is no one who remembers you in death, Lord.] Here David appears to be a materialist, like the other main authors of the Bible. It seems, indeed, from this passage, that this prophet-king might want to insinuate that after death everything is done and that even God is nothingness in the tomb. The Jews weren't much given to ideology.
7. Lines 13, 14 and 15 are lovely.
8. There is grandeur, nobility, and materialism, not to displease the translator Laharpe.[81] (The dead will not praise God.) David repeats the same heresy in psalm 113.
9. In line 5, Sacy translates *Qui judicas justitiam* as "You who judge according to justice". But the evident meaning seems bolder and more worthy of God: "You who judge justice itself".

    Verse 2 of psalm 10, according to the Hebrew, has a painful energy, all the more painful because it is only too true: *Dum superbit impius, incenditur pauper.* [While the evil man swells with pride, the poor is burnt up.] And divine justice permits, even authorizes this scandal! This scandal creates many atheists.
10. The opening is perfectly in the Oriental style: *Palpebrae ejus interrogant filios hominum* is of a fine boldness. [5. His eyelids interrogate the children of men.]

---

79   The numbering of the psalms may vary slightly from one Bible to another. For instance, the one Maréchal cites as #19 appears in some Bibles as #20.

80   Learn justice and do not despise the gods: Virgil, *Aeneid* 6.620.

81   J.-F. Laharpe's translation of Psalms appeared in 1797.

11. *Eloquia Domini, eloquia casta; argentum igne examinatum, probatum terrae, purgatum septuplum.* This is fine, too. [The Lord's words are chaste and pure, a silver tested by fire, purified in earth and seven times refined.]
12. Not important.
13. Everyone knows the beauty of the opening of this psalm: *Dixit insipiens*[82] *in corde suo: Non est Deus.* [The madman says in his heart: There is no God.] But perhaps not everyone has noted the beauty of this repetition: *Non est qui faciat bonum; non est usque ad unum.* [1. There are none who do good, not a single one.3.] David loved this image: *Sepulcrum patens est guttur eorum* [3. Their gullet is an open grave.] for he had already used it in psalm 5. What poesy there is in this passage: *Veloces pedes eorum ad effundendum sanguinem!* [3. Their feet run fast to pour out blood.] and especially in this other one: *Qui devorant carnem, sicut escam panis.* [4. Those who devour the flesh of my people like a piece of bread.]
14. What sweetness, what calm, what unction in this psalm, comparable to the *justum et tenacem virum* of Horace![83]
15. Not important.
16. This prayer of David's is a bit prideful. How did this despotic, cruel and adulterous king dare to say to his God, with well-considered confidence: *Probasti cor meum, et visitasti nocte; igne me examinasti, et non est inventa in me iniquitas?...* [3. You have put my heart to the test and visited it during the night; you have tested me by fire and no iniquity has been found in me.] This singer king certainly had impudence! Another verse well expresses the good cheer of his enemies: *Saturati sunt filiis, et dimiserunt reliquias suas parvulis suis* [13. They are gratified by the multitude of their children, and have left their remaining goods to their grandchildren.]
17. The opening is full of extravagant Oriental poetry. But how to explain this passage: *Cum viro innocente, innocens eris ... et cum perverso perverteris?* [You will be, Lord, innocent with the innocent man; and as to the one whose conduct is wrong, you will behave with some dissimulation and evasion. 27.] We see that the good Sacy was tortured here, but the theologian Laharpe is equal to everything; see his *French Psalm-book.* David painted his God in his own image. Nothing is more vindictive than the

---

82 SM's note: "Madman" and "atheist" are synonyms in the logic of King David and of the missionary Laharpe. [The Latin "insipiens" is often translated as "fool". New English Bible gives "impious fool"; Alter gives "scoundrel"; Tanakh, "benighted man" (in all three this is Ps. 14).—Trans.].
83 Horace (65 BCE–8 BCE), Latin poet and satirist. The line translates as "the just and resolute man" (Book 3, ode 2, line 13).

character of this tyrant prophet. His psalms revolve only around the vengeance he meditates against his enemies, and to which he makes his God the accomplice. And still he dares to repeat in this psalm: *Secundum puritatem manuum mearum ... ero immaculatus.* [21 and 25. The Lord will reward me according to my justice and the purity of my hands.] David a pure man!

18. The first seven verses sublime; the rest has no connection, only commonplaces of mysticism.
19. This is a prayer that David had composed for him the eve of a battle. Here we find this fine passage: *Hi in curribus, et hi in equis, nos autem in nomine Domini...* [8. Some rely on their chariots and some on their horses; but we invoke the Lord's name.] It's the last line of this psalm that has been consecrated in prayer for the kings of Christianity. One might have chosen better, for this verse is flat and says nothing. For example, *et nunc, reges, erudimini* [84] from psalm 2 would have been more appropriate.
20. This is like a sequel to the preceding. It renders thanks to God for the victory he has accorded to his anointed and because, as for his enemies: *Pones eos ut clibanum ignis, in tempore vultus tui.* [You will consume them like a burning oven when you show your face.]—and Lemaistre de Sacy adds, "fiery" to "face".
21. Recommended for details filled with poetic images.
22. Unimportant.
23. This should be read after Psalm 14; it is composed in the same spirit. The last lines have a pleasing turn.
24. Here David is more modest and presents himself to God for what he is: a sinner who needs every mercy.
25. In this one he resumes his presumptuous character, forgetting what he has been, probably to recall what he ought to have been; but only David would have the effrontery to say and repeat, after a life spent in all sorts of disorder and infamy: Ego, in innocentia mea ingressus sum ... pes meus stetit in directo. [1.11 and 12. As for me, I have walked in my innocence; my foot has remained firmly in the rightness of justice.] The hypocrite![85]
26. Unimportant.
27. Same. Commonplaces. However, we must except this pleasing expression: Refloruit caro mea. [7. And my flesh has as it were flowered again.]
28. Full of images.

---

84 "Now, kings, be instructed", rather than "May the king answer us when we call".
85 Hypocrite: SM has "le Tartuffe", citing the eponymous hypocrite in one of Molière's best-known comedies.

THE OLD TESTAMENT   77

29. Unimportant.
30. Same. Commonplaces.
31. Unimportant.
32. Somewhat better.
33. Superior to the previous one. I like this passage, which breathes feeling: Gustate et videte, quoniam suavis est Deus. [9. Feel and taste how sweet is the Lord. J.F. Laharpe's version.]
34. This turn of expression is bold: *Omnia ossa mea dicen: Domine, quis similis tibi?* [All my bones will render you glory, saying: Lord, who is like you? 10.] I like this one still better: *Et oratio mea in sinu meo convertitur*, which Sacy rendered well enough: [And I uttered my prayer in the secret of my bosom. 13.]
35. I rather like this line: *Iniquitatem meditatus est (injustus) in cubili suo;* [5. He meditated iniquity in the secrecy of his bed.] and even more this one: *Inebriabantur ab ubertate domus tuae; et torrente voluptatis tuae potabis eos, quoniam apud te est fons vitae.* All of it is lovely. [9 and 10. They will be drunk on the abundance that is in your house, and you will make them drink of the torrent of your pleasures because the source of life is in you.] And again this place: *Non veniat mihi pes superbiae!* [12. May the proud man's foot not come to me!]
36. One of the finest and the one with the most morality. Everyone knows the *vidi impium...* [I have seen the impious...] and the beautiful translation by Racine; but perhaps not everyone has noticed this other consoling, unctuous verse: *Junior fui, etenim senui; et non vidi justum derelictum, nec semen ejus quaerens panem.* [25. I was young, and now I am old, but I have not seen the just abandoned nor his offspring seeking bread.] Nonetheless such scandal is not rare in civil society organized as it is.
37. This one has other beauties. David confesses his iniquities with an uncommon energy: Non est pax ossibus meis, a facie peccatorum meorum, etc. etc. [4. In view of my sins, there is no peace in my bones.]
38. Same type as the previous one.
39. The author repeats over and over the same ideas, sometimes more feebly, sometimes proving the fertility of his imagination.
40. Unimportant.
41. The first half of this psalm is filled with beauties of detail. "My soul thirsts for the living God" is quite Oriental.
42. Almost nothing.
43. This bit is full of movement and energy. Why didn't Sacy deign to translate this strong expression, this picturesque image: *Inimicos nostros venti-*

labimus cornu?[86] What a fine apostrophe is *Exurge, quare obdormis, Domine? Exurge!* [Arise, Lord; why do you lag as if asleep? Arise! 23.]

44. This song, which contains a charming portrait of Solomon, must be astonished to find itself among the psalms and be numbered as one of them. The piece is full of graces; it would better be located next to the Song of Songs.
45. Repetition of the same images as are poured out with such profusion in the 149 psalms.
46. These are only words to be sung.
47. There are a few more ideas in this canticle: *Justitia plena est dextera tua* is fine. [Your right hand is full of justice.]
48. The beginning is imposing but isn't sustained.
49. The discourse that the prophet-king places in God's mouth is eloquent and elevated.
50. This psalm is famous, and several of its great features render it really worthy of its celebrity. What could be more poetic than *exultabunt ossa humiliate!* [10. My bones, broken and humiliated with sorrow, will tremble with joy.]
51. Unimportant.
52. Repetition of the 13th psalm.
53. Unimportant.
54. Only verse 7 is any good: *Quis dabit mihi pennas sicut columba?* [Who will give me wings like a dove?]
55. Repetitions and commonplaces.
56. Same.
57. The ferocious personality of David penetrates everywhere. He was far from understanding how to forgive injuries, who says: *Laetabitur justus, cum viderit vindictam; manus suas lavabit in sanguine peccatoris.* [The just man will rejoice to see the vengeance that God will take on the impious, and he will wash his hands in the sinner's blood.][87] If religion teaches the just man to dip his hands in the blood of the guilty, reason and philosophy preach that it is finer to heal the wounds of one's enemies and to stanch their blood.
58. It's still David proclaiming his innocence and enjoying the sight of his enemies crowded at his feet.

---

86 This line has been variously translated as: "We shall push down/upset/gore our enemies with our horn/bow/military might".

87 SM's note: Jean-François Laharpe finds this couplet not only very legitimate but very praiseworthy.

59. This little psalm has a lot of movement and rapidity: *Potasti nos vino compunctionis* [You have made us drink the wine of compunction] is quite Oriental, as is: *Fugiant a facie arcus!* [Let them flee from before the ark!][88] How this poor Isaac de Sacy murders Hebrew poetry!
61. 62.—63.—Unimportant.[89]
64. The end of this type of hymn is very poetic, particularly this expression in verse 14: "The countryside is dressed in flocks of sheep…"
65. The opening of this has something solemn and religious to it.
66. Unimportant.
67. This canto has pomp and majesty. One easily observes that it was composed for the Hebrew people: *Intingatur pes tuus in sanguine (inimicorum); lingua canum tuorum ex inimicis.* [24. Your foot will be dyed in your enemy's blood; your dogs' tongues will be slaked in it.] To justify these atrocious and disgusting details, here is the reflection of Jean-François Laharpe: "Such images of carnage have never spoiled poetry". We reply to this modern French translator of Psalms: Let poetry perish, if it requires human butcheries in order to have more power! May the book be condemned, branded, and thrown into the flames[90] that offers the people such atrocities to sing every week! If tigers had a religion, it would be that of David and his imitators.
68. One passage from this psalm has often been abused: *Zelus domus tuae comedit me.* [Lord, zeal for the glory of your house devours me.] The Church has inherited only too much of the irascibility of its prophet-king. And how should priests not be irascible? For their weekly work, they have had imposed on them the reading of 150 psalms of David, which revolve only around the pleasure of vengeance on one's enemies, marching in blood, etc.
69. Contains only repetitions.
70. Same. There is one distinctive passage: Quoniam non cognavi litteraturam. [15. Because I don't know the humanities.]
71. One of the good ones. It could be called the psalm of kings and sung every day in their chapels.
72. This one is again very fine and very moral. David perhaps didn't think he was stating something so philosophical when he said: Prodiit quasi ex

---

88 Ark: Not, of course, Noah's ark but the ark or container of Torah. Sacy's translation here, though conveying the sense, eliminates the personification (the "face") of the ark.
89 61: # 60, a prayer of a defeated king, is missing.
90 One of Maréchal's own books, his 1788 *Almanach des Honnêtes Gens (Almanac of Upright People)* was condemned by Parlement to be publicly torn and burnt; cf. Delany 2012, 6–7.

adipe iniquitas eorum. [7. Their iniquity is as if born of their fat.] The propter dolos, posuisti eis [18. This prosperity has become a trap for them.] is remarkable; the prosperity that God grants to sinners, which becomes a trap for them, is one of those too frequent and too necessary incoherencies in the absurd system of religions.

73. Contains superb things, among others, this: *Tuus est dies, et tua est nox.* [16. The day is yours and also the night.] Sacy doesn't seem to me to have given the right meaning for line 20.

74. This idea is pleasant: *Calix in manu Domini plenus misto; et inclinavit ex hoc in hoc, verumtamen fax ejus non est exinanita. Bibent omnes peccatores terrae.* [9. The Lord holds in his hand a cup of pure wine, full of bitterness; and although he pours it out sometimes to one and sometimes to the other, its dregs are not yet exhausted. All the sinners of the earth will drink of it.]

75. Full of warmth and movement.

76. Some grand images, but they are found elsewhere as well.

77. This long psalm of 72 verses is uneven, but in general it is fine. I like this paraphrase on manna: *Panem angelorum manducavit homo.* [Man ate the bread of angels.] All the Church fathers[91] (says Jean-François Laharpe) recognized the eucharist in these words. Fine, but it's far-fetched. In the energetic tableau of the misfortunes of Jewish people unfaithful to their God, there are features that reveal a great painter: *Juvenes eorum comedit ignis, et virgins eorum non sunt lamentatae. Sacerdotes eorum in gladio ceciderunt, et viduae eorum non plorabantur.* [63. Fire devoured their young men, and their daughters were not lamented. 64. Their priests were put to death by the sword and no one poured out tears for their widows.] Alongside these beauties are some images in poor taste; for example: 65. *Et excitatus est tanquam dormiens Dominus, tanquam potens crapulatus a vino.*[92] A modern book in which God was compared to a drunkard or to a cowardly father who strikes his ungrateful children from behind, would not pass the censure of certain purists. Finally, one admires the modesty of David, who says: *Eligit David*[93] *servum suum, et pavit (David) eos*

---

91 Fathers: major theologians whose writings helped establish the doctrines of early Roman Catholicism. Eucharist is the wafer taken at communion; Protestants say it represents God's body, Catholics say it is God's body.

92 The Lord roused up as if from sleep, like a strong man drunk from wine.

93 SM's note: There appeared at London, in 1761, a little English octavo volume entitled *The History of the Man after God's Heart*; it is David who is presented as the worthy model of men like Tiberius and Nero. [Tiberius and Nero: First-century Roman emperors noted, respectively, for moodiness and criminal brutality—Trans.].

THE OLD TESTAMENT   81

(*Judeos*) *in innocentia cordis sui.* [The Lord chose David his servant, and David raised Jacob and Israel in the innocence of his heart. 70, 72.]

78. Energetic tableau of the misfortunes of Jerusalem, in the genre of Jeremiah's lamentations.
79. A sequel to the preceding one. The extended comparison of God's people to a vine is touching and poetic.
80. The opening of this psalm has a festive air, and breathes a religious pomp.
81. This short psalm has something sublime to it.
82. At the end are a few images, perhaps a bit monstrous.
83. This one has unction, and gentle images, which relax somewhat the mind tired from the sentiments of hate and revenge to which the psalmist is only too faithful in the course of his prayers to his God.
84. The end is consoling: *Misericordia et veritas obviaverunt sibi: Justitia et pax osculatae sunt.* [11. Mercy and truth have met: justice and peace have kissed.] These images have double merit when one meets them in such a work as this collection.
85. Ordinary prayer of David, which doesn't say much.
86. This praise of the city of Jerusalem seems only sketched.
87. These are the usual jeremiads of the singer king.
88. Commonplaces. A suspicious praise of David.
89. There are some philosophical and well-said verses.
90. Occasionally one finds pleasant images, charming features of sentiment; for example, lines 11 and 12: *Quoniam angelis suis mandavit de te ... in manibus portabunt te, ne forte offendas ad ... etc.* [He commanded his angels to guard you; they will carry you in their hands lest you stub your foot against a stone.] If Jewish and Christian mythology were all of this type, it would create illusions, even for the sage.
91. I paid attention only to this passage: *Justus ut palma florebit.* [13. The just man will flourish like the palm tree.]
92. Repetitions.
93. There is a very fine movement of eloquence: *Viduam et advenam interfecerunt; et pupillos occiderunt et dixerunt: Non videbit Dominus ... Qui plantavit aurem, non audiet? Aut qui finxit oculum, non considerat?...etc.* [6. They have put to death the widow and the stranger; they have killed orphans. 7. And they said: The Lord will not see it ... 9. He who made the ear, he won't hear? Or he who formed the eye won't see?]
94. 95.—96.—Repetitions, but beautiful ones.
97. Same. Only the intoxication of a hymn can excuse the outrageous metaphor: *Flumina plaudent manu...* [The rivers applaud, clapping hands.]
98. All these hymns are only words, phrases suitable to putting into song.

99. Same. The simplicity of this verse shows something grand and sublime: *Scitote quoniam Dominus ipse est Deus: ipse fecit nos, et non ipsi nos.* [3. Know that the Lord is the true God; he made us; we did not make ourselves.]

100. Excepting the last couplet, which is harsh, this psalm is of a fine morality. In it, David paints himself not as he doubtless was in reality, but as he ought to have been.

101. The portrait of an unhappy man is drawn with true colors which draw forth tears; this psalm carries the title, in Hebrew: "The pauper's prayer". The unfortunate wise man (if he wasted his time in vain words) would perhaps not speak with such eloquence; but he would be able to find in the nature of things, consolations that religion doesn't always give.

102. In this type of hymn, sweetness and unction dominate. It was successfully retranslated by Jean-François Laharpe.

103. Pompous description of the creation and preservation of the world. Noble, grand, sublime details.

104. This hymn must have had for the Hebrews—whose marvellous history it recalls—a level of interest, which is nil for any other people. Nonetheless this rapid-fire narrative is read with some pleasure, although in it one may learn that God himself sometimes turns men's hearts to hate— which is not very admirable on the part of a "very good" God.

105. Almost in the same genre, but less fine.

106. Same. Some impressive features here and there. God repents of the evil he has done: this proposition, uttered in our day for the first time, could not avoid being treated as offensive.

107. Unimportant.

108. More jeremiads and, instead of pardon for injuries, curses.

109. This psalm, called figurative,[94] has obtained from the Church a preference that strikes me as gratuitous. It is perhaps the weakest of all.

110. Same.

111. In this one are two or three verses that say something.

112. Charming, a very pretty hymn. The Church hasn't many of this type, but it is very fitting to hear an eighteen-year old nun sing, at daily vespers, the 8th and last line of this psalm: *Habitare facit sterilem in domo matrem*

---

94 figurative: Psalm 109 (110 in some Bibles) was interpreted by some Christian theologians as prefiguring the arrival of the messiah (Jesus). Many other incidents and passages in Jewish scripture were also interpreted as prefigurations of events in Jesus's life or points of Christian theology. (See Auerbach 1959.).

filiorum laetantem. [He causes her who was sterile in her house to have the joy of becoming the mother of several children.]

113. The *in exitu* has beauties. The holy king David doesn't seem to believe in another life: (*The dead will not praise you, Lord.*)[95]
114. Sad commonplaces.
115. 116—117.—Unimportant.
118. This long, long, psalm has only words.
119. *Verba et voces…* This is where we find the phrases that Jean-François Laharpe can't tire of admiring: (Lord, have I not hated all those who hate you? Yes, I hate them with a perfect hate.) How charitable this is! How humane it is! How tolerant!
120. The prophet-king was a poor physicist, according to this verse: *Per diem sol non uret te, neque lumen per noctem.* [6. The sun will not burn you during the day, nor the moon at night.] But then, a psalter is not a treaty on fire and light.
121. *Sunt verba et voces praetereaque nihil.*[96]
122. Same.
123. 124.—Unimportant.
125. The last three couplets, and especially the fifth, are remarkable and praiseworthy: *Qui seminant in lacrymis in exultatione metent* [Those who sow in tears will reap in joy.] should be a consoling proverb.
126. A happy turn of phrase.
127. Verse 3 offers the most graceful image, very proper to making religion beloved, if that benefit were its purpose: *Uxor tua sicut vitis abundans in lateribus domus tuae* [Your wife will be like a fruitful vine within your house]; and *filii tui sicut novellae olivarum in circuitu mensae tuae.* [Your children will be like young olive trees around your table.]
128. Common places. Verse 6 has energy.
129. This is the famous *de profundis* that the Church recites for the dead; she could have chosen better. This psalm says nothing and is rather flat.
130. Almost nothing.
131. Unimportant.
132. *Ecce quam bonum et quam jucundum habitare fratres in unum* [Ah! How good and pleasant it is that brothers unite together!] is an axiom that can't be too often repeated, and to which it was good to give religious sanction. What follows is extreme and in bad taste.

---

95 The dead … From a different psalm (115 in some Bibles), with the sense that the dead have no voice, so it is up to the living to praise the Lord.
96 Not much more than words and sounds.

133. This is nothing.
134. Only repetitions.
135. Same. However, the refrain that terminates each couplet could produce an effect in the mouth of an entire populace. "Praise the god of gods", verse 2, isn't this a bit profane? The Greek poets also call Jupiter "the god of gods". The Holy Spirit and Apollo ought not to speak the same language.
136. This one has a reputation, and deserves it. The *super flumina Babylonis* is full of sentiment. Sorrow is characterized in profound strokes. Nothing more touching. David (if indeed he is author of all the psalms bearing his name) didn't create much like this. It is spoiled by the last couplet, which offers a terrible image: (Happy he who shall seize your children and smash them against a rock!) And they sing and repeat that every week!
137. Ordinary.
138. Verses 7 to 13 have a lovely movement.
139. 140.—141.—142.—Are almost nothing.
143. This one has something. The last strophes are well turned.
144. Unimportant, even though rather long.
145. Verses 7, 8, 9 are quite fine.
146. A less fine repetition of the previous one.
147. Same.
148. More repetitions, here with pomp.
149. Just words, lyrics for a song.
150. and last.—Same. [Praise the Lord with the drum; praise God enthroned...] The Church, which is not obliged to have good taste, considers this insipid translation by Isaac de Sacy to be a faithful one.

N.B. Jean-François Laharpe admits that he has no knowledge of Hebrew, and yet he has just expanded the list of translators of David. It must be that Jean-François Laharpe has received the gift of tongues, as he possesses that of slander, which he piously distributes to all who don't think the same way he does. See the preliminary discourse of his *Psalter*. As for his notes, the Louvre academician has become a village missionary. O fragility of human reason! If he is in good faith, that's a pity; if not, that's contemptible.

Long before Jean-François Laharpe, a society of Capuchins[97] published at Paris, in 1762, a "new version of the psalms from the Hebrew text". In 1677, a mayor of Étampes, Mr. Bredet, travestied "the seven penitential psalms of David in French Sapphic verses". Here is one of the better strophes:

---

97 A sixteenth-century order of friars, offshoots of the Franciscans whom they wanted to return to their original ascetic ways. So called after the hood (*cappuccio*) they wore.

> Don't demand repayment, Lord;
> Of all the mortals facing you, even the holiest
> Whether young or old, even the brave man
> Is not innocent.

One knows the psalms of David by Clement Marot and Theodore de Bèze.[98] Less known is the translation by Michel Marillac, brother of the beheaded Marillac.[99] Racan and Philippe Desportes[100] have also translated *all* the psalms of David. Wiser than his predecessors, J.B. Rousseau made a choice. His beautiful *odes* are still read—which doesn't, however, release one from rereading the originals. And there are a few tolerable strophes in the *Sacred Poesies* of Lefranc.[101]

We have the seven psalms of Anthony, king of Portugal, which are only feeble copies. They were translated and dedicated to Louis XIV in 1701, a very tiny volume of 150 pages. These seven psalms, and the hymn, are far from those of King David. There is some unction to them, but that's all: no movement, no spark, no nobility! The only tolerable verse is perhaps this: "The evils caused by pleasure are cured only by pain". The rest is the stupidest platitudes, nonetheless worthy of the author's spirit and the decrepitude of the monarch who accepted the dedication.

There appeared in Paris in 1784, with approval, a little work entitled *Book That Survived the Flood, or Psalms Recently Discovered*,[102] etc. It's not up to us to judge it. This little volume won its too candid author the persecution of priests.

Voltaire puts King David and King Frederick the Great[103] in the same line. Frederick made no psalms, but the public and private behavior of David was no less scandalous than that of Frederick. Moses, David, and Frederick were three statesmen, poets and conquerors, who regarded the rest of mankind as trash made for their petty pleasures. Another feature of resemblance between

---

98   A sixteenth century poet and a theologian, respectively.
99   Marillac (1569–1632) was an advisor to King Louis XIII; his brother, Louis, a general, was beheaded in 1632.
100 Honorat de Bueil, marquis Racan (1589–1670); Desportes (1546–1606). About Desportes' translation, the poet and critic F. Malherbe is reported to have said, "Your soup is better than your psalms".
101 J.-J. Lefranc (1709–1784), marquis de Pompignan, poet and scholar. About the work mentioned, Voltaire is reported to have said, "Sacred indeed, because no one will approach them".
102 Maréchal's *Livre Échappé au Déluge*, a parody of Biblical palms and prophets, cost him his job as a librarian at the prestigious Mazarin Library in Paris.
103 Frederick II ruled Prussia from 1740 to 1786. The scandal Maréchal refers to is the king's homosexuality including the erotic poems he wrote to his lovers.

the two last is that Frederick attached little more importance to philosophers than David to prophets, although they had them every day at their table.

Every week the psalms of David are recited in their entirety. Surely the Church ought to have preferred Proverbs or Ecclesiastes, where there is more morality. But there are more threats in the psalms, and they wanted to frighten grown children.

XXII   Proverbs, or the Wisdom of Solomon

Its beginning is fine, though a bit wordy. The first three chapters are filled with repetition, but these repetitions are all in imagery. The third chapter above all breathes poesy: *Dominus sapientiae fundavit terram; stabilivit coelos prudentia.* [10. The Lord founded the earth with wisdom; he established the heavens with prudence.] Verse 9, "Honor the Lord with your goods", motivated the honoraria of priests and numerous pious legacies. Everything needed is found in the Bible; it is a veritable Encyclopedia for priests.[104]

There is an interesting movement in the fourth chapter: *Nam et ego filius fui patris mei, tenellus et unigenitus coram matre mea, et docebat me et dicebat ... etc.* [3. For being myself son of a father who raised me and of a mother who loved me as tenderly as if I had been her only son. 4. He instructed me and said...] The rest offers only repetitions, which lose their force from that fact.

Chapter V is all in scenes. The portrait of the woman of ill repute is accomplished, and appropriately contrasted with that of the honest woman. I very much like this verse: *Ne des alienis honorem tuum et annos tuos crudeli.* [9. Do not prostitute your honor to strangers, nor your years to a cruel man.] I also like this passage: *Deriventur fontes tui foras, et in plateis aquas tuas divide.* [16. May the streams of your fountain flow out, and you distribute your waters in the streets.][105] But I don't like what the author of Proverbs adds immediately afterward—*Habete eas solus, nec sint alieni participes tui* [17. Possess them alone, and let foreigners have no part in it]—unless by "foreigner" he means "wicked". There is much sense in this other verse preceding: *Bibe aquam de cisterna tua et fluenta putei tui.* [15. Drink the water of your cistern and the streams of your fountain.] Was the pious Sacy afraid to tarnish his translation with the tableau of a good household that Solomon offers here? Why did he render *ubera sua inebriant te in omni tempore* by "may its sweetness intoxicate

---

104   Encyclopedia: The *Encyclopédie*, a massive multi-volume compilation of rationalist thought and social description from the mid- 18th century.
105   Translated differently, in the negative, in modern Bibles.

you always"?[106] I also very much like this phrase: *Quare, seduceris, fili mi, ab aliena, et foveris in sinu alteris?* [My son, why will you let yourself be seduced by a foreign woman, and why will you rest in another's bosom?]

Chapter VI is admirable for its expression, from one end to the other. It's too bad that its ideas are not connected. We see here an unusual expression: [30. "The thief steals to fill his *soul*".] *Soul* here stands for *stomach*. The Bible swarms with such synonyms. In the Hebraic language, *soul* and *dead body* are the same thing. *Flesh* signifies *man*, etc. *Blood* also means *soul*; they were the same for the Jews; they were materialists. They said *kidneys* to express thought, etc.

The following doesn't alter the argument. I like this turn of phrase: *Dic sapientiae: Soror mea es; et prudentiam voca amicam tuam.* [VII.4. Say to wisdom: You are my sister; and call prudence your friend.] What painter could ever represent a prostitute with colors as true as those employed in the rest of this chapter? It seems, according to this picture, that the customs in great cities have been the same everywhere and in every era, so that Paris can attest to the accuracy of the portrait of Jerusalem. But the latter city is more reprehensible in that its population was infinitely smaller.

The most sublime eloquence characterizes Chapter VIII: *Nondum erant abyssi, et ego jam concept eram ... etc. etc.* [24. Abysses did not yet exist when I was conceived...]

In 1595, the Proverbs of Solomon were put into French rhyme by Paul Perrot, lord of la Sale. Here is a sample of this old poet's talent:

> Exquisite beauty in a foolish woman
> Is like a ring in a pig's nose. *Chap.* 11, 152nd *quatrain.*

XXIII The Parables of Solomon

The nine chapters of the preceding Section (XXII) should rather bear the title of "Parables", and this, its Chapter X, which is not in the same style, be called "Proverbs".[107] It is composed of stanzas, each one of which contains a short

---

106 Sacy bowdlerized the phrase by using a metaphorical intoxication rather than the literal grape-wine (*ubera*) intoxication of the Latin.

107 In most Bibles, the section here called "Parables" and treated separately from the preceding one, is included as part of the book called Proverbs though set off by a break after Chap. 9 and treated as Chap. 10.

parallel of the sage with the fool. There are couplets full of energy: *Qui nititur mendaciis, his pascit ventos.* [4. Who relies on lies is fed on wind.] *Nomen impiorum putescet.* [7. The name of the wicked will rot *like them.*] The eleventh chapter continues in the same vein. Among other remarkable sentences, I noted this one: *Manus in manu non erit innocens, malus.* [21. The evil person will not be innocent, even with hands clasped together.]

Sacy may have given a contradictory meaning in translating the following passage: *Circulus aureus in naribus suis, mulier pulchra et fatua.* [22. The beautiful but foolish woman is like a gold ring in a sow's muzzle.] I believe the real sense was: *A beautiful but ill-behaved woman is, for the foolish man, what a ring is in a camel's nose.* The Orientals, instead of a rein, used a ring through the nose of this beast of burden to lead it where they wished. They still say of a woman who is mistress in her house: *She leads her husband by the nose.* And I also noted this other expression: *Qui conturbat domum suam possedebit ventos.* [29. Who makes trouble in the home will possess the wind.]

Chapter XII. What could be more pleasing than this figure of speech: *Mulier diligens corona est viro suo?* [4. The vigilant woman is her husband's crown.] What more terse than this: *verte impios, et non erunt?* [7. At the least change, the wicked fall and are no more.]

The opening of Chapter XIII is well done: *Filius sapiens, doctrina patris.* [1. The wise son is attentive to his father's teaching.] It seems that the proverb "Tell me whom you associate with, I'll tell you who you are" must be the same, though enhanced in this verse: *Qui cum sapientibus graditur sapiens erit.* [Who walks with wise men will become wise.] I dislike this sentence at the end: *Qui parcit virgae, odit filium suum.* [24. Who spares the rod hates his son.] I would willingly retort with this banal saying: *You catch more flies with honey than with vinegar.*

Again the more or less energetic, more or less new, moral antitheses, Chapter XIV. The prediction in verse 19 has not yet been verified: *Jacebunt mali ante bonos, et impii ante portas justorum.* [The wicked will be overthrown in front of the good, and the impious before the door of the just.] Let well-meaning folk await this miracle in order to believe! The following verse is unfortunately truer: *Amici vero divitum multi.* [20. The rich have many friends.] And here is a fine political maxim: *In multitudine populi, dignitas regis.* [28. The multitude of the people is the king's honor.] But only when this multitude has its liberties and manners; for a great population if degenerate and corrupted is not something so precious. It's especially in dealing with people that quality is more important than quantity. This further apophthegm has great meaning and great energy: 30. *Vita carnium sanitas cordis; putredo ossium invidia.* [The heart's health is the life of the flesh; envy is the rotting of bones.]

Chapter XV is similarly full of the soundest moral precepts: *Responsio mollis frangit iram.* [1. A soft word breaks anger.] What laconic style and fine choice of expressions! [7. The sages' lips will spread knowledge like seed. 15. A tranquil soul is like a continual banquet. 17. It is better to be invited with affection to dine on herbs, than to eat fat veal when one is hated. 25. The Lord will destroy the house of the proud and affirm the widow's heritage.] *Labia sapientium disseminabunt scientiam ... Secura mens quasi juge convivium ... Melius est vocari ad olera cum charitate, quam ad vitulum saginatum cum odio ... Domum superborum demolietur Dominus, et firmos faciet terminus viduae* ... And above all this passage: *Fama bona impinguat ossa.* [30. A good reputation fattens the bones.]

Chapter XVI contains only commonplaces or repetitions. The next one nearly the same, excepting a few verses, such as this: *Quid prodest stulto habere divitias cum sapientiam emere non possit?* [16. XVII. What good does wealth do the fool, since he can't buy wisdom?] Here is a nice turn in Chapter XVIII: *Qui mollis et dissolutus est in opera suo, frater est sua opera dissipantis.* [He who is soft and cowardly in his work is brother to him who destroys what he makes.] And this: *Mors est vita in manu linguae.* [Death and life are in the tongue's power. 21.]

In XIX there is nothing remarkable except for this truth touching the knowledge of the human heart and which is renewed nowadays: *Homo indigens misericors est.* [The unfortunate are always compassionate.] in Chapter XX, there are several sentences that would deserve to be remembered and considered proverbs: *Propter frigus piger arare noluit; mendicabit ergo aestate.* [4. Because of the cold, the lazy man doesn't want to labor; therefore, he will beg in the summer.] *Suavis est homini panis mendacii; et postea implebitur os ejus calculo.* [Bread of lies may be sweet to a person, but afterward his mouth will be filled with gravel.] *Qui maledicit patri suo et matri, extinguitur lucerna ejus in medii tenebris.* [20. Whoever curses his father and mother, his lamp will go out in the middle of the night.]

Chapters XXI and XXII offer little new. In the latter we find a proverb of the type *Qui seminat iniquitatem metet mala* [Who sows iniquity will reap misfortune]. The penultimate verse of the same Chapter is not correct in every sense: *Ne transgrediaris terminus antiquos quos posuerunt patres tui.* [28. Do not pass the ancient limits established by your ancestors.] XXIII is unimportant. The last three verses of XXIV are noteworthy: *Per agrum hominis pigri transivi ... etc.* [I have passed by the field of lazy men ... etc.]

Chapter XXV is even more filled with images and similitudes than the preceding ones. One senses, in the translation, that much of the finesse of allusions and exactitude of comparisons found in the original, must be lost: [The glory of God is to hide his word.] *Gloria Dei est celare verbum* is more philosophical than might be thought at first. There is profundity in this passage. Religion resembles love in that it needs shadow and mystery. Fanaticism of spirit and sense ignites in the depth of shade, and it is not without reason that the Catholic clergy recite their offices only in Latin. The people can only follow by groping along.

I am not of Solomon's opinion in verse 3 of Chapter XXVI: *Flagellum equo, camus asino, et virga in dorso imprudentium.* [A whip is for the horse, a bit for the donkey, and a rod for the fool's back.] But it is not with rods that one can correct a reasonable person who strays. Instruction in place of punishment, gentleness in place of intolerance, would have won more souls for the Roman church and for all other exclusive and fanatical sects.

Chapter XXVII is one of the best, full of well-rendered verities. What could be more attractive than this adage: *Ferrum ferro exacuitur, et homo exacuit faciem amici sui?* [17. Iron sharpens iron, and the sight of a friend stimulates the friend.] The last verse advises a Pythagorean regime; perhaps one would be obliged to come back to that in order to bring back health and manners.[108]

XXVIII and XXIX are weaker. In XXX there are fine movements and much imagination. The 4th verse of this chapter is rather sublime. The 9th is very philosophic; nothing more energetic than this portrait of the adulterous woman: *Quae comedit et tergens os suum, dicit: Non sum operata malum.* [20. Who, after having eaten, wipes her mouth and says: I've done nothing wrong.] The last verse is full of good sense.

The XXXIst and last chapter of Proverbs is the best of all, and the one with the most consequence. I have noticed this phrase: *Noli regibus, o Samuel! Noli regibus dare vinum ... etc.* [4. Don't give, O Samuel! Don't give wine[109] to kings.] The next one has a delightful moral about the weak man ... The portrait of a strong woman is painted with pleasant and well-chosen colors; but alas, *quis inveniet?...* [10. Who will find her?]

---

108 SM's note: On this subject, consult an excellent treatise by Ant. Cocchi, *On the rule of Pythagorean living*. This Italian physician, an atheist, was a meritorious man. His work has twice been honored with a French translation.

109 SM's note: What evils France was caused by all those laws made about the wine of Champagne under the reign of the Convention! [The National Convention governed France from September 1792–October 1795. It abolished the monarchy, established the Republic, and wrote a new constitution, which was suspended because of war; in July, 1794 a conservative reaction set in. Taxes on wine and other goods became an important economic issue during the 1790s (see Plack 2012).—Trans.].

Abraham Roger,[110] minister of the gospel on the coast of Coromandel, gave in his book entitled *The Open Door*, a translation of the *Proverbs* of Barthrouvherri, a Brahmin, which are absolutely in the genre of Solomon's proverbs. For example: "When a young woman sees an old man, she flees as if from a charnel pit. VIII.5. A clever man can make oil from sand. 1.5. He who is wise and can make books, fears neither age nor death. 11.10". Others of the same style can be found in the *Gulistan*:[111] Oriental literature, were it better known, would offer more than one rival to the Biblical authors. Perhaps they have all drawn from the same source, namely, those primitive people indicated by Plato and almost found by the unlucky and scholarly Bailly.[112]

One regrets the loss of more than three thousand parables and five thousand hymns composed all by Solomon. Abbé Timoleon of Choisy, countess[113] of Barres, composed a life of David and Solomon: the historian was worthy of his two heroes. The historical dictionaries have to be redone: no doubt all the scandalous names, such as these, will be pruned out.

XXIV Ecclesiastes, or the Preacher

The highest philosophy appears right from the first chapter. A carefree Epicureanism characterizes the second. It seems that the author (whoever he might be) counted little on another life: *Si unus et stulti et meus occasus erit, quid prodest mihi?...etc. Nonne melius est comedere et biber?...* [15. If I have to die just as the fool does, what's the good of applying myself to wisdom?...24. Isn't it better to eat and drink?] I liked the Oriental turn of the beginning: *Et gaudio dixi: Quid deciperis?...* [I said to joy: why do you fool yourself so vainly?]

Chapter III is even more precise than the second on the annihilation of a person after death, and on the necessity of enjoying life, after which there is

---

110 Dutch missionary (d. 1649) who lived in India and Indonesia. Coromandel is part of New Zealand. Roger's book was published in German and in French some years after his death.

111 Persian collection (1258) of stories and poems, translated into French and Latin during the seventeenth century.

112 Bailly: Jean Sylvain Bailly (1736–93), prominent politician, astronomer, poet and scholar; he wrote on Plato and on ancient Asian peoples. He was eventually guillotined. As members of the "Nine Sisters" lodge, he and Maréchal would have known one another personally (Mannucci 2012, 96 ff.).

113 Countess: This free-thinking priest (1644–1724), from a well-placed family, wrote a memoir narrating his adventures as a cross-dresser. He also wrote a history of the Church and was a prominent member of the French Academy. SM's apparent compliment is, of course, sardonic.

nothing more. Even the least rigid police censorship in Rome would not permit such a page in a modern pamphlet, and would consign it to the *index*.[114] Anacreon, Horace, Chaulieu,[115] have never gone so far.

Chapter IV is still finer and more moral. The opening breathes the profoundest sensitivity and the most majestic sadness: *Vidi lacrymas innocentium et neminem consolatorem, et laudavi magis mortuis quam viventes ... Vae soli!...*etc. [I have seen the tears of innocence flow without being wiped away by anyone, and I have said that it is better to be dead than to live. Woe to him who is alone.]

In the Vth chapter, Ecclesiastes broaches, in passing, the great objection against Providence, drawn from the oppression[116] of the just and the prosperity of the wicked; he responds by saying: *Non mireris super hoc negotio, quia excelso excelsior est alius.* [Do not let this astonish you, for someone high up has someone else above him.] Fine, but it's precisely because they say that there is an all-powerful and completely good God, that there should be no physical and moral troubles for the good.

> Why permit a crime? To punish it?
> Should a God be pleased to count victims?
> It would have been best to prevent these crimes.
> *Fragments of a Moral Poem on God,* or *The French Lucretius*[117]

The VIth chapter is also very good, and full of the same morality; namely, this wise indifference which, perhaps, is happiness for mankind. Chapter VII is a bit depressing and hardly gallant: *Melior est dies mortis die nativitatis; melior est ira risu; cor sapientum ubi tristitia est ... Inveni amariorem morte mulierem,* etc. [3. The day of death is better than that of birth. 4. Anger is better than laughter. 5. The sage's heart is where sadness is found... 27. I have found women's caresses more bitter than the cup of death.] It's also too much that the sage, in Chapter VIII, after having said *Sunt justi quibus mala proveniant ...* etc.

---

114 Index: the list of banned books and authors kept by the Vatican, updated and reprinted periodically for centuries until the Church suspended its publication in 1966.

115 Anacreon: sixth-century BCE Greek sensualist poet; Horace (65 BCE-8 BCE), Latin poet and satirist; Abbé Amfryde de Chaulieu (1639–1720), libertine poet.

116 SM's note: Unhappy virtue attests against the existence of a God, said a moral poet in his *Fragments on God.* [This moral poet is Maréchal himself, whose *Fragmens d'un Poème Moral sur Dieu* appeared in 1781.—Trans.].

117 Lucretius (99 BCE–55 BCE) Roman materialist philosopher and poet. Maréchal's book is the same one cited in the previous note, but in its 1798 re-edition with a new title, *Le Lucrèce Français.*

[14. There are just people to whom misfortunes occur], then concludes, *Laudavi igitur laetitiam. Quod non esset homini bonum sub sole, nisi quod comederet et biberet atque lauderet.* 15 [Therefore I have praised joy. The only good to be had under the sun is to eat, drink and rejoice.]

Same system in Chapter IX, where Ecclesiastes reveals himself more materialist than in the preceding ones: *Mortui nihil noverunt; nec habent ultra mercedem.* [5. The dead know nothing any more, there is no further reward for them.] Above he had just said: *universa aeque eveniunt justo et impio ... etc.* [Everything happens equally to the just and the unjust, to the good and the wicked...] and he concludes in his usual way: *Vade ergo et comede in laetitia panem tuum, et bibe cum gaudio vinum tuum; perfruere vita cum uxore, quam diligis, cunctis diebus...*[So go ahead, eat your bread with joy, drink your wine with good cheer. Enjoy life with the wife you love.] Lamétrie in our days has revived this convenient morality in his *Art of Enjoyment*.[118]

Chapter X is scattered; there are thoughts without order, without connection, without being introduced. Some of them are sensible. The XIth chapter is better digested. There are some odd things in the first half of the XIIth and last chapter. The rest is unimportant.

Voltaire, in his elegant verse paraphrase of Ecclesiastes, remained inferior to his model. Well before this brilliant poet, Paul Perrot de la Sale put Ecclesiastes into sonnets, in 1595. Here is some of the poetry of that period:

> There is a time to be born, as time to die.
> Time to kill and wound, time to heal...
> Time to say good night, time to say good day.
> Everything has its time, its season and its turn.
> VIIIth sonnet.

Ancient learned men, whom the Church treated as schismatics, attributed the book of Ecclesiastes to some materialist philosopher; and there is something convincing in this opinion.

XXV   The Song of Songs or the Song Par Excellence of Solomon

If one has to read the odes of Anacreon in Greek in order to feel all their charm, their pleasure, the pretty nothings that help create the genius of a language, one loses even more by not reading the Song of Songs in its original. One also

---

[118] Julien Lamétrie (1709–1751), physician and materialist philosopher.

has to be careful not to judge it from a translation. There one glimpses all the disorder of love, of Oriental love. The Orientals did not make love with madrigals or epigrams; they saw the beloved object in all objects; they expressed themselves only through more or less accurate comparisons, in accumulating epithets upon epithets, in multiplying the daintiest diminutives and all those little names that only passion can justify and ennoble.

Voltaire "frenchified" the Song of Songs in verse, and consequently gave it a different coloration. A bishop, Godeau, had taken that trouble before the author of "la Pucelle".[119] A prose imitation from the pen that gave us *La Nouvelle Héloïse* and the lyric scene of *Pygmalion*,[120] might have consoled us for not knowing Hebrew.

The Song of Songs is a type of pastoral in five scenes; it's not up to "le Devin du Village" or "Annette and Lubin".[121] At least mothers can take their children to a performance of these two pieces; but they couldn't, without some risk, allow their daughters to read the Song of Solomon. The Anabaptists regarded it as a libidinous production made for the harem. The Jews, more scrupulous than their Christian successors, forbade anyone to read it before the age of thirty. One circumstance worthy of notice is the place that the Song of Songs holds amid the holy books. It was inserted into the Bible precisely after Ecclesiastes and before the Book of Wisdom.

Wicked jokers have affected to take literally the 4th verse of Chapter v, which we will not translate: *Dilectus meus misit manum suam per foramen, et venter meus intremuit ad tactum ejus.*[122] The Holy Spirit, who dictated, as is known, all the books of the Bible, seems not to have supervised the editing of this and several others. Quite a few dirty jokes escaped the divine inspiration, which has been exploited. God, writing for human beings, ought, it seems, to have been more careful of their malice.

---

119   La Pucelle: Joan of Arc, known as "la pucelle" (the virgin or maid) of Orleans. Voltaire wrote a bawdy satirical poem about her. Antoine Godeau (1605–72), bishop and poet.

120   These are, respectively, a novel and a drama by J. J. Rousseau (1712–78), one of Maréchal's intellectual heroes except for his approval of religion. Maréchal implies in a rather contorted way that Rousseau was a better translator, or at least a better writer, than Voltaire.

121   "The village soothsayer", an operetta (1752) by Rousseau; "Annette and Lubin": tale of quasi- incestuous love between two cousins, perhaps based on a true story; it was represented in many different genres throughout eighteenth-century Europe.

122   "My beloved placed his hand on the opening, and my belly trembled at his touch". Maréchal, in rejecting a literal interpretation, follows the tradition, both Jewish and Christian, of reading the poem as an allegory of the love between God and his people. Or at least he seemingly does so in order to preserve the appearance of propriety: he was, after all, an atheist, and in the passage quoted further on he appears to reject the allegorical interpretation.

Mardochée Venture published in Nice, 1774, a new translation of the Song of Songs, with a Chaldaic paraphrase.

Here is the judgment of the author[123] of *The Golden Age* or *Collection of Pastoral Tales* about this poem a few years ago:

> "Considered simply as a work of literature, the *Song* is one of the most precious monuments of revered antiquity. The Greek and Roman muses produced nothing more imagistic, fresher, more tender, more delicate. Everything leads us to believe that it is an epithalamium composed by Solomon himself on the occasion of a wedding. The genre in which it is written is not uncertain; it is a pastoral. We still don't have a translation of it done in the true spirit of the original. Ascetic authors, having regarded this eclogue as a pious allegory, have not rendered its meaning completely; moreover, in a representation so far removed from our ways, there would have to be details somewhat strange for us. With some minor changes, the *Song of Songs* could be offered to all eyes and could satisfy the curiosity of those who might desire to know how people spoke of love three thousand years ago". S.M.

Saint Jerome, prescribing to Laeta the manner in which to raise her daughter, told her: "You must reserve for last the Song of Songs, in order to teach it to her without peril, for fear that if she read this holy book early on, the purity of her soul might suffer some blemish".

XXVI Wisdom

Chapter I is in a more tranquil, more mature style than that of Proverbs, its images less exaggerated and the wording less forced.

The speech placed in the mouth of the impious, Chapter II, is very well done. It seems that the way of thinking of the author of the Book of Wisdom is not the same as that of the author of Ecclesiastes. The portrait of the just man's happiness in Chapter III can hardly be by an equally brilliant brush, and IV, in an ascetic style, is similar.

---

123 As indicated by his initials at the end of this quoted passage, the author is Maréchal himself, whose *L'Âge d'Or, Recueil de Contes Pastoraux par le Berger Sylvain* appeared in 1782. "Le berger" (the shepherd) Sylvain was the *nom de plume* Maréchal took in his earlier, classicizing period.

The vth chapter is among the most poetic. There is a multitude of metaphors and comparisons in a Homeric manner. Several features breathe antiquity, among others this: *Spes impii, tanquam memoria sospitis unius diei praetereuntis.* [15. The hope of the impious is like the memory of a guest who passes through and stays only a day.]124

It is said in vain, as the sage says in Ch. vi: *Potentes potenter tormenta patiantur.* [9. The greatest men are threatened by the greatest torments.] It's only ordinary people who still have faith that the pains of hell are ordained against highly placed people; highly placed people let others believe it and don't believe it themselves. It's time to imagine a stronger leash to restrain the powerful people of the earth. A review of their conduct would be more frightening for them than the last judgment.

There is a fine expression at the end of this Chapter vi: *Multitudo sapientum sanitas est orbis terrarum.* [The multitude of sages is the world's salvation.] Perhaps only a single truly wise man would be needed to restore an entire nation. One really great man would suffice, he alone, to effect a happy revolution in manners, which so need it. *Quis inveniet?.*125

Chapter viii is completely ascetic, with some fine details in its portrait of wisdom. One is pleased to hear, from a king's mouth, the prayer in Chapter ix. The xth is a pleasing composition, for the history of the just is only the history of wisdom. Chapter xi continues the same subject. Chapters xi and xii contain good things, mixed with some repetitions and redundancies. In Chapter xiii, there is a very good irony against idolatry and superstition. How many people sing hymns every day, without fearing the verities which accuse them and predict their condemnation!

It's especially according to Chapter xiv that one might conjecture that the Book of Wisdom is not from as distant a date as other books of the Bible. In this chapter the origin of idols is discussed. They are given a respectable motive which touches the heart; but the Biblical sage goes perhaps too far in affirming that the father causes the cherished son, whose memory he wants to preserve in the bosom of his family, to be adored as a god. The inverse of this conjecture would be more realistic.

Chapter xv repeats the same ideas already seen in Chapter xiii. The sage's subject was to pour ridicule on the deformed tree-trunk or mud statue divinized by human beings; but while on the right track, he could have pushed his reasoning further, generalized his thought even more, to affirm that if human-kind

---

124 "sospitis" (of a savior, helper) is apparently a misprint for "hospitis" (of a visitor, guest).
125 Who will find him?

had stuck to its needs and to the morality which is its guide, it would not have given its consent to so many absurdities.

Chapter XVI proves mainly that this book is the work of rabbis, or of cenobites in the early days of the Church. Chapters XVII, XVIII and XIX are of the same genre. "Lord" (says he at the end), "you have lifted up your people". He appears no further.

This treaty of Wisdom, also called *The Book of All Virtue*, is attributed to the Jew Philo.[126] The children of Mahomet claim it back, to honor the wisest of their poets, the famous Locman.[127] The Council of Trent,[128] better advised, and to cut away every doubt, recognized it as a canonical book. Ever since, human beings have no part in it; it's the work of the Holy Spirit. It is only a question of knowing the name of the transcriber—which is not of the last importance! Nonetheless it is odd enough to see the Holy Spirit, already so rich in its own wealth, borrow from pagan mythology terms like *ambrosia, kingdom of Pluto*, etc.

XXVII   The Ecclesiasticus of Jesus, Son of Sirach

The prologue is only an ordinary preface, with nothing of the Oriental spirit. The opening of the first chapter has nobility and grandeur. Chapter II takes an ascetic tone. The part of Chapter III where filial piety is recommended, is touching. There are also excellent precepts in the following chapter, though drowned in a flow of mystical words that do them wrong. Chapter V has nothing striking. The VIth chapter is extremely wordy, but it has unction, and one reads it with interest.

The VIIth is one of the best, full of sensitivity: *Gemitus matris tuae non obliviscaris ... Cum lugentibus ambula.* [29. Do not forget your mother's pains. 38. Walk with those who weep.] The VIIIth is of the same type: *Noli de mortuo inimico tuo gaudere.* [8. Do not rejoice in your enemy's death.] Apparently, an old man was author of Ecclesiasticus; this is seen especially in this chapter. Perhaps this is why he is so ungallant toward women in the next chapter. There one also finds this axiom: *Vinum novum amicus novus.* [15. A new friend is a new wine.]

---

126   Philo (c. 20 BCE–c. 50 CE), Egyptian Jewish philosopher and historian, who attempted to reconcile Greek philosophy with Torah.
127   Perhaps Luqman, a legendary fabulist mentioned in the Qur'an.
128   Series of sixteenth-century councils held in the northern Italian city of Trent; convoked to address the threat of the Protestant Reformation.

Amidst many feeble, colorless passages with useless repetitions one occasionally meets energetic expressions. This, for example, from Chapter x: *Radices gentium superbarum arefecit Deus et plantavit humiles ex ipsis gentibus.* [18. God made the roots of prideful nations dry up...][129] Chapter xi is full of wisdom: *In die bonorum ne immemor sis malorum, et in die malorum ne immemor sis bonorum.* [27. Do not forget evil on a happy day, and do not forget happiness on an unfortunate day.] Here is another adage perfectly similar to the adage of Solon:[130] *Ante mortem ne laudes hominem quemquam.* [30. Praise no man before his death.] But the author of Ecclesiasticus adds a further idea: *Quoniam in filiis suis agnoscitur vir.* [30. For one knows a man by the children he leaves after him.]

Chap. xii is dictated by prudence. I would have wished nonetheless that the sage had not relied so much on the reward which the doer of good deeds can expect. He who does good ought to do it through love of good and of order, not in view of payment; the virtuous person is not a wage-earner.

Chapter xiii is admirable. Never have the great men of the earth been better portrayed, and never was a contrast better put than the one established here between poor and rich. Everything is of an uncommon truth and energy. The last verses of Chapter xiv are full of imagination. The next one is of the same type: at the end, one would like to infer free will: *Apposuit (Deus) tibi quam et ignem, ad quod volueris porrige manum tuam. Ante hominem vita et mors, bonum et malum; quod placuerit et dabitur illi.* [17. God has placed before you water and fire, so that you may put your hand on which side you wish. 18. Life and death, good and evil, are in front of mankind; what he chooses will be given him.] But alas! Man is the toy of circumstances; he is what he is forced to be by the elements composing him. The *fatum* of the ancients is the great law of all beings. God, nature and fate are perhaps only three synonyms.

Ch. xvi is completely mystical. The first part of the xviith is of a noble simplicity. Nothing more majestic and more imposing than the beginning of Ch. xviii. The xixth is weaker. Every verse of the xxth proves a great consciousness. The xxist, quite ascetic, nonetheless contains some quite accurate images: *Narratio fatui quasi sarcina in via* [19. A fool's conversation is like a heavy load as you go.] Chapter xxii is full of lively and touching images, and offers more poetic turns of phrase than the others do. The one after it does well and bursts with well-done movement.

---

129 Maréchal doesn't translate the second part of the sentence: and planted/cultivated the humble of those nations.
130 Athenian reformer and poet (c. 639 BCE–559 BCE).

Chapter XXIV is a superb piece, full of sublimity and imagination. It's already a mark of genius to have placed in the mouth of Wisdom herself her most majestic praise: *Sapientia laudabit animam suam.* [Wisdom will praise herself.] Is there anything grander than this opening: *Ego ex ore altissimi prodivi, primogenital ante omnem creaturam?* [5. I issued[131] from the mouth of the Most High; I was born before any creature.] And then, how well the author knows to change his tone and speak to the heart, when he has struck the spirit! *Ego mater pulchrae dilectionis ...* etc. [24. I am the mother of pure love...]

The XXVth chapter is of another kind; there is nothing more sensible than the beginning. It's doubtless on this chapter that Christ based his eight beatitudes, but the original remains superior to the copy. It seems that the author of this book knew the human heart; this is seen in the unflattering portrait he draws of women. How could he not persuade them that nastiness and bad habits change their appearance! *Nequitia mulieris immutat faciem ejus.*24. It is to catch them by their weak point—to forbid them to be ill-tempered for fear of becoming ugly. Nothing better done than the contrast between the good and the wicked woman.

The Church could have extracted from Chapter XXVI several energetic passages for the blessing of married people. *Mulieris bonae beatus vir; numerus enim annorum illius duplex.* [1. A good woman's husband is fortunate, for the number of his years will double.] Chapters XXVII and following are a bit weaker; nonetheless they contain fine details and imagistic statements. The XXIXth chapter offers moral verities that are good to know and especially to practise in private life.

Chapter XXX is remarkable: the sage, who at the outset showed himself so severe in the education of children, relaxes eventually and ends by recommending enjoyment to mankind. Nothing more tender than the praise he gives to the father of a family: *Mortuus est pater, et quasi non est mortuus, simile enim reliquit sibi post se.* [4. The father is dead, but he doesn't seem to be dead, for he has left behind a likeness of himself.]

The XXXIst chapter contains very salubrious precepts on sobriety and frugality—but too often repeated. The head of a household won't read the XXXIInd chapter without good results. The XXXIIIrd offers only repetitions. The next one has more new things; it breathes humaneness: *qui offert sacrificium ex substantia pauperum quasi qui victimat filium in conspectu patris sui.* [24. Who offers a sacrifice from the substance of the poor is like him who slits the son's throat in front of the father's eyes.] That is beautiful.

---

131   SM's note: Profane mythology meets that of the holy Bible: Minerva, goddess of Wisdom, issued from the brain of Jupiter.

It has been ascribed to Homer, as an aspect of his genius, that he personified prayers; what, then, to say about Chapter XXV of Ecclesiasticus: *Nonne lacrymae viduae ad maxillam descendant?...A maxilla ascendant usque ad coelum.* [18. Do not the widow's tears stream down her face? 19. From the widow's face they rise to heaven.] Same chapter: *Oblatio justi impinguat altare.* [8. The just man's offering enriches the altar.]

In Chapter XXXVI is a prayer perfectly in the Hebrew spirit: *Afflige inimicum ... contere caput principum inimicorum.* [12. Break the head of the enemy's leader.] The last part of this chapter is something different: the portrait of a good household. This disparate passage shows us that this book (like others in the Bible) is only a gathering of shortened passages without any connection. This is why there are so many double usages and why Ecclesiasticus (like the other wisdom books) has no fixed plan and does not form a consecutive and considered whole.

One often has occasion, in the business of life, to use the prudent advice given in Chap. XXXVII against false friends and opinion-givers. Chapter XXXVIII is much more extraordinary; it contains a complete and bizarre praise of medicine and the physician:[132] *Honora medicum, propter necessitatem.* [Honor the doctor because of necessity.] And then, right away, as if by analogy, the author treats death and funeral matters. Saint Jerome is a complaisant interpreter. *Honora medicum,* he says, does not signify sterile esteem or useless, frivolous honors, but rather effective assistance, honoraria, in short, money (Commentary, book II). Hippocrates the pagan is more detached from this matter than the Church father: *In medico sit argenti contemptus.*[133]

There is a great deal of mysticism in the XXXIXnth chapter, but finally the author adopts an inspired tone and becomes more poetic, warmer, and consequently more agreeable to read. The XLth chapter is one of the most likeable in the Bible and simultaneously one of the most philosophic. XLI isn't as valuable. What meaning can we give to this passage from XLII: *Melior est iniquitas viri quam mulier benefaciens*? [14. A man who does you ill is better than a woman who does you good.] XLIII would be fine enough were it not composed only of repetitions.

Chapter XLIV and the following would have had for the Jews a degree of interest that they have lost for us who are too distant and too foreign to the

---

132 SM's note: No doubt the author of Ecclesiasticus was a physician. This book was attributed, by Saint Cyprien and Saint Ambrose, to Solomon himself, that botanist king who boasted of knowing everything from cedar to hyssop. [Cyprian and Ambrose: Catholic theologians of the third and fourth centuries respectively.—Trans.].

133 A doctor should despise money. Hippocrates (c. 460 BCE–c. 370 BCE), Greek physician.

characters whose memory is recited here. The author, while praising the virtues of his nation's heroes, doesn't hide their vices. In Chapter XLVII he apostrophizes wise Solomon, daring to reproach him: *Et inclinasti femora tua mulieribus.* [21. You prostituted yourself to women.]¹³⁴ For the rest, there is a sort of imposing pomp. The prayer to God, in LI, the last chapter, has beauties and unction.

It seems that the author of Ecclesiasticus meant to create a kind of moral compendium and an abridged Jewish history, suitable for giving to young people to complete their education. This work, estimable in many ways, would be more suited to that purpose were it more systematic.

Claude Gauchet, great archdeacon and almonier of the king, in 1596 at Bayeux put the book of Ecclesiasticus into French stanzas. Here is how Claude Gauchet shapes a verse:

> O how happy is the man whose woman is good! Chap. XXVI. 1.
> The virtuous woman is a fine inheritance. 2.
> A woman's beauty cheers the face
> Of the faithful husband who believes her wise. XXXVI.13.

XXVIII Isaiah

What eloquence! Or, rather, what poetry! *Audite, coeli; auribus percipe, terra; Dominus locutus est: Filios enutrivi; cognovit bos possessorem suum; populous meus me non cognovit.* [2. Hear, heavens; earth, lend your ear: the Lord has spoken. 3. The ox knows to whom he belongs; my people do not know me.] What harmonious linking of sublimity and feeling! What movement and what rapidity and warmth in this movement: *Super quo percutiam vos ultra? Omne caput languidum ... Quo mihi multitudinem victimarum? Plenus sum. Quomodo facta est meretrix civitas fidelis?...* [5. What would be the use of beating you further?... Every head droops ... 11. What is this crowd of victims to me? It disgusts me. 21. How did the faithful city become a whore?]

The second chapter is less fine; its last verse is awkward: nonetheless, what wealth! What abundance! What profusion of imagery!

---

134 More literally: turned/bent your loins to women. Variously translated in a sexual sense or as inappropriate submission.

How well the IIIrd ends, after having given the tiniest details: *Et moerebunt atque lugebunt portae ejus, et desolata in terra sedebit Sion.* [28. The gates of Zion will mourn and weep, and she will sit desolate on the ground.]

The IVth chapter is unimportant and obscure; but the Vth compensates well for it. What poise and grace in the parable of the vine! And what finesse in this reproach: *An quod expectavi ut faceret uvas, et fecit labruscas?* [4. Was I wrong to expect that it would bear good grapes, but instead it only produced bad ones?] Poor Isaac de Sacy! There is so much energy in the tableau of vengeance and threats of the Lord against his ungrateful people! Sacy failed to give *lingua ignis* in translating *Sicut devorat stipulam lingua ignis* as [The way straw is consumed by fire.] [135] This *lingua ignis* comes from a great artist and reveals a great truth.

How majestic and imposing is the fiction or allegory of Chapter VI! What a grand composition! Only Michelangelo could have painted Isaiah's scenes. Chapter VII is not so beautiful, by far. The opening of VIII has solemnity: *Et dixit Dominus ad me: Sume tibi librum grandem, et scribe in eo stylo hominis.* [The Lord told me: Take a large book and in it write known, legible letters.] The rest reads a bit like a book of magic. Isaiah knew that in order to be prophet in his country, one couldn't speak too clearly.

Chapter IX, they say, is completely prophetic; Christ is depicted there in every detail. However this may be, one does occasionally find extremely energetic expressions: *Et devorabunt Israel toto ore ... Et erit populous quasi esca ignis*, etc. [12. They will fall upon Israel to devour it. 19. The people will be like straw to fire.]

Homeric heroes do not speak with more pride than the Assyrian king, in Chap. X. What image was more suitable to give the idea of a conquered nation than that which he uses, drawn from a bird's nest with its eggs abandoned by their mother! Chapter XI contains the very poetic portrait of a golden age expected with the coming of the messiah but which has not happened with the coming of the messiah. Alas! Wolves continue to eat lambs, and justice has not become the badge of judges. *Justitia cingulum lumborum ejus, cinctorium renum ejus.*[136]

Chapter XII is nearly nothing; it is an ascetic hymn, fortunately very short. XIII is a superb battle scene. Neither Homer nor Ossian[137] have any such

---

135 More literally: as a tongue of flame devours straw. As usual, Maréchal deplores Sacy's tendency to eliminate striking physical imagery in favor of something more trite or abstract.
136 Describing an ideal ruler (later interpreted as the messiah): Justice will be a belt around his loins, and a girdle for his waist (11:5).
137 Homer: reputed ancient Greek author of the *Iliad* and the *Odyssey;* Ossian: legendary Gaelic poet of the third century BCE; poems said to be by Ossian were fraudulently

descriptive pieces of such power. The beginning above all announces the catastrophe of Babylon; and nothing could better portray its ruin than the details at the end.

Chapter XIV is the response to Chapter X: the speech that Isaiah puts in the mouth of princes and peoples conquered by Assyria is in no way inferior to the one he gives to the conqueror. What poet has handled better than he the weapon of irony? What vehemence at the end of this chapter: *Ulula, porta; clama, civitas!* etc. [Gate, let your howls be heard; city, let your cries resound.][138] What a fine disorder, in Chap. XV, to announce the desolation of the house of Moab! What an effect this repetition produces: *Conticuit ... conticuit!...*[139]

Chapters XVII, XVIII, and especially XIX, offer some fine details, but also many repetitions and even monotony.

Chapter XX is certainly within the Oriental taste and breathes the highest antiquity. One finds some traces of it among the heroes of the Iliad: *Sicut ambuavit servus meus (dixit Dominus) Isaias nudus et discalceatus; sic minabit rex Assyriorum captivitatem AEgypti, et transmigrationem juvenum et senum nudam et discalceatam, discoopertis natibus ad ignominiam AEgypti...* [3. The Lord said: As my servant Isaiah has walked naked and barefoot, 4. So the Assyrian king will lead out of Egypt a mass of captives and prisoners of war, young and old, all naked and barefoot, without having anything to cover what ought to be covered...] This passage is characteristic.

The disorder of Chapter XXI is remarkable and expressive. Chapter XXII is not as good as XXIII; *Onus Tyri: Ululate, naves maris ...* etc. [1. Prophecy against Tyre: Cry and howl, ships of the sea.] It's bold. And the irony of the end! *Sume cythram ...* etc. [Take up the lute...]

Chapter XXIV is one of the richest and most superb in Isaiah; there is no expression that doesn't hit home, no word that doesn't create an image. Isaiah is as much a painter as Poussin, the Poussin who painted the Flood.[140] It's sad that all this display of genius doesn't have a more moral purpose, something more directly useful to humanity. Chapter XXV is like a pendant to the preceding one, though rather less rich and less energetic.

The hymn in XXVI has pomp; Isaiah here shows himself faithful to the spirit of his nation. Always the curses, always the spirit of vengeance: *Ignis hostes tuos devoret.* [Fire will devour your enemies.] And note, in passing, the manner

---

published as translations by a Scottish writer, James MacPherson, in the 1760s.
138   More literally: "Howl, gate; shriek, city!".
139   Conticuit: is silenced; variously translated as "meets her doom" (New English Bible); "was undone" (Alter); "is silent" (Catholic Family Edition); "was ruined" (Tanakh).
140   Nicolas Poussin (1594–65) made a set of seasonal paintings with Biblical characters; "The Flood" is the "Winter" panel.

of the Jewish nation, which seems to have at heart only the glory of its God and the zeal of the Lord's house—when it is concerned with its own interests.

The beginning of XXVII has something imposing to it: *In die illa visitabit Dominus in gladio suo, duro, et grandi, et forti.* [At that time, the Lord will come with his great sword, his penetrating and invincible sword...] Poor Mr. Lemaistre de Sacy, how you travesty the Bible!

In the prophecies of Isaiah, art rules—all the more artful because it is concealed under an apparent disorder: violent, sharp mixture of soft, consoling images, yoked to scenes of strong, dark colors. Isaiah understood the spiritual level of those to whom he spoke, and didn't trouble to explain the fine points. For crude people, an air of rusticity could only be more pleasing. A lot of motion, that's what was necessary to a fiery people, always ready to burst out. This chapter, among others, furnishes examples of it.

XXVIII has its beauties, which must have lost a lot in translation; same for XXIX and XXX. All this must be of the greatest interest for Jews. We can't find the same pleasure in it; we are too far removed from their culture, of which there remain hardly enough traces to understand the text of their books. Chapter XXXI, much shorter than the preceding one, struck me as much more energetic. In the following two, fine details but little coherency.

Chapter XXXIV is one of the most superb. What an ardent imagination Isaiah has! How vast are his scenes! How large his paintbrush! What could be more imposing than this piece? And—this can't be too often repeated—what a shame that Isaiah should have wasted such colors in painting objects with no purpose! His prophecies are sublime hints. Chapter XXXV shows that Isaiah was able to take on every tone. How softened his style is in this chapter! How calm he is! How he relaxes the reader fatigued by all that precedes!

Chapters XXXVI and XXXVII are purely historical; but history is treated here in the antique manner, that is, dramatically. Isaiah isn't satisfied with a simple story; he reports the very words of his principal actors, the harangues full of energy that were supposed to issue from the mouths of heralds or ambassadors. This is of the greatest interest. How is it that the Jewish people, who read the Bible every day, have not taken on the character of greatness that cannot be denied to this book? *Ubi est, Deus?* [Where is this God?] How beautiful this movement is! What action in all these conversations! Such authority in the speeches that the prophet places in the mouth of his God! One would think he had really heard them.

What beautiful simplicity in the beginning of Chapter XXXVIII! We love the good faith of the good Hezekiah! With what good nature, what candor, they tell of marvellous things! Fifteen years added to the life of a king on his death-bed! The hymn of Hezekiah is touching and worthy the miracle which has just been worked in him. The good Hezekiah doesn't play a good role in Chapter XXXIX; he displays, with vanity, all his treasures in front of Babylonian ambassadors. Isaiah reprimands him on God's behalf and announces that his treasures will be transported to the Babylonian royal palace, where his children will be eunuchs. Hezekiah replies to this prediction: *Bonum verbum Domini quod locutus est; fiat tantum pax et veritas in diebus meis.* [What the Lord has said is correct; may peace and truth only endure during my lifetime.] At least we owe him gratitude for his frankness. Our modern princes would perhaps be no less egotistical, but they would want to appear more generous.

Chap. XL includes the grandest ideas, ideas more than Homeric. Homer says that Jupiter takes three steps and arrives at the end of the universe. Isaiah says: *Appendit tribus digitibus molem terrae, et libravit in pondere montes, et colles in statera. Ecce gentes quasi stilla situlae, quasi momentum staterae. Insulae, quasi pulvus exiguus, omnes gentes quasi non sint, sic sunt coram eo, et quasi nihilum et inane.* [12. Who is he that by three fingers supports the entire mass of earth, who weighs the mountains and puts the hills on his scale? 15. Before him, all the nations are only like a drop of water falling from a bucket ... Before his eyes, all the islands are like a tiny grain of dust...]

> He sees as nothingness the whole universe;
> And feeble mortals, vain toys of death,
> Are all, to his eyes, as if they never were.
> RACINE[141]

Chapter XLI is a bit less fine. XLII the same, though we find nice features there among a lot of repetition. This apostrophe to idols is lovely: *Surdi, audite; caeca, intuemini.* [18. Listen, deaf ones; blind ones, open your eyes and see.] In Chapter XLIII: *Aliquando dormitat Homerus.*[142] Isaiah wakes up somewhat in XLIV. His piece on the making of idols is well done. There is a similar piece in the last chapters of the Book of Wisdom; but Isaiah's strikes me as superior: the details are strikingly true, and relevant to the narration.

It is in Chapter XLV of Isaiah that we find the famous line (verse 8) that is applied to Jesus Christ, I'm not sure why: *Roratae, coeli, de super, et nubes pluant justum...* [Heavens, send your dew from on high, and let the clouds send down the just man like rain.] The rest is noteworthy for its Oriental tendency. The apostrophe of God to Cyrus is noble.

---

141 Jean Racine (1639–99), tragedian and satirist.
142 Sometimes Homer sleeps, i.e., even the greatest writer occasionally lapses. Probably from a slightly different version in Horace, *Ars poetica*, l. 359.

Chapter XLVI again is about idols; Isaiah's imagination is inexhaustible on this subject, furnishing him with ever new and energetic imagery. In Chap. XLVII, the portrait of the city of Babylon is an exquisite painting. What resources Isaiah had in his genius to capture our attention, even while saying the same things! What fecundity of images, turns of phrase, movement! Chapter XLVIII proves it, as do others.

What pomp in the following chapter, to announce the claimed reign of Christ! Chapter L should have prevented any misunderstanding of it, and avoided attribution to Jesus of what Isaiah might have said himself. He knew, through the experience of others and his own, that those who, among the Jews, followed the profession of prophet, were exposed to upsets and discredit. The expression at the start of Chapter LI has come down to us; we still say today proverbially: "He's a man of the old rock". *Attendite ad petram unde excise estis.* [1. Recall to mind this rock from which you were carved.]

Chapters LII, LIII, LIV, LV contain only prophecies, or rather vague promises of future well-being for those who remain faithful to divine law. These chapters drag a little. The end of LV is more energetic: *Imber et nix de coelo INEBRIAT terram.* Sacy's "watering" does not give the *inebriat* of the original.[143]

LVI is consoling. God calls all men to him, even eunuchs: *Et non dicat eunuchus: Ecce ego lignum aridum. Haec dicit dominus eunuchis: qui custodierent sabbata mea dabo eis in muris meis nomen melius a filiis et filiabus.* [3. Let not the eunuch say: I am only a dried-out tree-trunk. 4. For here is what the Lord says to eunuchs: To those who keep my Sabbath day, 5. I will give in my house a name that is better than sons and daughters.] This is a curious verse. There are some good details in the portrait that God draws of people who fornicate, in Chapter LVII: *Suscepisti adulteram; dialtasti cubile tuum.* [8. You have received adulterers; you have widened your bed.][144]

LVIII is one of Isaiah's best, also one of the most useful and moral. Why did Sacy render *frange esurienti panem tuum* by these words: "Share your bread"? Why not have said, "Break your bread", which is more forceful and creates an image? LIX is remarkable for the multiplicity and singularity of turns of phrase to express the same thing; for example: *Conceperunt laborem, et pepererunt iniquitatem.* [4. They conceive affliction and give birth to iniquity.] LX contains details of an opposite sort; it is full of salient features that characterize the

---

143   The Latin means: "Rain and snow from heaven inebriate the earth". Maréchal complains that Sacy omits a vivid anthropomorphic image that might offend propriety or expectations about Biblical language. Maréchal's upper-case letters emphasize the Latin original, replaced in Sacy's translation by the weaker verb "to water".
144   Alter: made room in your bed.

abundance, grandeur and well-being of a nation; among others: *Suges lac gentium, et mamilla regum lactaberis.* [16. You will suck the milk of nations; you will nurse at the breast of kings.]

One could give no more favorable idea of the character of Christ than in applying to him the distinctive features contained in Chapter LXI. Saint Jerome claims that Isaiah in his prophecies is so exact that he seems to narrate past events rather than to predict future ones. Did he take as a sign of the new law, as proof of the messiah's arrival and the rehabilitation of the Jews, this verse and several similar ones in Chapter LXII: *Et gaudebit sponsus super sponsam?* Good old Sacy renders it thus: [5. The young husband will live with his virgin bride.]¹⁴⁵ Another Solomon, rather than Christ, might instead be recognized therein. Who can appropriately be described with the bloody features with which Isaiah delights to paint the conqueror of the Jews' enemies, dyed with carnage: *Sicut calcantium in torculari,* Ch. LXIII? [2. Why are your clothes like the robes of those who trample out wine in the wine-press?] Assuredly it couldn't be Jesus Christ that is meant; he was not a warrior by nature. The gentle, modest portrait in the previous chapter is more faithful.

In Chapter LXIV, a vehement prayer from the prophet. Why, when he speaks of God or to God, does he always seem angry? Why does he always aim to frighten? Would it be that people are more disposed to believe and convert when they are afraid? Indeed, that was the character of the nation he preached to, and of every ignorant, superstitious people. The same tone prevails in Chapters LXV and LXVI. In the latter, there is an effective repetition: *Ecce servi mei comedent, et vos esurietis; ecce servi mei bibent, et vos sitietis.* [13. My servants will eat and you will suffer hunger; my servants will drink and you will suffer thirst.] The beginning of LXVI, the last book, is fine, especially this verse: *Ad quem respiciam (dicit Dominus) nisi ad pauperculum et contristo spiritu?* [2. The Lord says, Upon whom should I cast my eyes, if not on the broken-hearted poor?]

Isaiah, they say, also composed an apocalypse; if there were not more logic in it, one would find more poetry and eloquence in it than in the apocalypse of John. Demosthenes is the only Greek orator whom one might compare to our prophet. Racine gives him poetic enthusiasm as a distinctive characteristic. Isaiah's father was not Amos the prophet but another Amos who was only a prince of the blood of the Davidic dynasty.

---

145   Sacy: more literally the Latin says "The husband will rejoice on/about his wife".

XXIX Jeremiah

The first chapter is a type of prologue; the prophet could not give a higher idea of his mission than through this dialogue between God and him.

Why did Sacy translate the beginning of Chapter II the way one opens a fairy-tale? "Once there was... The Lord spoke to me one day and told me..." This chapter, in the original, is full of beauty and movement. Nothing more animated than Jeremiah's style; it is at the same time more balanced than Isaiah's. The *dicentes ligno: Pater meus es tu; et lapidi: Tu me genuisti,* [Saying to the wood: You are my father; and to the stone: You have given me life.] is well invented.

One observes, especially in Chapter III, how closely the proprieties are observed; Jeremiah is very careful to draw his metaphors and comparisons only from the ways of the people he censures. The Jewish nation, which he wants to correct in the name of the Lord, had plunged into debauchery; he puts himself at their level and describes Jerusalem only with the features of a prostitute. Ch. IV continues in this way. One notes a number of bold figures that we would call, in our timid language, risky; for example: *Circumcidimini Domino; et auferte praeputia cordium vestrorum habitatores Jerusalem...*, which the timid translator renders this way: [4. Be circumcised with the Lord's circumcision; cut from your hearts what is carnal...][146] Admittedly it is not easy to put into good French "praeputia cordium".

Someone has claimed that Jeremiah was less vehement than Isaiah. Did Isaiah have anything stronger than this passage from Chapter V?: *Haec dicit Dominus, Deus exercituum:...ecce ego do verba mea in ore tuo in ignem; et populum istum in ligna; et vorabit eos. Ecce ego adducam super vos gentem robustam ... Pharetre ejus quasi sepulcrum patens.* [14. This is what the Lord said to me, the God of armies; I will make my words fire in your mouth, that this people will be like wood which this fire will devour. 15. I will bring a strong people against them. 16. Its quivers will be like an open grave.] This same chapter opens well: God tells the prophet to seek a single just man in all Israel, and that in his favor he will spare the rest. Jeremiah searches among ordinary people and finds no one; among the great ones, even less ... etc.

There is a lot of conflict in Chapter VI. There are also occasional false comparisons and poor taste; this, for example: *Sicut frigidam fecit cisterna aquam suam, sic frigidam fecit malitiam suam.* [7. As the cistern chills the water it receives, so this city cold-bloodedly performs the most criminal actions.]

---

146 More literally: Be circumcised by the Lord, and offer the foreskin of your hearts, Jerusalemites.

To compare a cistern, which gives cold water, to a city that coldly commits crimes, is neither accurate nor in refined taste. Chapter VIII, like others, has beauties despite its many repetitions. Jeremiah knows above all how to place himself in the scene. Here, he has God order him to hold on to the temple doors and preach there in his name. Further on in the same chapter, he has God tell him: *Tu ergo noli orare pro populo hoc.* [Do not presume to intercede for this people.] These oratorical turns are skillful and must have produced an effect.

What a frightening scene is presented at the beginning of Chapter VIII: *In illo tempore, ait Dominus, ejicient ossa regum, ossa sacerdotum, ossa prophetarum, et ossa eorum qui habitaverunt Jerusalem de sepulcris suis; et expandent ea ad solem ... Non colligentur, non sepelientur!...etc.* [1. In that time, says the Lord, the bones of the king of Judah, the bones of its princes, the bones of its priests, the bones of its prophets, and the bones of the inhabitants of Jerusalem, will be thrown out of their sepulchers; 2. They will be exposed to the sun and moon ... They will not be collected or reburied but left on the ground like manure.] What more appropriate images to announce the desolation of an empire! The seventh verse resembles a passage from Isaiah: "The ox recognizes its stable, but my people have not recognized me". Here Jeremiah says, less interestingly: *Milvus in coelo cognovit tempus suum ... populous autem meus non cognovits judicium Domini...* [The hawk in the sky knows when its time has come ... but my people do not know the time of the Lord's judgment.]

The movement that the prophet has kept throughout Chapter IX is fine: *Quis dabit ... oculis meis fontem lacrymarum? Quis dabit in solitudine diversorium viatorum, et derelinquam populum meum? ...* etc. [1. Who will give my eyes a fountain of tears?...2. Who will show me a traveler's hut in the desert, that I may abandon this people?] How powerful this expression is: *Et extenderunt linguam suam, quasi arcum mendacii!* [3. They use their tongue like a bow, to launch lies...] Chapter X is remarkable, especially for a prosopopoeia against idols, very similar to the one I noticed in the book of Wisdom and in the prophecies of Isaiah.

At the beginning of Chapter XII, the prophet nearly reduces God to silence. One enjoys hearing good Jeremiah demanding of God why there are wicked people and why they prosper. God answers him rather vaguely and in an unsatisfying way; he seems pressed to his last resources.

If one wishes to have an idea of Oriental genius in all its sublimity, one need only read Jeremiah's Chapter XIII, the story of his linen sash. The prophet well understood how to exploit its possibilities, and what an effect his words have: *Haec dicit Dominus: sic putrescere faciam superbiam Juda!...* [9. This is how I will cause the pride of Judah to rot.] Further on, what a touching image! *Sicut enim adhaeret lumbare ad lumbos viri, sic agglutinavi mihi omnem domum Israel ... ut essent mihi in populum.* [11. For as a sash is wound around a man's loins, so I have tightly tied to me the entire house of Israel...] Further still, the image of the bottle full of wine is of the same type; but not quite as good. And, at the end of the chapter, how well he paints the shame and punishment of Jerusalem! *Ego nudavi femora tua contra faciem tuam et apparuit ignominia tua, adulteria tua, et hinnitus tuus, scelus fornicationsi tuae.* [26. This is why I lifted your robe up to your face and your shame was seen, 27. Your adulteries, your excesses, and the crime of your fornications.] Our modern literary folk may find this image poorly chosen, but how expressive it is!

Chapter XIV offers the scene of aridity, painted in three strokes of the brush, but they are master-strokes. Further on, Jeremiah puts into God's mouth invectives against false prophets—probably his rivals, who could reciprocally say the same about him. Chapter XV is full of powerful details along the lines of this verse: *Et dispergam eos ventilabro, in portis terrae.* This is a grand image. [God who disperses an entire nation on a winnowing basket and scatters the chaff to the four ends of the earth.] The first half of Chapter XVI is also full of affecting images. Jeremiah understood how to move the human heart. What could be more touching, to portray a desolate, ruined city, than what the prophet says in the Lord's name! *Et non frangent inter vos lugenti panem ad consolandum super mortuo, et non dabunt eis potum calicis ad consolandum super patre suo et matre. Ecce ego auferam de loco isto vocem sponsi et vocem sponsae.* [7. No one will give bread to him who mourns the deceased, to comfort him, and no one will give him drink to console him for the death of his father and mother. 9. In this place I will put an end to the husband's hymns and the wife's songs.]

Our classical poets, Greek and Latin, are no more classical or poetic than Jeremiah, when he wants to be. See, as proof, the first verse of Chapter XVII: *Peccatum Juda scriptum est stylo ferreo in ungue adamantine; exaratum super latitudinem cordis eorum, et in cornibus ararum eorum.* [1. The sin of Judah is written with an iron pen and diamond nib; it is engraved on the tablet of their heart and at the corners of their altars.] This entire imposing apparatus, all these terrible threats, aim at making people observe the Sabbath. Jeremiah got along with the priests, and probably made common cause with them: between priests and prophets there is only a hand's breadth. It is annoying that Isaiah and the other prophets did not use the sublimity of their talents to raise the abased spirit of their nation and to give it culture.

The fine metaphor of the potter, Chapter XVIII, is of the same type and perhaps even better than the one of the linen sash, which we mentioned above. The *numquid sicut figulus iste, non potero vobis facere*, is sublime. [6. Can I not do with you what the potter does with his clay?] In the rest of the chapter, Jeremiah speaks of the persecutions he has suffered, and displays a personality too irascible, too vindictive, for a man of God. Always many repetitions, but they are a bit less tiresome than in Isaiah because they are all dramatic.

In Chapter XIX, Jeremiah takes up again his fine comparison of the preceding chapter, and gives it a further degree of force. The sack of a city has never been better depicted than in this chapter: *et non vocabitur amplius locus iste Topheth, et vallis filii Ennom, sed vallis Occisionis* is a great stroke of the paintbrush. [6. The time will come when this place will no longer be called Topheth nor the valley of the sons of Hinnom, but the valley of Carnage.] The *sic conteram populum istum et civitatem istam, sicut conteritur vas figuli, quod non potest ultra instaurari* [I will break this people and this city as an earthen vase is broken and can never be put together] is the pendant to the *numquid* ... of the preceding chapter.

Chapter XX contains the most wonderful curses. XXII is full of fine details and traits of sensibility. The *vivo ego, dicit Dominus* [I swear by myself, says the Lord] of verse 24 is surely the etymology of the type of modern oath that our Henry IV often swore: "Vive Dieu..."

The chapter where Jeremiah struck me as most truly a prophet is the XXIIIrd. The clergy must recognize itself there, feature for feature, as in a mirror: *Et in prophetis Jerusalem vidi fatuitatem et in prophetis Samariae vidi similitudinem adulterantium, et iter mendacii; a prophetis Jerusalem egressa est pollutio super omnem terram.* [14. I have seen the prophets of Jerusalem like adulterers; among them I have seen the path of lies. 15. Corruption has spread from the prophets of Jerusalem over the entire earth.] Our preachers, our ministers of the Gospel, believe themselves (at least so say their heirs) the successors of the biblical prophets; they could be, except for the talent.

Isaiah began several chapters of his prophecies with *onus Aegypti, onus deserti maris, onus ... etc.* Did Jeremiah have him in mind when rising up against prophets *dicentes onus Domini* [speaking of the burden of God]? Might there not have been between them some professional rivalry? What happens today must have happened then. People are always the same.

The parable of the good and bad figs in Chapter XXIV produces little effect and is not as good as the preceding apologues. This Oriental fable is in a minor style.

Chapter XXV is one of the most superb in Jeremiah; it is very long but perfectly sustained from one end to the other. It is sublime, especially for this passage: *Sic dicit Deus: Sume calicem vini furoris de manu mea, et propinabis de illo cunctis gentibus ad quam mittam te; et bibent et turbabuntur, et insanient a facie gladii ... Et accepi calicem de manu Domini at propinavi cunctis gentibus,*

Jerusalem, et civitatibus Juda, et regibus et principibus ... etc. [15. This is what the Lord said: Take from my hand this cup of the wine of my fury and make all the peoples to whom I will send you drink it. 16. They will drink it and be troubled and they will be beside themselves with fear at the sight of the sword ... 17. I received the cup from the Lord's hand and I made all the peoples drink ... 18. and Jerusalem, and the cities of Judah, their kings and princes...] *Bibite et inebriamini, et vomite, et cadite, neque surgatis a facie gladii, bibentes, bibetis...* [27. Drink and get drunk, vomit what you drank, fall down and don't get up when you see the sword...] And at the end: *Et conticuerunt arva pacis a facie irae furoris Domini.* [37. The fields of peace are sadly silent before the anger and fury of the Lord.] Demosthenes has nothing approaching this thunderous eloquence.

Chapter XXVI has some relation to the passion of Jesus Christ, "the God who made Jeremiah prophesy", as the theologians say. We think—we who are neither theologians nor academicians—that Jeremiah speaks on his own behalf, and very eloquently reproduces a scene that could well have happened to him.

In Chapter XXVII, would he not be the tool of Nebuchadnezzar? Did not the prophet have an understanding with the conqueror? One can hardly explain otherwise this strange exhortation to servitude. Why distribute chains, on God's behalf, to the minor principalities of the Hebrews? We must admit that here Jeremiah plays an unattractive role; I barely recognize him. Instead of using his influence to rally his compatriots' courage, and reignite in them the love of liberty at the torch of religion, he preaches slavery and exhorts them to submit to it under pain of fire and famine; as if fire and famine were worse torments than the loss of liberty! One notes that Jeremiah, as much as he can, addresses the eye the better to reach the heart. Here, it is real chains he shows his compatriots, to make them submit more quickly to the yoke of the great king of Babylon.

Chapter XXVIII is still more strange. Another prophet comes to contradict, in the Lord's name, what Jeremiah predicted in the Lord's name. To prove that Hananiah is a false prophet, Jeremiah predicts his death: *Et mortuus est Hananias propheta in illa anno, mense septimo.* [And in fact Hananiah died the seventh month of the year marked for his demise.] What are we to think of such arguments? We must render justice to Jeremiah's genius and remain silent about the rest.

In Chapter XXIX, Jeremiah pushes his plan to its conclusion. He has urged his compatriots to a cowardly captivity; here he exhorts them to keep their chains and to multiply under the yoke of slavery. He is careful at the same time to denounce those of his colleagues who, more generous and better citizens than he, advocate the contrary. There is a fine expression in this chapter, which would cease to be so fine in the mouth of anyone but a God: *Ego sum judex et testis, dicit Dominus.* [23. I myself am judge and witness, says the Lord.] Nonetheless, it is not good to accustom the people to see, in one and the same person, an entire tribunal. This person, true enough, is the divinity; but since heads of state usually call themselves representatives of their gods, one must consider the consequences of illegal attributions given to God. His images on earth benefit from this in order to govern arbitrarily and absolutely, in his name.

Chapter XXX is more reassuring; it has warmth and rapidity. The next chapter is more pompous. I don't know what Jeremiah meant to say with these three words: *femina circumdabit virum*, nor why they are printed in capital letters. Isaac Lemaistre de Sacy has quite adequately translated them as: "A woman will surround a man". Apparently there is some mystery hidden beneath this.[147] This *circumdabit*, could it be a synonym for the *obumbravit* in an odd incarnation? Would these three words designate the conception of a savior in the belly of a virgin? Why taint the beautiful poetry of the Bible by making it an accomplice to the indecent mysteries of Gospel? Among the imaginative details of this chapter, there are some of quite bad taste, and not only this passage: *seminabo domum Israel ... semine hominum et semine jumentorum.* [The time is coming when I will scatter the house of Israel; I will populate it with men and beasts.] The translator blushed at this.[148]

The story of the sales contract, in Chapter XXXII, is another rhetorical figure along the lines of the linen sash, the earthen vase, etc. It creates a big effect and certainly demonstrates all the resources of the fine genius of its author. XXXIII contains only repetitions. XXXIV is similar. I was pleased to find in it an expression I had already noticed previously. The better to frighten King Zedekiah, here is how Jeremiah proceeds: *Et oculi tui oculos regis Babylonis videbunt, et os ejus cum ore tuo loquetur et Babylonem introibis.* [Your eyes will see the eyes of the king of Babylon, and you will speak to him mouth to mouth, and you will enter Babylon.]

Chapter XXXV is again a type of parable, Jeremiah's favorite rhetorical figure. One observes, too, that most of the chapters of his prophecies begin with this imposing formula: *Verbum quod factum est ad Jeremiam a Domino.* [1. Here is the word that the Lord addressed to Jeremiah...]

All the details of Chapter XXXVI are odd. It's only in Hebrew books that one finds their like. The Jewish people had its own particular physiognomy, customs

---

147 Alter explains by relating the line to the preceding image of Israel as a rebellious daughter, reversing the usual gender roles. *Obumbravit* in SM's guess is to shadow, darken, conceal.
148 Because Fr. "semer" can mean sow, scatter or inseminate.

belonging to them which the good man must observe; like the skillful chemist who renders the most toxic plants salubrious by separating their components. However, despite the system that the prophets put into their predictions, despite their fulminating rhetoric, picturesque poetry and ingenious parables, despite the God in whose name they speak, one does not see that they often persuaded the people to whom they spoke. Perhaps their lack of success must be attributed to the many charlatans who harangued the people.

In Chapter XXXVIII, there is a noteworthy expression. The elite of the people demand justice from King Zedekiah against Jeremiah who, through his predictions, removed the Hebrews' courage and urged them to submit to the yoke of Nebuchadnezzar. King Zedekiah answers them: *Ecce ipse* (Jeremiah) *in manibus vestris est; NEC ENIM FAS EST REGEM VOBIS QUIDQUAM NEGARE.* [5. I place him in your hands, for it is not just that the king should refuse you anything.] Kings of that time did not resemble their successors. "Such is our will, it pleases us" is today, in many countries, the response ordinarily made to the respectful remonstrances of the nation.

XXXIX and XL are remarkable in that they inform us that no one was spared in the sack of Jerusalem except Jeremiah, the same prophet who had exposed himself to ill treatment by his compatriots by stubbornly continuing to preach a prompt submission to Nebuchadnezzar. The conqueror was grateful for the service that his sworn prophet wanted to render him. In Chapter XLII, Jeremiah perfectly sustains his role, exhorting the conquered to kiss their chains rather than flee slavery and go to Egypt. Nebuchadnezzar had a faithful and zealous agent in Jeremiah. In Chapter XLIII, Jeremiah uses the figure so familiar to him, threatening his fellow citizens, who had considered him a liar, with the anger of the God whom he makes speak. He is careful, though, to speak to the eyes, using as imagery the stones that he says will soon serve as steps toward Nebuchadnezzar's throne.

Chapter XLVI offers a superb piece of poetry, a war scene done with a master's hand. What warmth! What rapidity in the seven lines composing the following chapter! What fine disorder! *Non respexerunt patres filios, minibus dissolutis ... O mucro domini! Usquequo non quiesces? Ingredere in vaginam tuam, refrigerare et sile.* [3. Fathers have not looked at their children, so beaten down are their arms. O sword of the Lord! Will you never rest? Return to your sheath, grow cold and *strike* no more.] "Strike", to translate *sile*[149]! How Sacy murders Jeremiah! How ill-inspired he is!

In Chapter XLVIII, Jeremiah swarms with images, turns, all the tricks of the most fertile and expressive imagination. XLIX is in the same style. Several of

---

149   sile: Be silent or still.

these chapters could have begun with the formula familiar in Isaiah: *Onus Ammon, onus Moab,* which is the same as *Ad Ammon, Ad Moab.*[150] But Jeremiah had loudly criticized the *onus* of his rival, so he can't use the same word. These chapters have been poorly arranged by the copyists or editors of the Bible. This one, XLIX, could make two or three; the division is indicated quite clearly. These different pieces, which owe a lot to the odes of Pindar,[151] are all in praise of Nebuchadnezzar, whose consecrated singer and devoted orator Jeremiah seems to be.

Chapter L is another superb piece, full of movement ... *Quomodo confractus et contritus malleus universae terrae?* [23. How did he who was the hammer of the whole earth get broken?] *Gladius ad divinos ejus ... gladius ad fortes ... gladius ad equos ... currus, ad vulgus, ad thesauros ejus ...* [36. The sword is drawn against his holy ones, against his brave ones, 37. against his horses and chariots and the entire people; the sword is drawn against his treasures.]

But Chapter LI, the last, is still more beautiful. The disorder of vengeance reigns there in all its horror, and Jeremiah terminates this grand composition with a stroke of the most profound energy: *Et dixit Jeremias ad Saraiam: Cum veneris Babylonem et videris et legeris omnia verba haec ... cumque compleveris legere librum istum, ligabis ad eum lapidem et projicies illum in medium Euphratem, et dices: Sic submergetur Babylon et non consurget a facie afflictionis.* [Jeremiah said to Saraiah: When you are in Babylon and you have read every word of this book ... then tie it to a stone and throw it into the middle of the Euphrates and say: This is how Babylon will be submerged...]

Chapter LII, which is not thought to be by Jeremiah, contains only details of the Jews' captivity in Babylon; it is a very simple account of the destruction of Jerusalem.

In this book, as throughout the Bible, one finds transpositions and contradictions among which it is difficult to orient oneself. The prophets, like the Pythian oracle and its priests, gave themselves a lot of trouble without much result, agitated in every sense, according to the winds of favor or circumstances.

XXX   Lamentations of Jeremiah

The Greek and Roman poets left no monuments surpassing this beautiful poem by Jeremiah. The richest imagination, the most touching sensibility are here displayed. The author of these Lamentations, a model of the elegiac

---

150   onus: load, burden, message.
151   Pindar (c.518–c. 438 BCE): Greek lyric poet.

mode, was a fine spirit. What truth in its scenes! Every image is well chosen! Not only poets but all artists should study and meditate on this great composition which is worthy of its fame and too well known to put forward all its beauties here.

This type of poem was cultivated in Egypt, Phoenicia, Greece and by the Romans. All peoples have losses to deplore, but none has painted its sorrows with as much energy as the Jews, thanks to the talent of their Jeremiah. This great poet prophesied for forty-five years, lived celibate, and died by stoning at the hands of his fellow citizens. His Lamentations have been scarcely better treated in the French translation by Arnaud Baculard,[152] around the middle of the century that has just ended.

XXXI   Baruch

The first two chapters are only ascetic commonplaces. The IIIrd starts to get interesting at verse 14. At the end are a few large strokes in the Oriental manner: *Stellae vocatae sunt, et dixerunt: Adsumus.* [God called the stars and they said: Here we are.] There is unction in Chapters IV and V.

The VIth and last chapter is the best and most important in this book. It contains instructions in the form of a letter which Jeremiah addresses to his captive compatriots in Babylonia, to protect them against the cult of idols, whose complete inanity he makes them feel. He ridicules the idols in every way and with every image he repeats this refrain, which is brought in gracefully: *Vade, sciatis quia non sunt dii; ne ergo timeatis eos.* [22. Go, and recognize that they are not gods, and do not fear them.]

The prophet Baruch, pupil and copyist for Jeremiah, stole a ray of his master's halo for his own head.

XXXII   Ezekiel

Ezekiel tells us in which year, in which month, and on which day he had the vision contained in his first chapter; he forgot to tell us at what time of night he had this dream, in which one recognizes only a prophet fast asleep in a troubled, agitated state. If this chapter expresses his mission, it doesn't give a very healthy idea of it; and if all these wheels, all these animals with four faces and

---

152   Baculard (1718–1805), novelist and dramatist.

calf's feet, represent the glory of God, one ought not be astonished by people's lack of haste to enjoy celestial blessedness.

Chapter II returns to antique simplicity, immediately becoming more interesting and more imposing. God, in Chapter III, gives his prophet a book to eat. If this is a sacred fact, there is nothing to say; if it is a metaphor, as would appears from these words: *et comedi illud, et factum est in ore meo sicut mel dulce* [3. I ate this book; it became sweet in my mouth, like honey], then it is rather extreme, a bit forced. The rest of Chapter III is of the same type; though one has to set apart the place where God gives the prophet *faciem adamantem et ut silicem* [A forehead of brass and hard as a stone] so that he may resist the opposition of those to whom he has to speak the truth. The meaning of this verse is fine, and even a sage could and should apply it to himself.

Stercore quod egredietur de homine operies panem tuum, Chapter IV. [12. You shall cover your bread with human feces.] Without claiming to justify this bit, which is no longer part of our culture, it must be admitted that the prophet Ezekiel couldn't better paint the desolation of a people reduced to feeding on its own excrement. This passage, which characterizes the Hebrew spirit, has its eloquence and its sublimity. The *fimum boum*[153] which comes afterward, weakens the metaphor. *Ecce ego conteram baculum panis in Jerusalem*[154] is superb. Never has a poet used a bolder or, at the same time, more precise expression. *Baculum panis* is not accurately rendered by "the power of bread" in Sacy; it would rather be "the sustenance, the support".

The curses of Chapter V are wonderful, but the preceding ones do them wrong. The metaphor of the shaven beard, etc. is ingenious but lacks great qualities. One is too aware of the author turning his idea every which way. The opening of the next chapter is much more imposing. There is something elevated in this apostrophe to the mountains and the rocks: *Ecce ego inducam super vos gladium, et dispergam excelsa vestra.* [3. Mountains of Israel, I will drop the sword on you and destroy your high places.] Poor Isaac de Sacy! Much movement in Chapter VII: *Finis venit; venit finis, afflictio ecce venit.* [The end is coming; the end is here, with affliction.] All the details of this scene are suitable to inspiring fear. The *certe vides, certe vidisti* [17. Indeed! You see, you have seen...] shows a beautiful simplicity. In Chapter X, veritable visions of a brain either sick or overstimulated. XI and XII contain only repetitions that become tiring and monotonous. Chapter XIII the same—and, moreover, much

---

153 Cow dung. The *New English Bible, Tanakh* and Alter translate this passage as referring to the kind of fuel used to bake the bread, whether human or animal dung.
154 I will break the staff of bread in Jerusalem (bread having been elsewhere called the staff, or support, of life.).

obscenity, many allusions lost to us and that we probably shouldn't regret. It seems that prostitutes were mixed up in this business and made fools of the prophets. The long Chapter XIV is nothing but words. If comparisons such as the vine in Chapter XV were less extravagant, they would be more effective.

Perhaps we are no better than the children of Jerusalem portrayed in Chapter XVI; but at least we have learned to put decency in our public behavior and in our books, if not in all our actions. This chapter will therefore revolt our chaste ears; but, apart from any idea of propriety, it can't be denied—if we care more for the spirit than the letter—that Ezekiel's long metaphor is perfectly sustained throughout this chapter, in which the most fecund imagination rules along with the most imagistically rich poetry; it is true to say that they are not all well-chosen. But other times, other customs.

Chapter XVIII is a complete refutation of original sin, and it could be parodied thus: "The sons of Adam should not have their teeth set on edge by the apple that Eve gave their father to eat".

Chapter XX, filled with repetition and boredom, has some fine features; for example, at the beginning: *Haec dicit Dominus Deus: Numquid ad interrogandum me vos venistis? Vivo ego, quia non respondebo vobis, ait Dominus Deus.* [Here is what the Lord your God says: Have all of you come to interrogate me? (And not "to consult me", as Sacy expresses it.) I swear by myself, says the Lord your God, that I will not answer you.] The last verse is remarkable; after a long litany of threats that Ezekiel places in God's mouth: *Et dixi: A! a! a! Domine Deus, ipsi dicunt de me: numquid non per parabola loquitur iste?* [Then I said: Alas! Alas! Alas! Lord my God, they ceaselessly say to me: Doesn't this person speak in parables?] Which seems to show that the people were not always so credulous.

Chapter XXI is one of the most extraordinary in the Bible; this long apostrophe to the avenging sword is full of movement and warmth. An intoxication of the brain dominates here, which must be highly valued in the original but seems very strange in the Latin and French versions. There is energy in the portrait of the bad customs of the Jews in Chapter XXII.

XXIII is absolutely in the style of XVI. The colors are even more vivid: *Carnes asinorum, fluxus equorum.* [20. She has abandoned herself to shamelessness to join those whose flesh is like the flesh of asses and whose friendship is like what one would have with horses...] How embarrassed was poor Sacy![155] These words are not the most edifying; but the letter kills and the spirit gives life, says the Bible in another place, doubtless to justify this one.

---

155 Because the line refers to the penile size and ejaculatory flow of donkeys and horses.

Chapter XXIV. To compare Jerusalem to a stew pot is not the noblest metaphor. But what does it matter, if the prophet makes himself understood? And it is not his fault if he doesn't succeed, for there is nothing he won't try to that end. His predecessors were stricter in their choice of means. Isaiah and Jeremiah had more tasteful style and more elevated spirit, but God uses all sorts of means to achieve his ends. A nightingale's song and an ass's bray are equally part of nature.

Chapter XXVI contains a fine curse against Tyre. The next chapter continues it and includes a number of details useful to history. The end is in the beautiful genre of Jeremiah's Lamentations. The apostrophe to the king of Tyre, Ch. XXVIII, is lively and of a noble simplicity. A despot's pride is well portrayed in these words from Chapter XXIX: *Meus est fluvius, et ego feci memetipsum.* [3. The river is mine, and it is I who created myself.]¹⁵⁶ XXX has no less energy and force: *et confortabo brachia regis Babylonis, et brachia Pharaonis concident.* [24. I will fortify the arms of the king of Babylon, and break the arms of Pharaoh.]

XXXI is full of poetry. Again the king of Egypt in XXXII, and thus the same ideas return with the same words. There is a strong hyperbole in verse 6: "O Pharaoh! The Lord says: With your blood I will soak the place where you swim, up to the mountains..." Chapter XXXIII only repeats an earlier one—XVIII, I believe. Chapter XXXIV is full of unction and must have made a strong impression on the Hebrew people. This didn't escape Christ, who used it in his evangelical mission; this choice shows the gentleness of his character, worthy of a better destiny.

Chapter XXXV, a curse! This chapter is another proof of the fecundity of imagination of the Orientals: one finds in the Bible curses on almost every page; yet each one has its particular character. The timid Isaac Sacy didn't dare a literal rendition of this truly bold and picturesque expression: *Concluseris filios Israel in manus gladii.* This passage certainly deserved that the translator should struggle with its original and not make it say flatly in French: "You have pursued them, sword in hand".¹⁵⁷

Much movement in Chapter XXXVI; but, to experience all its special beauties, one would have to be transported into the midst of an enslaved people to whom liberty has been promised. Chapter XXXVII is one of the most beautiful in the Bible. Homer and all of pagan mythology have no fiction approaching

---

156   SM follows older Catholic versions with God as speaker asserting his creation of nature and himself. But God is quoting Pharaoh's prideful assertion of having made the Nile, hence "I created it myself" or "for myself".

157   Maréchal's objection is probably that the Latin verb "concludo" would, in this context, mean something like "finish them off".

this vision for its sublimity, and even for the manner in which it is told. Cadmus's "teeth" are not worth Ezekiel's "bones".[158] Nothing more animated or more affecting had ever been said to the Jews in their captivity. This chapter alone puts Ezekiel in the rank of the most sublime poets.

There is much warmth, rapidity and power in Chapter XXXVIII and above all in XXXIX. The nine last chapters are filled with details that could not have been meaningless to the Jews. Ezekiel prophesies their reestablishment, the return to their country, the rebuilding of their temple and their religion. All of this is very skillful and must have had a powerful effect. Ezekiel was a fine genius. Born into a priestly family, he embraced, at the age of thirty, the profession of prophet, and practised it for twenty years. The reading of his prophecies was forbidden to Hebrews who had not yet reached the age of thirty.

XXXIII Daniel

The first chapter has only a small miracle to pique our curiosity; it must flatter those who hold with Pythagoreanism,[159] for vegetables and water procure for Daniel and his three companions a physique that they would scarcely have obtained from the succulent dishes served at the table of the king of Babylon.

In the second chapter, Nebuchadnezzar shows himself a strange sort of despot, and Daniel quite a subtle courtier for his age. What! To have all the sages of the empire killed because they couldn't guess the dream that his majesty had forgotten! What! To burn incense for an adroit flatterer and give him second place in the kingdom because he knew how to stroke the egoist on the throne!...For the rest, the diction of this chapter is remarkable for the air of sincerity dominating this sleep-inducing fantasy; still, it has its morality which could be applied to events in modern history.

Chap. III is no less odd. God still owes a miracle to those today who, following the example of the three young men in the furnace, dare to refuse incense to the divinized caprice of their prince; but the season of miracles is past. As for the literary merit of this long chapter, it has the merit of simplicity; but the prayer of Azariah and the hymn sung as a trio amid the flames are just words and do not support the justified celebrity of other biblical hymns. One notes

---

158 Cadmus: mythical Phoenician prince who sowed dragon's teeth from which grew warriors with whom he founded the Greek city of Thebes.

159 Pythagoras (c.570 BCE–c.495 BCE), Greek philosopher and mathematician said to have traveled widely and to have recommended a vegetarian diet. Maréchal became vegetarian and wrote a book (*Voyages de Pythagore*, 1799) about Pythagoras's travels and reform projects.

the absolute silence that the author of this chapter maintains about Daniel himself, during the torture of his three young companions.

This moral fairy-tale gets better in Chapter IV. Only a skillful narrator would place in Nebuchadnezzar's own mouth the tale of his humiliating metamorphosis. The allegory is obvious, and Daniel plays a fine role here. We don't mention the proprieties violated in every chapter; one ought not to be difficult with a tale of a thousand and one nights.[160]

What is more admirable in Chapter V: Daniel's courage in telling hard truths to his king, or the king's generosity in rewarding him for telling the truth? This trait merited a pardon from Balthazar. The end of this apparently simple chapter conceals a very skillful bit of rhetoric. There is an advantage to suppressing all detail, all commentary, and sticking closely to the fulfillment of the prophecy. For the rest, there is more than one difficulty to resolve in this narrative, which is regarded as a true story. It's extraordinary that at the death of Nebuchadnezzar, Daniel should have been completely forgotten by the king's successor. The tale of the lion's pit is in the style of the preceding ones. All these little stories must have amused the good Israelites.

Chapters VII and VIII are filled only with pointless visions. However, what have people not imagined in order to give them meaning? Daniel's prayer in Chapter IX is verbose and timid. The seventy weeks of this chapter are famous among theologians and definitely for no good reason. All the details of Chapter X are pretentious; they serve to show just how far, beneath an apparent cheerfulness, the prophets hide the art of giving an air of truth to the most absurd visions. La Fontaine[161] would have made a good prophet; he made animals speak as if he believed in animals' language.

In Chapters XI and XII are prophecies that have only the virtue of having been imagined long before those with which Matthew Lansberg every year enriched his almanac.[162] Then comes the pretty little novella of Susannah, which everyone knows, but which it's best to read in the original. It has a charming simplicity, which our songwriters ought to have kept in adapting this Biblical

---

160   *A Thousand and One Nights* is the title of a collection of tales from Persia, India and elsewhere, compiled perhaps as early as the eighth century and added to later. It became a generic term for fantasy narrative and the prototype of "Oriental" style.

161   Jean La Fontaine (1621–95), poet and fabulist.

162   Almanac: an annual calendrical document with various information whether medical, agricultural, predictive, etc.; a much-used genre, especially among rural populations. The almanac published annually from 1626 to 1951, usually at Liège, under the name of Matthew Lansberg (a seventeenth-century astrologer and mathematician) was popular throughout Europe (see Dagenais 2016).

anecdote to the Vaudeville theatre.¹⁶³ Few books lend themselves to parody better than sacred books.¹⁶⁴

The xivth and last chapter is in the style of the first few. It appears that Daniel had good sense, and an even more liberated spirit. His writings have tormented many an ecclesiastical Saumaise¹⁶⁵ and blackened plenty of paper. As for himself, one presumes he was a eunuch at the court of the king of Babylon, and that he prophetized very comfortably during his eighty-year long life.

xxxiv Hosea

What to think of the opening of Hosea's prophecies? *Et dixit Dominus ad Osee: Vade, sume tibi uxorem fornicationum, et fac tibi filios fornicationum, quia fornicans fornicabitur terra a Domino.*¹⁶⁶ This verse, which I will not translate, cannot be proposed as a model of taste, sublimity or decency, whether it is taken symbolically or at face value. The copyist, under the dictation of the Holy Spirit, experienced unusual distractions—and that's what they still call nowadays the divine scripture!

Chapter ii is in the same style. It might once have had, for the Jews, local beauties; but assuredly these strange parables cannot please everyone and are not of an eternal beauty. All the details of Chapters iii and iv are equally worthy of the b—¹⁶⁷ and indicate either an extreme corruption or extreme simplicity among a people who couldn't be made to understand reason except through the use of such means. And even nations that call themselves civilized, that have famous scholars and that respect themselves, continue to echo the obscene songs of a demi-barbaric, shameless horde! And our temples still resound every day with the filthy phrases of the Bible! And our pure virgins repeat them in our religious solemnities, under the eyes of their mothers!

---

163   The Vaudeville Theatre opened in Paris in 1792, specializing in light or sentimental performances, often with music.
164   As Maréchal well knew, having published a parody legendary, *La Nouvelle Légende Dorée* (1790), as well as parodies of other religious genres such as the catechism.
165   Claude Saumaise (1558–1653), Protestant classicist and Bible scholar.
166   "The Lord said to Hosea: Go, take for yourself a wife of fornication, and make for yourself sons of fornication, because by fornicating, the land has fornicated away from God".
167   Maréchal has "worthy of the b....l". The missing word is probably "bordel" (bordello).

Chapter v is everywhere quite obscure and consequently very prophetic. Chapters vi and vii the same. Here and there one finds a gleam of light which justifies the placement of Hosea right after Isaiah, Jeremiah and Ezekiel; for example, Chapter viii: *Quia ventum seminabunt, et turbine metent.* [7. They have sowed the wind and will reap tempests.] *Israel nunc factus est in nationibus quasi vas immundum.* [Israel is now treated, among the nations, like a vessel soiled by filthy uses.] And Chapter ix: *Area et torcular non pascet eos, et vinum mentietur eis.* [2. Israel will find nothing to eat in its barns or wine-presses, and its vines will disappoint expectation.] There is still more poetry and movement in x. Chapter xiv, the last, offers a sweet picture contrasting with what precedes it, and gives a bit of rest to the exhausted reader.

Theologians find very extraordinary things in the prophecies of Hosea. One must suppose, they say, that God is not ordering him to commit adultery but rather to marry a prostitute; this is the feeling of Saint Augustine and Saint Basil. What an edifying book, where God himself orders one to visit party-girls, and even to take them as wives! If one tore out all the indecent and immoral pages from the Bible, it would no longer be so voluminous.

xxxv Joel

Joel is more of a poet than Hosea. Has anyone ever better described an epidemic or a year of sterility than this prophet in his first chapter? The figures are grouped with maximum effect. His exclamations terrify. His frequent apostrophes communicate alarm even to the coldest reader, the reader most wary of prophecies.

Chapter ii is full of rapid movement and warmth. What imagination! What fire! What precision! And at the same time, what a profusion of images! How the scenes are both hurried and fulfilled at once! Sometimes he falls into exaggeration: grasshoppers that fly up do not make as much noise as chariots.

Chapter iii, the last, cedes nothing to the two preceding. Joel takes every tone; he multiplies himself. What an overexcited mind this prophet must have had! His little work is a model of the oriental style, exemplifying it more than any other book of the Bible; and reading it would make one a poet, if one could become a poet by reading.

We know nothing personal about this vehement prophet. We don't even know which tribe he came from. From his style it doesn't seem that he frequented bad places after the example of Hosea his contemporary. The spirit of God inspired him with more honest but no less poetic terms. The rhetoric he uses is more chaste and does not cause a blush.

XXXVI Amos

The first two chapters have the usual character of prophecies, but there is vigor only in a few spots of the second: *Pro eo quod vendiderit pro argento justum, et pauperum pro calceamentis ...* etc. [Israel has sold the just man for money, and the poor for the vilest things.] Chapter III has nothing very remarkable; the prophets have accustomed us to piled-up comparisons, often to good effect.

The end of Chapter IV has nobility and grandeur: *Quia ecce formans montes et creans ventum, et annuntians homini eloquium suum, faciens matutinam nebulam, et gradiens super excelsa terrae.* [13. Here is the one who forms the mountains and creates the wind, who announces his word to mankind, who produces the morning clouds, and walks on the highest places.] There are fine things in Chap. V, if only the second verse, and also a lot of repetition at the beginning.

Chapter VI, against the rich and fortunate of the time, has power: but the rich and fortunate of the time are normally deaf to all these fine declamations; the joys of the moment prevent them from considering future dangers.

The shepherd Amos shows firmness in Chapter VII. All these little quarrels between prophets are pitiable; but from this ridiculous conflict some flashes jump out, which slightly diminish the boredom of the rest. Chapter VIII contains another fine curse against the evil rich and bad people; the prophet ends it this way: *In die illa deficient virgines pulchrae, et adolescentes in siti.* [At that time, beautiful virgins will die of thirst, and with them the young people.] The eight first verses of Chapter IX, the last, are beautiful; the rest is ordinary.

The prophet Amos was a shepherd, gathering berries among the thorns; as he guarded his animals on the outskirts of Bethlehem, God chose him to increase the herd of his prophets.

XXXVII   Obadiah

The single chapter of twenty-one verses which makes up the prophecies of Obadiah, is too trivial to merit much time. Still, verse 4 offers a fine poetic image, and 18 has pathos. This prophet was the chief officer in the house of King Ahab. In those days, God found his servants everywhere, even at court.

XXXVIII   Jonah

This prophet, son of a prophet, was a bastard born of a widow. According to God's commandment to Hosea, Jonah's father settled for concubinage to avoid adultery, with a woman who no longer had a husband.[168] Whatever ... let's talk about his book.

The narrative of the first chapter is amusing. Jonah's hymn in the belly of the whale is worthy of the place that inspired it. Chapter III must make the wise man smile. Actually, it is pleasing to see, through Jonah's voice, the king and inhabitants of Nineveh cover themselves in sacks, they and their mares; a great fast is commanded, even for the herds of animals: *Homines et jumenta et boves et pecora non gustent quidquam nec pascantur, et aquam non bibent; et operientur saccis hominis et jumenta.* [7. Let people, horses, cattle and sheep eat nothing; they are not to be taken to pasture and not to drink water; 8. Let men and animals be covered with sacks.]

Chap. IV shows Jonah's good heartedness. What! He is angry with God because God has pardoned Nineveh! Let us also pardon the prophet on account of his confession of anger; let us admire above all the compliance of God, who deigns to account to Jonah for his conduct. "In Nineveh (says the Lord to his servant) there are 120,000 men who don't know their right hand from their left; and I should punish them?...They are more stupid than wicked". It's only in the Bible that we find this sort of naiveté.

It's interesting to read in the "Prologue" to Jean-François Laharpe's *Psalter*, how this converted literary man tortured himself trying to find something sublime in Jonah's Oriental fable; he admires above all the familiarity established between the man and his God—which, according to him, could only be inspired. But we profane types whom grace has not yet illuminated, in spite of our good will we are unable to see anything here other than the language of an Asiatic poet who, to place himself at the level of simple people, and to give himself importance in their eyes, relates to his divine master informally as an equal companion and uses conversational style. This observation should be applied to all the parables with which both Testaments abound.

XXXIX Micah

The first chapter contains types of lamentations, less fine than Jeremiah's. In Chapter III, Micah scolds false prophets. Would he be engaging in a bit of professional rivalry with this holy curse? Chapters IV and V are full of vague allusions, which some have not failed to connect to Jesus Christ. There are also passages imitated from his colleagues. Chapter VI has more originality. I like to

---

168 The story of Jonah's parentage is rabbinic legend, not scriptural.

see God humanize himself and play the interlocutor with his people. The portrait of Jewish iniquities is strongly portrayed in the VIIth and last chapter.

We know that the root of the word "Micah" means "like God". Mankind is so little in a position to test or verify this illustrious etymology that he has given this name a quite contrary specific meaning; it has been made an injurious expression, a term of contempt, to designate a good animal, a good Israelite, a good apostle, a foolish husband, etc. There have been many Micahs.[169]

XL   Nahum

This second prophet against Nineveh is much more a poet than the first. The scene he has left us of the sack of this city is from a master's hand. Nothing more animated, more rapid, can be found in Homer or Ossian. Art has never attained this fine disorder. Every word is an image or a sentiment: *Vox flagelli, vox impetus rotae.*[170] Nahum is a great painter. He is thought to be a contemporary of King Sardanapalus.[171]

XLI   Habakkuk

The two chapters of Habakkuk are quite fine. The prophet confronts God with his responsibilities: *Quare taces? Devorante impio justiorem se ...* etc. [13. Why do you remain silent, while the impious man devours those who are more just than he?] It was difficult to respond to this lively apostrophe. Without completely justifying himself, God replies in grand style: *Vae qui aedificat civitatem in sanguinibus ... Quia lapis de pariete clamabit ...* etc. [12. Woe to him who builds a city with the blood of men! 11. The stone will cry out against you from within the wall.]

Here it was a case of resolving the famous problem of good and evil under a God both good and all-powerful; we have to believe, according to these fine chapters of Habakkuk, that it is insoluble. The name "Habakkuk" signifies "struggler", doubtless because of his courageous struggle with God himself. The hymn which terminates these too-short prophecies is less beautiful than they, although it certainly has the exalted character suited to this sort of production.

---

169   In French, the name is *Michée*. A slang word, *miche* or *michet* meant a prostitute's client or someone who pays out or is taken advantage of.
170   The voice (noise, i.e., crack) of the whip, the violent voice (noise) of (chariot) wheels....
171   Assyrian monarch of uncertain historicity.

Saint Jerome attributes to Habakkuk, Daniel's contemporary, the little anecdote of the chaste Susannah. Theologians admit freely that the prophecies of Habakkuk are obscure and difficult to reconcile with events. We can confirm this declaration.

XLII   **Sophonius**

This excellent prophet (according to Saint Cyril) has somewhat of the style of Jeremiah. His prophecies, vehemently spouted in the crossroads, must have made a great impression on the mind of the Jews. He predicted the happiness that the messiah would procure. The messiah has arrived: so when will we be happy?

XLIII   **Haggai**

His two chapters are unimportant; however, they do have the prophetic character and breathe antiquity. The word was put into Haggai's mouth to incite the Jews to rebuild their temple, for they were hardly in the mood for this expense. The first temple, which had cost so much, had not preserved them from captivity. God had already gone back on his word several times; despite his fine promises, he had abandoned his cherished people. Haggai's eloquence restored a little courage to his unfortunate compatriots.

XLIV   **Zachary**

The visions of the first chapter are not well done: talking horses, horns that attack people—all this is definitely sublime!
　　There are two better-done touches in Chapter II, which must have been consoling for the Jews. Zachary has them spoken by God himself, on the topic of a surveyor whom he sees in a vision, measuring the borders of Jerusalem: *Et ego ero ei, ait Dominus, murus ignis in circuitu.* [5. I myself will make a wall of fire to surround it.] The other feature is about sentiment; it's still God who is made to speak: *Qui enim tetegerit vos, tangit pupillam oculi mei.* [8. Because he who touches you, says the Lord, touches the pupil of my eye.]
　　The meaning of Chap. III is up to the speaker. Same for Chapter IV. In Chapter V, what is the meaning of a flying book, a woman seated at the bottom of a bottle, and a bottle for which a house is built? All this is an enigma, or rather

the fantasies of a prophet either fasting or drunk. What poverties, what foolishness in this Bible which is sometimes so fine! Chapter VII at least has a moral purpose; it implies that a good action is worth more than a long fast. The only satisfying thing in Chapter VIII is this: *Veritatem tantum et pacem diligite;* [19. Love only truth and peace] "and I forgive you the rest", says the Lord to his people. The Lord's ministers are more exigent and harder to please than their master.

The 9th verse of Chapter IX is a quite clear prophecy of the advent of the messiah: *ecce rex tuus veniet pauper et ascendens super asinam, et super pullum filium asinae.* [9. Here is your king coming to you; he is poor; he is mounted on a donkey and on the donkey's foal.] This isn't the place to sing with the Church: *Rex celestis, rex gloriae.*[172] The last verse is completely pleasing: *quid enim bonum ejus (Domini) est et quid pulchrum ejus, nisi frumentum electorum, et vinum germinans virgines.* [17. For what has the Lord to give that is good and excellent, if not the grain of the chosen and the wine that makes virgins bloom?]

Chapter X has rapidity and an air of inspiration glimpsed through the obscurity and disconnected ideas it is full of. For instance, what can this mean, placed in God's mouth? *Et super hircos visitabo* ?[173] You have to be a prophet, to have the privilege of speaking this way without understanding it oneself, as also in Chapter XI. Chapter XII is more intelligible and also finer. This image has grandeur; it has wonderful simplicity, albeit a bit ferocious: *In die illa ponam Jerusalem lapidem oneris cunctis populis; omnes qui levabunt eam concisione lacerabuntur.* [3. In that time, I will make Jerusalem like a heavy stone for all the peoples; all those who want to lift it will be killed and torn apart.] And this verse as well: *In die illa ponam duces Juda sicut caminum ignis in lignis, et sicut faciem ignis in foeno; et devorabunt ad dexteram et ad sinistram omnes opulos in circuitu.* [6. On that day, I will make the chiefs of Judah like charcoal placed under firewood, like a torch lit amid the straw; and they will devour, left and right, all the peoples around them.] God treated the Hebrew nation like a starving mob, a pack of dogs. The last two chapters are quite prophetic, that is, full of vague details that could produce an effect only on Jewish souls.

According to Saint Jerome, Zachary was the natural son of Barach, and son of Addo according to the law. Here is a rather curious observation: It is that from Moses to Christ inclusive, almost all the slightly famous people in the Bible are bastards. Their words and their behaviors show the effects of their birth.

---

172 Heavenly king, king of glory.
173 I will visit (punish) the goats: Zachary X, 3. This is, of course, metaphorical: the Jews are a flock without an adequate shepherd.

XLV Malachi

This prophet's name signifies "my angel". In fact, if we must trust Tertullian and the voluntary eunuch Origen,[174] Malachi was an angel incarnate. However, the Seventy[175] and the Church fathers maintain that Malachi was only an angel by function, not by nature. But you know, honorable readers, that priests are not all angels by function; this is the view of Malachi himself.

In his first two chapters, he inveighs courageously against priests. He reproaches them above all for living badly with their wives. The modern clergy is sheltered from this suspicion but is no better. The two other chapters contain only prophetic commonplaces. "Awaiting", he says, "the terrifying day of the Lord", that is, the arrival of a messiah.

Nonetheless there is a noteworthy passage; here it is: "The priest's lips will guard knowledge, and it is from his mouth that you will ask to learn". Where would we be if we had never been to any other school?

N.B. Extract from the Catechism of Curé Meslier[176]

QUESTION. What is it to lie?
ANSWER. To act like a prophet.

"The Oriental style is that of the prophets", says Jean-François Laharpe in his *Psalter*, p. 56. This assertion strikes us as a bit immoderate, and injurious to God; it attributes to him very little taste, for who doesn't know that the Oriental poets are more inflated than sublime, have more emphasis than eloquence and don't always trouble to put justice, truth, and nature into their frequent extended metaphors?

The Jews attached little importance to all these prophecies, as this proverb testifies: *Producentur dies, et peribit omnis visio.* [Prophecies envisage only distant times; thus, they are useless.] There is good sense in this impious saying. The prophets riposted with another proverb: *Ubi non est visio, profligabitur populus.* [When there is no prophetic vision, the people are fallen.] We must

---

174   Tertullian (c. 155–c.240), Carthaginian Christian scholar; Origen (185–254), Greek theologian said to have castrated himself in order to remain chaste.
175   The group of seventy Alexandrian scholars credited with translating Jewish scripture into Greek, between the third and second centuries BCE.
176   Jean Meslier (1664–1729), a priest, revealed his atheism and anti-clerical views in a long posthumously discovered "testament". Maréchal appropriated Meslier's name for the title of his own parody of Catholic catechism (a series of questions and answers about the faith).

regret the loss of some prophecies, despite the divine inspiration from which they emanated. Human books are not the only ones that are lost.

The Greek also had their prophets, but we must agree that the Apollo of Delphi did not furnish his ministers with inspirations as sublime or poetic as the Jahweh of Jerusalem.

Honorable readers, we appeal to your goodness and wisdom: Is it not true that the "seers, men of God, envoys of the Most High, indeed angels"—for holy scripture freely gives all these magnificent titles to the prophets—is it not true, we say, that men worthy of these fine titles would have spoken, would have written, if not with more poesy (there couldn't be more), at least with more consequence, more logic, more wisdom, and above all with more decency and humanity? The divine inspiration that possessed them resembles all too closely the disorder of an ill-organized brain, a mind ill-made or ill-furnished. Honorable readers, you have just gone through the prophetic books with us; tell me, can they be good for anything other than to be occasionally consulted by poets?

The Bible itself doesn't give a very elevated idea of its prophets since, in its style, "prophetize" is used for "sing, dance, play instruments". This grammatical observation, though serious enough, doesn't come from us; it belongs entirely to the Reverend Father Dom Augustin Calmet. [177]

Saint Augustine—not the Benedictine just mentioned, but the bishop of Hippo—claims that the prophets were the philosophers of Judea. To complete this assertion by a Church father, one could find some analogy between our holy prophets and the Cynic philosophers;[178] they too wore the cloak, the big sack, the cane and the beard: they had all the prophets' slovenliness. The Capucin Bolduc[179] claims that the profession of prophets goes back to the deluge.

Among the Jews can be counted ten or so prophetesses, of whom Sara is the first and the virgin Mary the last. Why not go all the way back to Eve? These prophetesses all seem to be copies of the sibyls.[180] Most of these claimed prophetesses did not know how to read, and died without doubting the role they had played or that it was suggested they play, unknown to them, for posterity.

---

177 Calmet (1672–1757): monk, Biblical translator and commentator.
178 Cynics: a Greek school of philosophy from the fifth century BCE, emphasizing reason, nature and virtue; often they practised asceticism.
179 Jacques Bolduc (1580–1646): monk, theologian, church historian.
180 Ancient Greek seers or women prophets with oracular powers, who lived at specific shrines.

XLVI   Maccabees,[181] or the Murderers: Book I

The first chapter could serve as a model for writing history; a fine simplicity prevails, and an attractive air of veracity. Our interest grows significantly in the next chapter, whose hero is Mattathias. His speech is excellent and very suited to what he is thinking: *Vae mihi!...Templum ejus sicut homo ignobilis ... Vasa gloriae ejus captiva abducta sunt.* [7. Woe is me! 8. His temple is treated like a disreputable man. 9. The vessels consecrated to his glory have been stolen like captives.] I don't at all like to see him kill with his own hand both his compatriot sacrificing to false gods, and the conqueror's envoy; he ought to have remained on the defensive and never attacked. His fine zeal degenerates into rage, especially when *circumdederunt (Mattathias et amici ejus) pueros incircumcisos quotquot invenerunt.* [46. They circumcised all the uncircumcised children they found.] A hero making war against babies!

It's good to see, in Chapters III, IV, V, a people fighting for their homes, their gods and their liberty. The Jews play a truly honorable role only in the books of the Maccabees. In the style there prevails a rapidity which depicts quite well the conquests of Judah; the most marvellous thing is that all these narratives are not accompanied by any miracle or magic. The Jews owe their victories to nothing but themselves. On that topic, we note how proprieties are observed in the Bible: when it's a question of establishing religion, miracles are multiplied; but in this book, which treats the liberty and life of the Israelites, the author of this part of Jewish history had the good sense to not throw in magical events but to leave all the honor to the Jews.

As for the rest, we must pardon the annalist for making Antiochus die of regret for having profaned the holy places, Chapter V. The grandeur of the Romans is painted with broad strokes in Chapter VIII: *Et in omnibus istis nemo portabat diadema.* [14. Not one of them wore a diadem.] It is also odd to read, in the same chapter, the treaty of alliance made between the Romans and the Hebrews.

Up to the XVIth and last chapter of this book, all goes well; and the history of the Jews is that of a brave people led by skillful and prudent generals. The nation ascends to a degree of power and well-being that it had not been able to obtain up to then, Chapter XIV: *Et sedit unus quisque sub vite sua et sub ficulnea sua.* [12. Each one sat beneath his vine and his fig tree.] In any language, nothing

---

181   SM's note: *Per me plaga*, word for word from the Hebrew name. [There is much scholarly discussion about the meaning or even original language of the name Maccabee. Maréchal probably relies on the 1777 *Tractatus de Divinitate et Canonicitate* of J.F. Marcini.—Trans.].

better than this verse can be found; it admirably portrays the calm and security of a people free because of its courage, and sheltered by its laws.

The last chapter spoils everything. We see with dismay old Simon allow his enemy to get him drunk, and to die shamefully at the table.

The original of this first book is in Hebrew; that of the second is only in Greek, but not the best time of the Greeks. The spirit of God was not eloquent in all languages, as we will see.

XLVII   Maccabees, or the Murderers: Book II

This second book opens with a miracle: this thick liquid drawn from the pit where the sacred fire had been hidden, this troubled water which catches fire in the sun's rays, definitely seems like a priestly invention. Chapter II especially does not bear the antique character that we have observed in the first book: the writers are clever; comparisons are multiplied; in a word, it is a preface such as is too often placed in modern books.

How slow-paced is the narrative of Chapter III! It is a dull scene that would have taken livelier colors under the brush of prophets. We can judge from this dragging phrase: *Sed spiritus omnipotentis dei magnam fecit suae ostensionis evidentiam ita ut ...* [24. But the spirit of all-powerful God made itself visible through perceptible marks, so that...] Can there be anything more cowardly? Assuredly the Holy Spirit did not inspire the author with this description; or rather, *aliquando dormitat.*[182] As for the miraculous torture of Heliodorus, if we reduce it to its proper value, it is perhaps again only a little priestly ruse. Two of the Levites[183] would have dressed up as "angels of office" (see *Malachi*) and, proving their audacity, come in to whip Heliodorus, etc.

King Antiochus was not whipped, Chapter V; however, he did even worse than Heliodorus. This whole narrative is flat and boring, written without warmth or movement. Still the same style in Chapter VI. The narrator interrupts himself to give in to monastic reflections. Please: more nerve, more precision, more nobility! The martyrdom of Eliezer is interesting despite its poor diction, and his death shows to what point people can carry stubborn opinions, even for the most futile or pointless things. To eat pork! The old man had constancy worthy a more important cause. The rest is of the same type. Perhaps they ought to have been content with the first book of Maccabees and not

---

182   Sometimes he slept (i.e., made a mistake).
183   Levites: assistants at the shrine.

put this one among the canonical books; it devalues this fine set of antique monuments.

Lamothe-Oudart shod the Maccabees in French tragic sandals, in 1721, with a bit more success than J. Virey in his 1596 *Maccabee* and Abbé Nadal in his 1722 *Antiochus*. These three dramatic authors drew their subject from Chapter VIII of the second book, which is much more atrocious and distasteful than tragic. It is not natural that a mother should applaud the dismemberment of the bodies of her seven sons. Racine made better choices from the Bible.

N.B. Extract from the Catechism of Curé Meslier

QUESTION. What is the Bible?

ANSWER. It is a book that today would be banned from publication for the sake of maintaining good behavior.

And nonetheless Jean-François Laharpe claims that sacred books contain God's knowledge! If that is true, God has genius, no doubt—but neither logic nor morality. Let us read the last lines of a decretal of the Council of Trent[184] on the Bible: "If someone does not accept all these books as sacred, with all that they contain, let him be anathema!"[185]

We say: How could there be found, how can there still be found, men sufficiently deprived of good sense and modesty to preach to the simple the turpitudes that abound in the two testaments, and which the literary beauties found there do not redeem? This book from on high is often in the lowest style. If a quill pen, plucked from an angel's wing, wrote Boaz and Ruth, Tobias, even the Song of Songs, an iron blade hacked out the rest. The worst tone prevails in the works of David, Solomon, the prophets, and Moses himself. The Bible cannot become a classic work without serious drawbacks; reading it corrupts youth. "What one reads of the Old Testament (says Saint Basil,[186] in his "Letter to Chilon") can often create damage". Let us cite, in support of this observation, Rule IV of an index to the Council of Trent itself:

> "Bookshops that sell books of the Bible, in the vernacular, to those who don't have the ability to read them, will lose the price of their books and

---

184 SM's note: We note in the history of this council an unusual circumstance: that it began with a ball. [The Council of Trent—actually a series of meetings between 1545 and 1563— was convened to combat the Protestant Reformation and establish some reforms within Catholicism—Trans.].
185 An ecclesiastical curse of excommunication or doctrinal unacceptability.
186 Greek theologian, c. 330–c. 379.

will be punished".[187] So we see that even priests were sometimes embarrassed by the contents of their books; that's what they were reduced to! Someone composed a work entitled *The Sanctuary Closed to the Profane*; deliberately to demonstrate that they must forbid the people to read the sacred books. In the preface to a picture-book Bible, without text, that appeared in 1728 in Paris, the publisher motivated his decision by saying: "It is not appropriate for everyone to read holy scripture".

---

[187] For centuries, the Bible was available only in Latin; translation into vernaculars was forbidden by the Church. The inability to read, in the rule quoted, meant inability to read Latin.

PART 2

Christian Scripture

∴

The New Testament

I   The Holy Gospel of Jesus Christ According to Saint Matthew

The first chapter is divided into two sections: the first has the genealogical tree of Christ. Fine, although it may be a poor example to display one's ancestors this way. The second part narrates the story of Jesus's birth; it is hardly normal and edifying, this birth of the legislator for Christians. If we require marvels to make people better; if we have to ornament the truth to help it find favor in people's eyes, at least this first chapter in this special code of laws should not be sullied by an indecent and scandalous mystery! What to think of a moral book that begins with adultery? A bastard is a person like any other, no doubt; but why list among his perfections the illegitimacy of his birth?

One is revolted in reading, in Indian mythology, that Brahma, the supreme god, finding himself alone with his daughter, conceived and executed the project of incest. Must one be more edified, in reading Christian mythology, that God the father meditated from all eternity an adultery, and consummated it through the operation of the Holy Spirit, by impregnating the married Mary with God the son? It is true that they call her a virgin, even after having been a mother. Thus, Asia consecrates a religion to incest, and Europe one to adultery.

We must admit that the universe has been very lucky. The redemption of the human race, salvation of the world, fulfillment of prophecies, literal and figurative senses of the Old Testament, miracles of the new; the dispersion of the Jews, conversion of gentiles, destruction of idolatry, etc.—what did all this depend on? On a word. The destiny of the world depended on a "yes" or a "no". If the virgin had not had such an easy virtue; if she had responded flatly "no" to the fine promises and insinuating propositions of the messenger of the Holy Spirit, that would have been it. What would we have become? Alas! We would have had no Church, no pope, no cardinals, bishops or priests, no masses or councils, no indulgences, inquisitions, crusades, no Saint Bartholomew,[1] no Carmelites, Jacobins or Capuchins; Mary would have been simply a carpenter's wife and the mother of a little apprentice woodworker. This is where we read the history of great events through small causes.

---

1 In 1572, Catholic mobs, encouraged by nobles and royalty, massacred thousands of Protestants (Huguenots) in Paris and other cities across France. This particularly violent episode in the religious wars of the period began on St. Bartholomew's Day (August 24), commemorating one of the original twelve apostles of Jesus, sometimes known as Nathanael.

A married virgin[2] who finds herself pregnant without her husband's knowledge, and through the work of another agent; an angel who comes to explain everything to the deceived husband[3] and to forbid him to lament or complain—all this doesn't seem like too much for evangelical purity. Genuinely admirable, or rather genuinely singular, is the good-natured tone and the air of truth that the chronicler puts into his narration of such an extraordinary event; he doesn't deign to motivate anything or justify anything. Apparently, he takes his readers either for idiots or for libertines.

Honorable readers! We will spare you the household quarrels that must have surfaced between Joseph and Mary when she became pregnant, to his great surprise. Among the fifty or sixty existing gospels, the Church has prudently recognized only the four that are silent about all these unedifying details: it has already let only too many slip through in its canonical books.

Let us nonetheless notice Joseph's moderation: 19. *Joseph vir ejus, cum esset justus, voluit occulte dimittere eam.* [Joseph her husband, being just and not wanting to dishonor her, resolved to send her away secretly.] In spite of religion and its mysteries, here one renders homage to the eternal principles of honesty that nature engraves in the hearts of all people, and which nothing can entirely efface. Joseph, not completely reassured by the angel Gabriel, feels the affront he has suffered; for to be dishonored by the deed of a God or by the deed of a simple mortal, it is still an affront. It is not in the power of a God to purify the conjugal bed that he has just sullied.

Chapter II is even more filled with absurdities, worthy of the *Thousand and One Nights*. The miraculous star that leads the three kings or mages of the Orient to the crèche of Bethlehem: wouldn't that be a warmed-over version of the star of Venus which, according to the learned Varron (*rerum divinar.* II) guided the pious Aeneas to Italy, *ad agrum usque Laurentum*?[4] While reading these fantasies, I admire the precaution of the Church, which has been very careful to recommend to its grown children the non-use of reason, *in obsequium fidei.*[5]

---

2 SM's note: Niu-oua or Niu-va, sister or wife of Fohi, an ancient legislator of the Chinese, obtained, through her prayers, the status of both virgin and wife. This is how queen Kiang-yuen became the mother of Heon-tsi and remained a virgin. Cf. the *Chou-king. Nil sub sole novum.* [The Latin phrase means "Nothing new under the sun".—Trans.].

3 SM's note: It is a major question among the Greek and Latin Church fathers as to whether Joseph was a virgin or a widower when he married the good virgin Mary. See the "Remarks" of Saint-Réal on the *Life of Jesus Christ.* [César Vichard, abbé de Saint-Réal (1643–92), novelist and historian.—Trans.].

4 Varro (116 BCE–27 BCE), Roman poet and scholar, author of *On Divine and Human Matters*; Aeneas: Trojan hero who became the mythical founder of Rome, led by his mother, Venus (goddess and star), to the territory/fields of Laurentum.

5 In deference to faith.

How the historians of Jesus have done him wrong! And must one be of bad faith to warn against a mission announced under such auspices? And the gospel of Matthew is still the least ridiculous of them all!

John the Baptist, in Chapter III, proclaims Jesus in rather too strong terms: *Cujus ventilabrum in manu sua, et permundabit aream suam; et triticum suum congregabit in horreum.* [He has his winnowing pan in hand, and will perfectly clean his threshing floor; he will gather his wheat in the loft.] *Paleas autem comburet igni inextinguibili.* This metaphor is fine; but "to burn the straw in an inextinguishable fire" is extreme and far from realistic. But this proclaims Christ as a pitiless God, eternal in his vengeance. I still don't find any model of behavior in the Holy Gospel. Jesus Christ finally appears, and fortunately he contrasts completely with his precursor. I suppose that one of his faults was poor judgment in choosing his people. But the first phrase he utters expresses modesty and balance.

The first part of Chapter IV—the story of the temptation—honors the goodness and moderation of Jesus. Under this somewhat crude allegory (though more suited to the people), he gives lessons full of sense; he instructs us that it isn't enough to care for the body but it is also necessary to nurture the spirit with useful truths, etc. etc. It's too bad that he soon forgets his serious personality; or rather, Jesus Christ shows us that the sage can sometimes enjoy himself. It is doubtless in this spirit that we should read the word-play from his divine mouth when he addresses the brothers Simon and Andrew, both fishermen: *Venite post me, et faciam vos fieri PISCATORES hominum.* [Follow me and I will make you *fishers* of men.]⁶ However, I don't approve Jesus tempting the son away from the father: *Illi statim relictis retibus et patre, secuti sunt eum.* [22. At the same time, they left their nets and their father, and they followed him.] Today one would blame this person as anti-moral and anti-social. Here, Jesus behaves like a true bastard.

It's in Chap. V that Jesus begins to be really interesting; not in spouting his eight beatitudes—a vague sermon, disconnected, inconsequential, and susceptible of contrary interpretations; but especially from verse 33 to the end. That is where he deploys all the sweetness, all the simplicity, all the good nature of his character. For those who have studied the ancient moralists, he says nothing new; but it must have seemed new to the Jews to hear one of their compatriots exhort them to virtue with this wise moderation, so much more expressive than miracles. The last half of this chapter is admirable and can hold its own even next to the finest maxims of wise antiquity.

---

6 SM's note: Besides, we find word-play even in the *Odyssey*. Jesus could certainly allow himself a freedom that Homer had taken.

The same can be said about the whole of Chapter VI, a continuation of the preceding one, with the exception of the model of prayer that Jesus proposes. I don't care for the *pater noster*.[7] Others grant it a beautiful simplicity; I find it flat, just a set of words. There is much more substance in the rest of the chapter, where it appears to be inserted or intercalated, perhaps by another hand. *Nesciat sinistra tua quid faciat dextera tua.* [3. When you give alms, let not your left hand know what your right hand does.] There is something fine and worthy of being retained and, above all, practised. There is a good deal of philosophy in several verses of this chapter, notably the last.

Continuation and end of the "sermon on the mount", Chapter VII. The preachers who came after Jesus Christ said, and still say every day, more pretty things than their model; but they are far from putting into their brilliant academic phrases and their numerous clauses, the unction and substance found here! Here, everything is in action, in images, in feelings. The translators, commentators, theologians, ascetics, and other authors, spoil everything with their interpretations; let them stick to the letter! But to try to give spirit to Jesus Christ, who had only good judgment, a healthy mind, a sensitive heart and a gentle character! It's in the sermon on the mount that I recognize his evangelical morality, which will be fine in every century, in every country, and which needs no miracles, prophecies, or divine inspiration to be appreciated and felt. Jesus Christ is doubtless quite innocent of everything attributed to him after his death; he didn't try to pass himself off as the son of God; but he called God his father, just as philosophers call nature the common mother of all beings.

There is a similar ineptitude in the ritual of the Holy Sacrament, when a priest applies to the host this passage of Chapter VII: *Nolite dare sanctum canibus* [6. Be careful not to give holy things to dogs] as versified in bad Latin:

Ecce panis angelorum,
Non mittendus canibus.
[This is the bread of angels; don't throw it to dogs.]

---

7 SM's note: The frequent practise of prayer, so strongly recommended in all religions, is an act of servitude which has not been able to raise people from the yoke they bear almost everywhere even now. The ruling spirit of resignation, the terms of lowness and abasement that are used, the humble posture required in reciting the prayer—all this smells of slavery.

Temples are like so many horse-training rings, where priests, as skillful and perhaps as deceitful as horse-dealers, control credulous people and train them for slavery. If we imagine a God as a father shared by all, isn't it insulting to him to prostrate ourselves before him, join our hands, cover our head with ashes, in order to obtain our daily bread? What would I suffer if my children embraced my knees and kissed my feet to remind me that they have needs and that I owe them their daily bread, *panem quotidianum!*

They should have seen that the application is not fitting, and that it gives rise to many well-deserved ironies. This symbolic word of Christ—*Nolite dare sanctum canibus*—is doubtless only a variant of an ancient proverb: *Margaritas ante porcos* [pearls before swine]. Christ, who appeared in public only at the age of thirty, spent those thirty years in retreat; and, in the spare time that his manual labor with his mother's husband allowed, it is likely that he studied and, like the bee, created evangelical honey from what he considered best in the moral works known up to that time—unless, of course, Jesus uttered words put into his mouth, for there are scholars who persist in seeing him only as a historical mannequin, dressed in borrowed clothes.

The narrative in Chapter VIII has a sort of sublimity: *Domine, si vis, potes me mundare; et extendens Jesus manum, tetigit eum, dicens: Volo mundare; et mundata est lepra.* [2. Lord, if you will, you can cure me. Jesus, extending his hand, touched him and said: I wish it, be cured. And the leper was cured.] "At the same instant", adds Sacy, who translates without intuiting the merit of his original.

The centurion tells a candid story, and Jesus could not help admiring it. But I don't acknowledge his benign character when Jesus tells one of his disciples who wants permission to go bury his father, *Sequere me, et dimitte mortuos sepelire mortuos.* [Follow me, and leave to the dead the duty of burying their dead.] This stoicism is revolting. One tries in vain to find a hidden meaning in it, an excusable palliative, but I see only an unpardonable rudeness with a very bad effect, for it violates one of the most sacred duties of nature and society. One might suspect Jesus of having been afflicted with the mania for singling himself out by displaying outrageous principles and wanting to surpass the Cynic philosophers. It's likely that he didn't have an orderly plan; he lived from day to day, improvising—sometimes well, sometimes poorly. Hence the unevenness of his style and the contradictions in what is called his morality. Fine, this life-style worked for him. "Men of the people" are not difficult. Priests haven't thought they had to espouse their master's bad moods. Far from abandoning the care of the dead to the dead, ministers of religion have always been jealous of playing a role at funerals; it is true to say that their presence is not completely free of charge.

Chapter IX is filled only with miracles, the telling of which one reads with pleasure, as it is more admirable than the marvels themselves. They seem to be no harder to perform than to write about. The historian who relates them has a charming confidence.

The reading of Chapter X distressed me. I was beginning to enjoy the genius of Jesus Christ. His speech at the mountain had given me pleasure. Could Jesus Christ have been only a hypocrite? The public man is not the private man;

what he says to his apostles does not at all resemble what he preached to the dumfounded multitude. *Beati mites! Beati pacifici!* [v.4. Blessed are the gentle! 9. Blessed the peaceful!] he repeated to the people. But here, he blows hot and cold. This Janus[8] Jew advises his people to be "sly as the serpent" and "simple as the dove", depending on circumstances. He adds: *Non veni pacem mittere, sed gladium; veni separare hominem adversus patrem suum, filiam adversus matrem suam.* [34. Don't think that I have come to bring peace on earth. I have not come to bring peace, but the sword; 35. For I have come to separate a man from his father, a daughter from her mother...] Is this a demon speaking? Alas! The clergy has taken this infernal passage only too literally. Is that the language of a God or a sage? Did Socrates, above whom J.J. Rousseau[9] thoughtlessly wanted to place Jesus Christ, ever permit himself such a morality? No commentary can possibly palliate these lines. It is certainly appropriate here to say that the letter kills. Is it for this that we have seen so many miracles, so many martyrs, so many prophets? *Vae! Vae!* And that's what is called *sanctum evangelium*! Good news? Well, certainly news! *Vae! Vae!*[10]

However, there could be two extreme sides to take on this subject. One, to conjecture that gospel (like the entire Bible) is only a mosaic composed of various pieces, incoherent maxims taken indiscriminately from here and there in the ancients, and placed under the name of an imaginary being called Jesus Christ. (The same could be said of Moses.) The other side, which doesn't exclude this first one, is that the Essene[11] sect, which seems to have authored this book, wanted to explain that Jesus came to combat tyrants, awaken the human race from the soporific servitude in which it vegetated in stupefied peace, and give it a sword against despotism. Which can't be achieved without setting father and son of different opinions against each other, etc. etc. etc. But isn't this doing too much honor to the Bethlehemite?

Ulphilas, bishop of the Goths, was more peaceful than Jesus: having undertaken a Gothic version of the Bible, he could never resolve to translate the four books of Kings, fearing that the recital of wars described in them might heat the temper of his nation, which was already too prone to war. It is so true that the Bible is not, like the sun, for every time and every place.

---

8   Two-faced Roman guardian of doorways, looking both forward and back. The month of January is named after him.
9   Jean-Jacques Rousseau (1712–78), novelist and philosopher whom Maréchal generally admired.
10 Vae: Woe! Both "gospel" and "evangelium" mean "good news".
11 A Jewish ascetic sect from about the 2nd century BCE, to which some scholars believe Jesus belonged.

Jesus is right to say, Chapter XI: *qui habet aures audiendi, audiat;* [Let him hear who has ears to hear!] for most of this chapter is unintelligible and is not worth a single line of the sermon on the mount. But the last couplet is only too clear to convict Jesus Christ of a striking contradiction. He has said above, Chapter X: *Nolite arbitrare, quia pacem venerim mittere in terram.* [34. Don't assume that I have come to bring peace on earth.] Here he says: *Tollite jugum meum super vos et discite a me, quia mitis sum et humilis corde; jugum meum suave est, et onus meum leve.* [29. Take my yoke upon you and learn from me that I am gentle and humble at heart; 30. For my yoke is easy and my burden is light.] Which to believe: the Jesus of Chapter X or the Jesus of Chapter XI? Those who make a philosopher of him might place him in the sect professing a double doctrine, one for the people, another for the adept. It is time to return to Reason; she doesn't wear two coats.

They say that theologians manage to reconcile everything wonderfully. It follows at least that gospel, fallen from heaven to earth for the entire world, needs all the subtleties of the Sorbonne[12] to not offend good sense. The sage of Bethlehem thus had two weights and two measures, which would not be good in the behavior or in the principles of a human legislator.

The end of Chapter XII proves that heads of religion have no parents. Jesus Christ renounces his family and, in his heart, prefers his disciples to his mother.

Chapter XIII is filled with parables; but the kingdom of heaven, which they prefigure, meant little to the Jews, who up to that point had the intelligence to attach themselves to the things of this lower world, to temporal goods, to all that is ruled by the senses. People are born materialists; they require a morality and a happiness founded on what they can touch. No metaphysics! The kingdom of heaven is too elevated for their earth-bound spirit; they take the short view.

Chapter XIV. To cure the sick, to satisfy 5,000 people with five loaves and two little fish, are miracles admirable in themselves and at least have a useful purpose; but to walk on water and make poor Peter Bar-jonas do the same—though he was never brave and still lacked the requisite faith—this is a bit of mischief whose telling could amuse a village gathering, but wouldn't make as much of an impression on the mind of a thinking man as the sermon on the mount. And then, while Jesus is killing time by walking on water during the night, he had an even better subject for a miracle: his relative John the Baptist

---

12 Sorbonne, founded during the thirteenth century as a college within the University of Paris; it became a center for theological scholarship.

was the victim of two women, and his head became the price of a contradance.[13] What a book the gospel is! You find everything in it.

Chapter XV offers a repetition of the miracle of Chapter XIV. This double use doesn't suggest much orderliness on the part of the editor of the gospel. In this same chapter as well, Christ shows himself a bit imprudent: the priests do not pardon him; he who knew everything could not have been ignorant of this; and in what follows they remind him only too well. For the rest, he gives good enough precepts, which Horace[14] had already clothed in beautiful verse before him; but Horace addressed the court of Augustus, and Jesus, the poor people of the port.

Bar-Jonas, man of the people that he was, does not come off as credulous in Chapter XVI. "A starving belly has no ears"; the proverb might add, "no eyes either"; for the prince of apostles, witness to the miracle of the five or seven loaves that fed 5,000 souls, is no less worried about the food he forgot to take with him. Nonetheless it is he whom Jesus chooses as head of his church, a church based on faith. Perhaps he owed this honor only to his name, which lent itself to a pun, and to the pleasure that the good Jesus took in making or saying riddles. People try to save the honor and gravity of gospel by saying that these puns and riddles are not in the original text. That is possible; but then, why permit them in translations? Is it to make the profane reader laugh? Yet this wordplay has contributed not a little to the propagation of Christianity. People like to see them in books and repeat them with pleasure. Once more let us admire the great events that come from small causes.

It must be that Peter, the fisher, was strong-minded, to deserve his master's reproach of not having faith even the size of a mustard seed—even after having witnessed the transfiguration. But why does this transfiguration take place in private, in front of only six eyes? This miracle, performed before the eyes of the whole universe, would have been decisive. The rest of Chapter XVII is full of little marvels, hardly worth being included in this supreme book that was made to eclipse all the writings of wise antiquity.

In Chapter XVIII there are several moral commonplaces that can never be repeated too often.

Jesus had already said: *Qui habet aures, audiat.* [Let him hear who has ears to hear.] He repeats it here, in Chapter XIX, about voluntary eunuchs wishing

---

13   Literally, a country dance, but Maréchal refers to Salomé's dance of the seven veils. The two women are Herodias, whose marriage to Herod John the Baptist had criticized as incestuous, and her daughter Salome, who insisted on John's death as punishment.
14   Horace (65 BCE–8 BCE): Roman lyric poet and satirist.

to gain the heavenly kingdom: *Qui potest capere, capiat.* [12. Whoever can understand this, let him understand.] What is the point of all these mysteries? Ought morality be expressed in enigmas? To make oneself a eunuch in order to go to heaven! Is that how the regulator of morals ought to express himself? The Church has made marriage indissoluble, according to this not very edifying chapter. However, the Church has gone further than her legislator, for he imagines cases where divorce could be permitted: *Nisi ob fornicationem.*[15] In this same place, Jesus adds: [Let man not separate what God has joined. 6.] The words of Christ: *What I have joined, no one can separate*, appear to be recycled from the Egyptians. An inscription found at Nisa, an Arabian city, on a monument consecrated to ancient Isis, appears thus:

I AM ISIS, QUEEN OF ALL LANDS; MERCURY HAS OPENED ALL KNOWLEDGE TO ME, AND NO ONE CAN SEPARATE WHAT I HAVE JOINED.

Not to displease those who admire everything in gospel, the conduct of the father of the family is normal but harsh, according to this axiom: *Summum jus, summa injuria.*[16] Here it's a case of repeating this French proverb: *Comparaison n'est pas raison.*[17] And then, once again, what is the kingdom of heaven, in the last analysis? A good definition of two or three lines would be worth more and be more beneficial than a whole volume of ingenious parables.

The curse on the fig tree, Chap. XXI, made me smile. Chapter XXII proves that Jesus Christ was never short of words with the Pharisees; but it doesn't prove that gospel should be the rule for our behavior; it can suit only the kingdom of heaven, which is not of this world. Consequently, it must be completely foreign and a matter of indifference to honest folk who have both conscience and reason.

Chapter XXIII has energy; the portrait that Jesus draws of the Pharisees and preachers has kept all its resemblance if we apply it to modern ministers of temples. The apostrophe to Jerusalem at the end is beautiful and full of feeling. Such bits are rare in gospel. Jesus's style is a bit more elevated in this passage.

What morality is to be drawn from this parable of the destruction of the world, in Chapter XXIV? There are some great strokes, some fine moments, but *cui bono*? [18] And then, what incoherence! No plan, no connection, we don't know where we are.

---

15 Except for fornication.
16 *Summum*: Ultimate law, ultimate injustice. A classical phrase or proverb suggesting that inflexibly rigorous law may not provide real justice.
17 Comparison is not the same as reasoning.
18 *Cui bono:* to whose good, who benefits?

Chapter XXV is one of the best-written in gospel. The parable of the virgins is valuable for its narration. The one following it is quite moral. The last is one of the finest precepts of human life put into action. Nothing more affecting than this scene of the last judgment, and the prize awarded him who has given a glass of water. Perhaps it came from the dignity of the reformer of the human race that he prescribed good actions more for themselves than for the advantage that could result from them. The attraction of the beautiful, taste for the good, love of order, should be the only determinants for the honest person. Punishment and reward ought to be reserved for slaves, and there ought not to be a single slave among human beings. Only honor should be the sole motivation for persons of every social class; nothing great or durable will ever be done without this sacred fire that must be carefully nurtured in every soul. This fine moral revolution was not beneath the son of God, and was worth the pain to which he was martyr:

> What first deceiver, to give us law,
> Covered our eyes with the blindfold of faith,
> Degraded the virtues by a shameful wage,
> Made the generous man a vile mercenary
> And, showing him his paymaster above,
> Dared to suggest reward outside his heart?
> *Fragments of a Moral Poem on God*[19]

The last three chapters contain the death and passion of Jesus Christ. This would furnish a mass of reflections if there remained time to lose in reflecting on such a monument. One might limit oneself to this single observation: What is the point of all this machinery? Are people better since the torment of Jesus Christ than they were before his conception in the womb of a virgin?

Nonetheless the inventors, or the first defenders, of Christianity, knew the human spirit. Pagan mythology was more ingenious, more cheerful, but not as engaging as Christian mythology. What spectacle is more able to move the people than that of the virgin and baby Jesus in the stable! The last stroke of genius was to ceaselessly display the image of Christ on the cross: on one side, maternal love; on the other, innocence condemned to the most cruel and shameful of tortures; was anything further needed to capture the multitude? A man with a dog's head, a dog with a man's head,[20] repel homage; a white

---

19 Maréchal's own work, *Fragments d'un Poème Moral sur Dieu* (1781), reprinted in 1790 and, in 1798, under a different title, *Le Lucrèce Français*. (See Karmin 1911, 263–64).

20 Anubis, the Egyptian god of the dead, had a dog's or jackal's head.

pigeon, a tender lamb, call forth trust. Why is it necessary that the Christian religion should have joined indecency and atrocities to this silliness?

II   Holy Gospel of Jesus Christ, According to Saint Mark

This is almost a repetition of Saint Matthew. However, we don't find here the beautiful sermon on the mount, or the *pater*,[21] or the instruction given to the disciples. There are also a few small additions; here is a rather odd one, Chapter IX to the end: 46, 47, 48, 49 ... *In gehenna ignis, ubi vermis eorum non moritur et ignis non extinguitur. Omnis enim igne salietur, et omnis victima sale salietur. Bonum est sal, quod si sal insalsum fuerit, in quo illud condietis? Habete in vos sal et pacem habete inter vos.* [It is better for you to enter life having only one hand than having two and going to hell, where the gnawing worm does not die and the fire is never extinguished; for they must all be salted by fire, just as every victim must be salted with salt. Salt is good; but if it becomes tasteless, what will you use for seasoning? Have salt within you and keep peace among you.] Good God! What a mix-up in Latin as well as French. This is where we have to say again, with Jesus Christ himself, in Saint Matthew and Saint Luke: *Qui potest capere, capiat;* or with Saint Jerome, in his *Epistle to the Galatians* 1.1.: "According to interpretation, God's gospel is made the gospel of humanity or, worse, the devil's gospel". Bad luck to the book susceptible of many interpretations! The science of salvation ought to be, one would think, an exact science.

In Chapter VII, verse 10, there is a pleonasm[22] which gives much force to the thought: *Who curses his father and his mother MORTE MORIATUR!* This fine locution is not from the evangelist; Mark borrowed it from Moses. Isaac de Sacy, as usual, has enervated this passage; he translates: *Let him be punished with death!*

Let us come back to Saint Mark's Chapter VI for a moment, related to Chap. XIII of Saint Matthew; he tells us that Christ practised a mechanical profession for some time: 3. *Nonne hic est faber?* [Isn't he the carpenter?] In a little work entitled *Manual Labor Recommended to All Ecclesiastics,* and dedicated to Jesus Christ himself, Paris 1680, we read: "The Jews testify to having seen him work with his own hands with Saint Joseph". We will observe on this subject how much more pure and edifying Christ's life would have been had he modestly followed his father's trade instead of trying to be head of a religion. An honest

---

21 *pater noster:* Our father, who art in heaven, etc.
22 pleonasm: excessive, unnecessary or redundant words; here the pleonasm is "morte moriatur" (to die by/with death or will die the death). Sacy eliminates the pleonasm.

carpenter is a useful man; the same cannot be said of a heavenly figure. To adjust a mortice is more profitable to the world than to found a religion. A hardworking and peaceful artisan deserves our respect; let us keep our disdain and indignation for these turbulent innovators who, incapable of fulfilling a man's duties, try at all cost, even to endangering their lives, to pass as heroes or demi-gods.

Mark wrote his legend a bit later than Matthew wrote his, ten years after the piteous catastrophe suffered by their master.

III   The Holy Gospel of Jesus Christ, According to Saint Luke

The simplicity and good nature that dominate in the first chapter disarm even the most severe critic. Besides, to take some pleasure in reading a fairy-tale, *obsequium rationis sub jugo fidei* is required.[23] Let us note nonetheless that the little anecdote of Zachariah and Elizabeth seems like a recycled version of the story of Sara and Abraham who became fertile in their old age. The origin of "Saint John's fire"[24] is found in verse 14 of this chapter: *Et multi in nativitate ejus gaudebunt.* [14. And many people rejoiced in his birth.] The Church has taken advantage of everything. The virgin's *magnificat*, in a revolutionary style, seems apocryphal to us; and Zachary's hymn weak and unworthy of the beautiful hymns in the ancient Bible.

Let us pause for a moment on this first chapter to cite a few lines from a *Physico-theological Dissertation of the Conception*, 1742. We read on page 101: "The Lord Jesus was conceived in the flesh in an egg of the Virgin Mary. All the Old Testament saints (says Abbé Rupert) asked for and sought Jesus Christ. They asked for this egg which the prophetic oracles had announced as a certainty and without any doubt; this egg, which the Holy Spirit would cover with its shadow, arriving in it as a bird rests on its egg until the chick it encloses is completely formed. This is what was to happen and this is what was done. The Holy Spirit, o Virgin Mary! arrived in you, and the power of the Most High covered you with its shadow; and it is thus that you conceived and bore your son". (Book 7, *On the Gospel*).

---

23   The obedience/subservience of reason under the yoke of faith.
24   Fire: The eve of Saint John's birthday on June 24 is celebrated with a bonfire replicating the legend that his birth was accompanied with a celestial fire display.

And it is near the middle of the 18th century that someone wrote like this! But let us not leave this chapter, the strangest in all the Bible and of all known books, without adding:

> Honest wives and whomever you respect, we make you the judges! If an angel, even if God himself in person, descended from the sky expressly to propose adultery, saying to you: 28. *Ave, gratia plena*, etc. 31. *Ecce concipies in utero.* [I greet you, (who are) full of grace!...You will conceive in your womb, etc.] Honest wives, and whomever you respect, tell us! Would you reply with Mary, Joseph's wife: *Ecce ancilla Domini; fiat mihi secundum verbum tuum?* [I am the Lord's servant; let me be treated according to your word!]

Good mothers, there is the basis of the religion preached to your children! No, one wouldn't want to believe it for a single day; or rather, one doesn't know which to wonder at more: the immodesty of priests offering, every morning and every evening, such a tawdry mystery (the *ave Maria*) for the veneration of wives and virgins; or the docility of women, and even men, in believing and revering such monstrous dogmas. Does the Bible concordance speak of adultery, punished by death in the Old Testament but honored with a religion in the New?

The episode of Simeon, in Chapter II, is good; one enjoys hearing this old man call out, while carrying the child-God in his arms: *Nunc dimittis* ... etc. [Now you will let your servant die in peace.]

From the age of seven, little Jesus showed himself an arguer; this is noticeable in his rather harsh response to the tender solicitude of his mother and of the good Joseph—a response that ought to have earned him a whipping; but he was a spoiled child. The following chapters are, as in Saint Mark, only a repetition of Saint Matthew, with more or less unimportant variants.

Verse 4 of Chapter x contains a short version of the Quaker doctrine: *Et neminem pervias salutaveritis* [Do not greet anyone in the street.] But I have not found in the gospel the origin of the titles "Eminence" and "Holiness" that are freely given to heads of the Church. What must make this chapter precious is the affecting story of the good Samaritan, a parable that deserves to be in all the gospels. The little tale that follows is not quite so well done; I'm referring to the two sisters Martha and Mary. Of two women who both loved me at the same time, it seems to me that I'd prefer the one who proved her love through her efforts, rather than the one who spent the whole day doing nothing and let me do without everything. This fable could refer to theory and practise.

Jesus Christ declares himself for theory; but the wise man would hold with the practise of good works. Verse 9 of this chapter is noteworthy. Christ enjoins his apostles to cure the sick before preaching to them. Whence one might conjecture that Christianity begins with empiricism. This, no doubt, caused Paracelsus[25] to say: *Theologia et medicina sunt inseparabiles*, Book 1, *Origin of Diseases*, Chapter 6.

Saint Luke, Chapter XII, has Jesus Christ say, even more positively, what was already so repulsive in Saint Matthew: *Ignem veni mittere in terram; et quid volo, nisi ut accendatur ... Putatis quia veni pacem dare in terram? Non dico vobis, sed separationem ... etc.* [I have come to bring fire on earth; and what do I wish if not that it should catch? 51. Do you believe that I have come to bring peace on earth? No, I assure you, but, on the contrary, division.] It wasn't necessary to suffer death and the passion for that. Christ justifies himself in another place. One of his pupils called him "his good master": "Why do you call me that? (replied Jesus) only God is good". Necker[26] will never persuade us, in his thick volume, *The Importance of Religious Opinions*, that the spirit of charity is characteristic of gospel and its hero.

Chapter XV is among the finest, perhaps the finest, of the entire Old and New Testament; it contains the parable of the good pastor and the prodigal child. The Bible would doubtless merit the title of "holy writ" if it were written like that from one end to the other.

Chapter XVI is consoling for the unfortunate. Gospel is not a book for the rich; but alas! We must repeat, it is not with parables that the wealthy will be made to understand reason or that the poor will be fed. A good code of law, based on justice, would constrain people better than hell or paradise seen from afar. Such legislation will never exist, since he who is said to be the source of all justice has not deigned to give us anything better than gospel; the all-powerful Being thought there was nothing further to do for humanity, after he dictated a book for them.

The gospel of Saint Luke is much more complete than those of Saints Matthew and Mark. His Passion especially is accompanied by various circumstances which he was not neutral in reporting.

The Hebrew race has been regarded as the outcast among nations. However, there is a people even more vile than the Jews. The Chinese, for centuries, have

---

25   Paracelsus (1493–1541): Swiss physician, astrologer, botanist. ("Theology and medicine are inseparable".).

26   SM's note: It is suitable that a financier took up the defense of a Jew. [Jacques Necker (1732–1804): Swiss banker who became finance minister to Louis XVI. He wasn't Jewish, but apparently Maréchal associated Jews with financial matters. The Jew is, evidently, Jesus.—Trans.].

had the cowardice of adoring their king as a "son of God". The man, on the contrary, who dared to take this title for a moment among the Israelites, his compatriots, was punished for it by the torture of slaves.

Saint Luke, said the editor of an ancient Bible in pictures and quatrains,[27] printed at Lyon in 1583, is the one who, among the evangelists, best represented the historical style. We read in another illustrated Bible, from 1637 in Paris, "Luke never had a wife or children, and he lived 74 years, and left the world, full of the Holy Spirit, in Bythinia". Luke practised medicine; Saint Paul, writing to the Colossians, speaks of him this way: *Lucas medicus carissimus.*[28] However, good physicians do not attach themselves to miracle workers. Wouldn't Luke have been only an empiricist following another one? Christ, his master, touched the sick.

The gospel of Luke dates from the twenty-third year after the torture of his hero. Christ did not lack chroniclers; at that time there were more than fifty of them. *Enumerare longissimum est*,[29] says Saint Jerome, in his *Commentary on Matthew*.

IV   Holy Gospel of Jesus Christ, According to Saint John

The first chapter is famous; it won its author the surname of theologian.[30] But to deserve the name of sage and philosopher, more evidence is needed. *Fiat lux, fiat lux* [Let there be light.] I said when I finished reading this chapter, so worthy of the author to whom we owe the *Apocalypse: Et tenebrae non comprehenderunt.* [5. And the shadows have not understood the light.]

Chapter II is less unintelligible; there one sees with pleasure that Jesus is humanized, that he deigns to attend a wedding, and that for his first miracle he metamorphosizes six pitchers of water into six flasks of wine. This marvel is not completely worthy the majesty of a God; but Jesus doubtless does it to place himself more on the level of human beings. The response of Jesus to his mother, in the same chapter, is a bit brusque, to say the least: *Quid mihi et tibi est, mulier?* [Woman, what is there in common between us?] In our primary schools, a son who responded thus to his mama would certainly be punished. Whatever the interpretation of this unedifying passage, the divine model for

---

27   quatrains: a popular type of sixteenth-century Bible showed a pictorial scene on each page, with an explanatory quatrain (four-line rhymed verse) beneath.
28   Luke, our dearest physician.
29   To enumerate/list is very tedious.
30   SM's note: Saint Chrysostom, in his homily on Saint John, describes this evangelist as an uneducated man.

men, if he returned among us, would have to agree that this is not the finest moment of his life. Jesus would not be more excusable, even if we suppose he knew about his illegitimacy; for Mary was no less his mother even if she was the adulterous wife of Joseph.

The first part of Chapter III doubtless gave the idea of introducing baptism in the Church; but this idea was not new: all antiquity practised ablutions. We must admit that there is good reason why Nicodemus has been made the patron saint of all simple-minded folk. Jesus had every advantage in disputing with him; he does it willingly and at length. The rest of the chapter is full of mysticism.

The IVth is even stranger. The episode of the Samaritan and her well is odd. It is pleasing to see Jesus act like a gallant with a woman, and play with words: *When you have drunk* (he says to her, 13 and 14) *from my living water which bursts forth, you will never thirst again*. It would be difficult to find a book with more platitudes and more impertinences than the gospel—"this divine book, the most useful of all", according to J.J. Rousseau. The rest of the chapter is in the same tone. "I have some meat to eat by the will of God", 32, etc. Nothing more pitiful than the gospel! One wants to repeat this exclamation on practically every page.

The Samaritan did not always have the right word in her mouth; she calls Jesus Christ a "prophet", and he was just a soothsayer. The prophet is for the future, the soothsayer for the past.

The five first chapters of Saint John do not at all resemble the three preceding gospels, especially for style. Saint John makes his hero speak a great deal, presenting him as a wordy and vigorous theologian. The three other evangelists were more sober, so the words they put into their master's mouth have accordingly more weight.

It is not possible that Jesus Christ would have been enough of a scholar or academic to say all the fine things about the eucharist[31] that John has him spout in Chapter VI, and that Jesus probably never thought. Jesus was not

---

31   SM's note: In 1607 in Paris, a priest of Barenton—Montruelx, lord of Mont-Sacré—published, with the approbation of doctors in theology, a "spiritual poem" entitled "The Holy Eucharist", or "Jesus Christ on the Altar and on the Cross" of which here are the first two lines: "I sing a great banquet, a gourmet feast/ whose chef is God-man, and his flesh the meat ... etc". Page 1. As for the rest, this bad poet merely translates the Bible word for word. In *Leviticus* and *Numbers*, "sacrifice" and "God's meat" [*viande*] are synonyms.

The prose translation of the Bible lets us guess that Isaac de Sacy would not have been a good poet; this guess becomes certainty if one has had the patience to read a few lines of his poem on the Eucharist.

Christian; that is not the concise and sententious style of the sermon on the mount. I very much like the naïve observation of a good Capharnaite on these words of Jesus Christ: "If you don't eat the flesh of the son of man and don't drink his blood, you will not have life within you". 54. *These words are harsh; who can hear them?* 61. He replies to Jesus Christ, abandoning him.

At the beginning of this same famous Chapter VI, there is a scene which spoils the image of Jesus's divine character. What! Jesus, following the devil's example, tempts his disciple Philip? All this strikes me as a pious ruse of John. Chapter VIII is justly famous because of the adulterous woman: Jesus Christ is nowhere in the gospel as grand as at this moment. The rest of the chapter is verbiage from John and Paul, that is, mystification.

The laconic narrative of the miracle in Chapter IX has beauty: *Vade et lava. Abiit et lavit, et venit videns ... et abii et lavi et video.* [11. This man, whom they call Jesus, told me: Go and wash. I washed myself and I see.] The parable of the good pastor, Chap. X, would be better were it not held back by a flood of words. Saint John was talkative and didn't know that "The secret of boring others is to tell everything". Nonetheless, through his verbiage he lets out some curious details for those who want to study the character and conduct of Jesus Christ. Here, for instance, he is strongly pressured; and he responds to objections only with subterfuges or concessions, which show the resources of his intelligence rather than the authenticity of his mission. We need not be astonished that his favorite rhetorical figure is the parable; under this veil, he could say everything with impunity. He gave them to fools, and was not without an answer for more educated people. Similitudes, symbols, parables have done as much wrong to morality as allegories have done to the arts and to history. Figurative language in both Old and New Testaments has let loose the priests, given them every license. The explicit word kills them; they can save themselves and take credit only in speaking with double meaning. If one reproaches them for figurative language, they take refuge in the real, and vice versa. They only go from literal to spiritual, from spiritual to literal. By this sleight-of-hand, they can do everything with confidence and make the plebeians, who love the marvellous, believe whatever they want them to. In this, the priests have perfectly studied and grasped the *sacred poetics* of their master. A religion clear as day has not yet been seen and probably never will be seen. The sacred books of every religion are collections of enigmas for which theologians have only the words, which they skillfully accommodate to circumstances and to their own profit.

Ancient philosophers were not immune from this accusation; but they lacked courage, and did through fear what priests permit themselves through more criminal motives, no doubt.

If ever a miracle has been described in detail and attested, it is the miracle of Lazarus, Ch. XI. What a scandal for truth is an impossible thing! Even a lie may have its proofs! It can make the weak change their mind and get unbelievers stoned to death. But Jesus, pardoning the adulterous woman, is more sublime than Jesus resuscitating Lazarus, dead for four days and already fetid.

Chapter XIII. Simon-Peter is charmingly naïve: *Non lavabis mihi pedes in aeternum ... domine, non tantum pedes meos, sed ut manus et caput.* [8. You will never wash my feet ... 9. Lord, not only my feet but also my hands and head.] For the rest, Jesus's banquet is well told. One can never overestimate the bonds of fraternity and favors among men. The story of Judas Iscariot is of another type; this poor, miserable man makes us pity him; he is more to be pitied than blamed. Jesus gives him a bit of moistened bread; in swallowing it, he swallows the devil and becomes a traitor: could it be otherwise? Has anyone the choice between good and evil when the devil is in his soul? And then, it had to be: *Scriptura impleatur* [scripture is to be fulfilled]. These two words recall the "fate" of the ancients.

The next eight chapters are a bit wordy; but they have unction and do not at all resemble the teachings that Saint Matthew ascribes to Jesus after his sermon on the mount. Chapter XVII contains a prayer from Jesus Christ to God, his so-called father. This prayer seems to have been paraphrased by Saint John; it includes only words, repetitions, commonplaces in saints' lives.

What a loss we have had! In Chapter XVIII, Pilate asks Jesus Christ: *Quid est veritas?* [What is truth?] and turns his back quickly before hearing the definition. Having missed this unique occasion, ought we not to give up hope of ever knowing the truth?

Saint John, who tells everything, has left us many details about what follows his master's death, but they are so mean-minded that they compromise it. He ends with these curious words: *Sunt autem et alia multa quae fecit Jesus; quae si scribantur per singula, nec ipsum arbitror mundum capere posset eos, qui scribendi sunt libros.* [I don't believe that the world could contain the books that could be written about it, if one were to report in detail all the things that Jesus has done.]

And there it is, this "word of God", this "gospel", this book that is put up with confidence against the moral systems of Pythagoras, Confucius, Saadi, Socrates, Plato, Cicero, Epictetus, etc.! That is the divine book that for eighteen centuries has been preached every day and for which so much blood and bitter bile has been spilt! That is whence people have drawn a code of behavior, a universal legislation—in a word, the general rule of heart and mind! This book, where there is no unity, no two similar ideas, not even any consistent style, where we find hardly four or five features worthy of being quoted and remembered; this is the book to which, they say, the human race must submit its reason! This book, the work of a few dusty copyists, has obtained preference over the immortal productions of Athens and Rome! An obscure society of narrow-minded[32] people, whose only excuse would be their good intentions, wrote with no purpose the tales of a few idlers; they sprinkled throughout some moral ideas stolen from here and there; and this book becomes the mirror of wisdom where the human race is to reform its abuses and acquire perfection! This is the book which was to turn old mankind into the new man! Xenophon wrote a life of Socrates and did not make a religion of it. Matthew, Mark, Luke and John write the adventures of Jesus, and voilà, a religion! Fanatics will shout "Miracle!" The sensible person will keep quiet and avoid the crowd, smiling in pity.

How can it be that the crucified Jesus could have founded a religion which still endures, and that Epicurus[33] never even founded a school (he who concealed duty under the lure of pleasure)? Apparently, reason is not within the scope of human beings, while they are a multitude.

We have to regret above all the small success of the efforts of a certain Jovinian, a monk of Milan in the fourth century; it's irritating that his party did not survive him. His enemies gave him the glorious name of "the Christian Epicurus" for having attempted to reconcile religion and pleasure. He deserved to have proselytes: he wanted to reduce every devotional practise to a simple act of charity. He is scarcely known, this friend of humanity, though he had their well-being at heart, and honored mothers of families rather than sterile virgins. Instead, our schools echo with the names of Saint Jerome, Saint Augustine and Saint Ambrose, who exiled him.

The wise author of the book *On Wisdom*, P. Charron, said: "All religions share this: that they seem strange to nature and horrible to common sense; an even slightly vigorous mind mocks them and is offended by them". Book II, Ch, V, p. 357 (1601, Bordeaux). The people would not be so stupidly attached to the Christian religion if they knew that they are designated in this proverb taken from sacred books: *Asino gramen et baculum.* [Grain and a stick for a donkey.]

Christ says plenty of bad things about contemporary priests; he calls them whited sepulchers. Is it from professional jealousy? One has to decry those who occupy the place where one wants to be. Moreover, priests have always

---

32 SM's note: Antoine Couillard, lord of Pavillon, says in proper terms in the proem to his *Singularities of the World* (Paris, 1557): "The only son and eternal word wanted to set the first foundations of his church on ignorant people". [Couillard's phrase is "gens idiots", which for a Latin-speaking writer of the sixteenth century would mean ignorant or uneducated, rather than the much more derogatory meaning it would acquire by Maréchal's time and in our own.—Trans.].

33 Epicurus (341 BCE–270 BCE): Greek philosopher.

bad-mouthed each other, and they have all been right. In a little-known book of "Selected Proverbs", we read; "There is no church in which the devil doesn't have his chapel".

Like Alexander, Jesus died at 33 years of age; he did not die in his bed. No doubt he would have lived longer if—contenting himself with the title of citizen of the small town of Nazareth and with being a craftsman—he had not wanted to imitate Moses on a larger scale. Ambition ruins gods and men. Jesus died on a scaffold, but today he still has altars and sacrificial victims. Christ did not write, and a taste for it did not prevail among those whom he chose as secretaries.

Saints Irenaeus and Augustine agree in giving a rather pleasing reason why there are four gospels; few of our readers, even the most sagacious, will guess: "It is because there are four parts of the world and four principal winds". Voltaire,[34] in his *The Bible at Last Explained* and elsewhere, jokes about all these things: it would surely be time they were properly judged.

Beyond the four or five main gospels, there is also the gospel of Saint Thomas the incredulous; one of Judas Iscariot the traitor; those of saints Bartholomew, Thaddeus, Barnaby, Andrew, Timothy, Nicodemus. This last gospel, worthy of its author's name, contains a pile of such absurdities that the most shameless scholars have not dared take it upon themselves to rank it among the orthodox books of the Bible. Here is one of the thousand comical things in this book: "When the dead arose and when Jesus Christ arose, the first thing they did was to make the sign of the cross". Even so, such a book is still not placed on the list of apocryphal books.

Of the four main evangelists, chosen among fifty, one was a tax clerk (Matthew); another the son of a fisherman; a third a physician. But physicians are not ordinarily so credulous, if we think of the Latin proverb: "Duo medici tres athei" ["Two physicians, three atheists".] Twenty-five years ago, a *Critical History of Jesus Christ*[35] was published, with this epigraph: *Ecce homo* [This is the man.] Few readers know the *Testament* of Jesus Christ in one hundred and twenty-five articles, among them these:

> "My dear brothers, I leave you, as sign of my love, my hatred of the world. I rise to my father and leave you my tears, my rods, my chalice, my cross and nails ... etc. I leave you the blindfold that was placed on my eyes;

---

34 Voltaire, pen name for F.-M. Arouet (1694–1778), rationalist philosopher, critic, dramatist.

35 *Critical History ...* (1770) , by the atheist Baron d'Holbach. The following quotation is presumably from that text, though not attributed.

I leave you the holy blindness of spirit; I leave you sacred madness..."
Faithfully taken from the edition of 1709 at Bar-le-Duc.
Epitaph of Jesus-Christ: Here lies a God made man, who died for an apple.[36]

v   Acts of the Apostles

We would bless the sacred reveries contained in the gospels and the Acts of the Apostles, had they produced over the ages fruits as sweet and customs as pure as those briefly sketched at the end of Chap. II and Chap. IV: *Omnes erant pariter et habebant omnia communia.... Frangentes circa domos panem, sumebant cibum cum exultation et simplicitate cordis ... Neque quisquam egens erat inter illos.* [44. They were all equal and possessed everything in common. 46. Breaking bread in their houses, they took their meal with joy and simplicity of heart. 34. There was no poor person among them.] But all this is only a plagiarism unskillfully made from the school of Pythagoras: he is the philosopher who first instituted the agape.[37] The first Christians got hold of it and abused it so soon that Saint Paul disapproved of them. The habits of the agape girls resembled only too well those of the virgin Mary, their founder.

It strikes us as quite harsh and contrary to this maxim of Jesus Christ—"I do not wish the death but the conversion of the sinner"—to have Ananias and his wife killed (Ch. V); for, after all, what they did was not a crime; it was at most only an excess. This act of severity is perhaps only a warning to the avaricious reader. We note, for style, a stroke worthy of antiquity: *Ecce pedes eorum qui saepelierunt virum tuum, ad ostium, et efferunt te.* [9. Those who are coming to bury your husband are at the door, and they will also put you in the ground.] Poor Isaac de Sacy![38]

As for the miraculous deliverance of Peter from prison, it seems as if it's nearly the same with miracle-workers as with alchemists: they have the secret of converting everything into gold, but they starve to death. The apostles make the crippled walk straight but can't prevent themselves from being whipped and crucified, like Saint Peter, prince of the apostles, and Saint Steven, the first deacon.

---

36   Apple: the reference is to the fruit that Eve gives Adam in Genesis and which is considered by Christians to be the original sin that taints all mankind; to expunge this sin is said to be why Jesus died. In French this is a rhyming couplet (homme/pomme).
37   Greek word for spiritual love; also a communal meal among early Christians.
38   Because "effero" means to carry away or carry out. In fact, though, she is carried out dead, and then buried.

Their successors did not imitate them; they were not embarrassed to sell holy things at a high price; they ought to have recalled this fine response of Peter to the magician Simon, Chapter VIII: *Pecunia tua tecum sit in perditione, quoniam donum dei existimasti pecunia possideri.* [May your money die with you, you who have believed that the gift of God can be acquired with money!]

All the little details of the following chapters characterize the apostles[39] perfectly; they show themselves worthy of their master especially according to the vision of their leader housed with a leather-worker. I like very much the *pertransiit bene faciendo.*[40] X.36. This bit is fine. The naïve narrative of the second deliverance of Peter, Chapter XII, perfectly fulfills this precept of wholesome literature: "The art is to hide the art".

Without pausing over all these wonders—which can no more be proofs for us than they were safeguards for those who performed them—we will point only to Chapter XVII as the oddest of the Acts. It shows us Saint Paul in Athens, preaching his God before the Areopagus;[41] what he says to the grave senators isn't new, for he admits to using expressions from their own poets. It seems to us that there is a bit of Spinozism[42] in his doctrine. Furthermore, if ever a miracle would have been well placed, surely it would be before the Areopagus; but this wise group wasn't worthy of it: God and his apostles displayed their miracles only for the simpleminded and for those lacking perspicacity. God only lets himself be seen by the blind. So Saint Paul succeeded with his speech, which is quite good.

According to Chapter XX, it seems that it isn't only today that one sleeps through sermons. They were fast asleep during those of Saint Paul, for he had the kindness to revive a young man who had died from a fall while listening to him, *mergens somno gravi.* [9. Fallen into a deep sleep.] That is a well-placed miracle; Saint Paul had caused a bad thing so he had to remedy it. At the end of this chapter, he copies his master quite well in the farewells he addresses to his neophytes.

---

39 SM's note: Fontenelle said: "Give me four people persuaded that night fell at noon, and I will demonstrate it to two million". So Jesus was dealt a good hand, since twelve apostles were at his service and blindly submitted to his orders. The witticism of the Norman philosopher encapsulates a brief history of all world religions past, present, and future. [Bernard de Fontenelle (1657–1757), speculative rationalistic scholar.—Trans.].

40 He (Jesus) went about doing good.

41 Areopagus: a hill in Athens, site of a tribunal for trying murder cases; also a council of city elders.

42 Benedict (Baruch) Spinoza (1632–77), Dutch Jewish rationalist theologian, one of Maréchal's intellectual heroes and a pioneer of rationalist Bible criticism.

Saint Paul has a rather imposing attitude in the rest of the chapters. He had an ardent and opinionated temperament—in a word, a true missionary. The Christian religion owes him more than it does to its founder. The good[43] Jesus knew only how to die. Paul died only after taking the trouble (in every sense) to give a sort of existence to the obscure sect he adopted. This tent-maker felt himself capable of a less secondary role. Perhaps, on mature reflection, one might wish for peaceful philosophers a little of this ardor which seems to be the specialty of fanaticism. Superstition, lies, and prejudice have had their apostles; now it's time that truth has its apostles too.

The Acts of the Apostles are attributed to Luke, who was an apostle, evangelist, and physician; those of the clergy have nothing in common: these two works are not inspired by the same Holy Spirit. The symbols of the Apostles (there are four of them) are far from being worth the symbols of Pythagoras, even though this latter work is fairly insignificant on its own.

VI   Epistle of Saint Paul to the Romans

From this title, one expects something grand, something worthy of the nation that the apostle wants to convert to Jesus Christ. One is deceived in expecting ideas or style. Here are no more of the strong images or fine movements encountered frequently enough in the Bible, above all in the prophets whose successor Paul claims to be.

In the first chapter, after a wordy preamble which offers no clear meaning, the apostolic author inveighs against philosophers in a scandalous and trivial way. First, he attributes to them unnatural behaviors of which the ancients were suspected to be guilty; then he dares to argue that these abominable customs were given them by God himself, to punish them for having failed to recognize him. That would be a very strange paternal correction: *Propter quod tradidit illos Deus in desideria cordis eorum, in immunditiam, ut contumeliis afficiant corpora sua in semetipsis;* [This is why God delivered them to the desires of their heart, to vices of impurity, so that they themselves dishonored their own bodies.] *qui commutaverunt veritatem Dei in mendacium* ... And he repeats further down: *Propterea tradidit illos Deus in passiones ignominiae.* [25. They who had taken lies in place of God's truth. 26. That is why God delivered them to shameful passions.] Then the holy apostle goes into details that never sullied the writings of those against whom he argues so incongruously. Paul's logic resembles his style. We note in passing a little fraud by the translator Sacy,

---

43   SM's note: Our blessed Christ (said Saint Francis of Assisi) prayed more than he read.

which the venerable pastors of Geneva[44] have not imitated. *Vocatus apostolus*[45] is rendered, in Sacy, with these words: "Apostle by divine vocation". Why "divine"? This word is not found in the text.

Chapter II. What a style! So many words to specify a trivial truth, one that the sages of antiquity had so fully and so eloquently developed! He could have done it with this one verse: *Cum gentes quae legem non habent, naturaliter ea quae legis sunt, faciunt, ejusmodi legem non habentes, ipsi sibi sunt lex?* [1. When the gentiles, who do not have the law, do by nature what the law commands even while not having the law, they themselves take the place of the law.][46] *Qui ostendunt opus legis scriptum in cordibus suis, testimonium reddente illis conscientia ipsorum.* [15. Showing that what is prescribed by the law is written in their heart, as their conscience testifies.] This passage is intelligible and beautifully simple; but Paul resented the Jews, and his animosity did not allow him to leave it at that. However, one observes that here he gives, to honest people, weapons against himself. Fanatical missionaries, close your books and your temples! *Ipsi sibi sunt lex.* [They themselves are the law.] These philosophical ideas, which one would not have been tempted to seek in the epistles of Saint Paul, are found in the work of several Church fathers.

"Why (says Tertullian) go to the trouble of seeking a divine law, when you have the one shared by the whole world and which is written on nature's tablets?" If only the Church fathers had always written the same way! "Those who follow reason can be regarded as very religious, even if they may be atheists". This thought, so fine and so accurate, is from Saint Justin martyr. If only all the saints and martyrs had always thought that way!

The following chapters are a double and triple mess. However, we must except a few passages drawn from the Bible, and a few unorthodox propositions such as this one, which is pure Spinozism—if indeed we may suppose Paul's mind capable of such profound ideas. *Quoniam ex ipso (Deus) et per ipsum et in ipso sunt omnia.* And this would be the right place to exclaim, with the same Saint Paul: *O altitudo divitiarum sapientiae et scientiae Dei! Quam incomprehensibilia sunt judicia ejus et investigabiles viae ejus!* Chap. XI. [33. O depth of the treasures of God's wisdom and knowledge! How impenetrable are his judgments and his ways how incomprehensible!]

Chapter XII is filled with moral commonplaces collected from one place and another, including gospel and elsewhere. Chapter XIII has more than once served as a safeguard for despotism and tyrannical troublemakers. From Saint

---

44   Geneva, center of Protestant theology.
45   He was called "apostle", or, was called to be an apostle.
46   Law: here, the law of Torah is meant.

Paul onward, kings have added to their titles, "by the grace of God", in agreement with the apostle's reading: *Non est potestas nisi a Deo; qui resistit potestati, Dei ordinatione resistit. Dei minister est; non sine causa gladium portat. Idaeo necessitate subditi estote. Reddite, cui timorem, timorem.* [1. There is no power that doesn't come from God. 2. So whoever opposes powers is resisting God's order. 4. The prince is God's minister; it is not without cause that he carries a sword. 5. Therefore submit to necessity. 7. Give fear to whom you owe fear.] Saint Paul, who called himself a Roman citizen, preached only for slaves; and there is probably no need to seek elsewhere the reason for the progress of newborn Christianity than the trouble taken by its founders to flatter power and to train people to the yoke. Christian religion is neither the cult of republicans nor the morality of free men.

One could take, in Ch. XIV, arguments for and against abstinence from this or that food at certain times of year. Pythagoras is more eloquent in Ovid.[47]

VII   First Epistle of Saint Paul to the Corinthians

What jargon! *Placuit deo,* 1st ch., *per stultitiam praedicationis salvos facere credentes...*[21. It pleased God to save, through the folly of preaching, those who believed in him.][48] And it is in this flow of words that our preachers, for more than a thousand years, continue to seek the text of their sermons and take their authority.

The apostle, Chapter II, warns the Corinthians that in writing to them he is not using eloquence and human wisdom; he even has the good faith to agree that what he preaches might look like folly; he could add, and like a platitude in the eyes of people of taste and sensible minds. The miserable man is right; the Holy Spirit that possesses him has nothing in common with the genius of Socrates or Plato. He was clever not to want any parallel with such men, and to distance himself from anyone who might have been tempted to establish one.

The same mess in Chapter III: *Adhuc carnales estis ... Dei agricultura estis; Dei aedificatio estis ... stultus fiat ut sit sapiens.* [1. You are still carnal. 9. You are the field that God cultivates and the building that God builds. 18. If someone wishes to be wise, let him become a fool!] This is not how the seven sages of

---

47   In his great collection of Greek myths, the *Metamorphoses* (Book 15: 60–142), the Roman poet Ovid (43 BCE–17 CE) summarized the life and teaching, including vegetarianism, of the earlier Greek philosopher and mathematician, Pythagoras.

48   The apostle is being sarcastic with "folly", using his opponents' term.

Greece spoke; and Jesus Christ himself used better-founded, more poetic and better motivated parables. In Chapter IV, Saint Paul plays the good apostle.

Chapters V and VI are filled with completely strange details that give a very poor opinion of the Corinthian neophytes: *Tollens ergo membra Christi, faciam membra meretricis ... glorificate et portate Deum in corpore vestro.* [VI, 15. Should I rip off Jesus's limbs to make them become the limbs of a prostitute?] The aim of these instructions was praiseworthy, to make the body be regarded as the sanctuary of Jesus Christ, in order to keep it free of fornication; but all this perverted morality can suit only a crude and ignorant people. One has to speak another language to honest people and enlightened spirits. On the example of his boss, Paul preferred to address the lowest sort in all the cities where he preached, at Rome, at Corinth. At least—or so we may conjecture—according to the mule-drivers' language he adopts in order to make himself understood and well received: *Membra meretricis!* But who obliges us to continue even today to soil the hearing and the mouth of our sisters, wives, and daughters? What do these priests take us for? Let them remain alone in their temples if they persist in making them dangerous places!

One could fill an entire volume with remarks on Chapter VII. It contains a matrimonial code in the bachelor Saint Paul's style. In effect, he takes on the tone of a legislator, contrasting even with his master. In Genesis, God had said and ordained: *Crescite et multiplicamini.* [Grow and multiply.] The apostle Saint Paul permits only what God himself has positively ordained: *Hoc autem dico secundum indulgentiam, non secundum imperium.* [6. I say this as something to be pardoned, not something commanded.] And he modestly adds: *Volo enim omnes vos esse sicut me ipsum.* [7. For I want you all to be the way I am.] and he repeats a line further on: *Dico non nuptis et viduis, bonum est illis si sic permaneant, sicut ego.* [8. As for unmarried women or widows, I tell them that it is good to remain in that condition, as I myself do.] Nonetheless he admits: *Melius est nubere quam uri.* [9. For it is better to marry than to burn.] He advises virgins and widows not to think of marriage. He tells fathers: *qui matrimonio jungit virginem suam, bene facit, et qui non jungit melius facit...* [38. Thus, he who marries off his daughter does well, and he who does not marry her off does even better.] He ends these fine teachings with this humble phrase: *Puto autem quod et ego spiritum dei habeam.* [40. And I believe that I also have God's spirit.] If we join to this chapter the treaty *On Matrimony* by Sanchez[49] we will have a very edifying and reasonable matrimonial code! However, it's according to such authorities that we dispose of the human heart in the most delicate circumstance of our life. Yet in this chapter, a sentence did manage to escape

---

49   Thomas Sanchez (1550–1619), Spanish Jesuit who wrote on the role of sex in marriage.

Saint Paul which is worthy of being written in letters of gold, but which has scarcely been noticed: *Nolite fieri servi hominum.* [23. Do not become a slave to men.] But perhaps the apostle's intention was that one might be a slave to priests, in the name of God.

Chapter VIII is more or less a repetition of Chapter IV of the same author's Epistle to the Romans. Socrates often said: "I know that I know nothing". Isn't it a reminiscence of the wise Athenian's maxim that made Saint Paul say: *Si quis existimet scire aliquid, nondum cognoverit quemadmodum oporteat eum scire?* [2. If someone flatters himself that he knows something, he still doesn't know how one must know.] But the spirit that blows upon the apostle from Corinth is more cowardly, softer, than the familiar daemon of the sage of Athens.

The successors of Saint Paul and the clergy have not shown themselves as generous, or at least as tactful as he is in Chapter IX. Here he presents himself as a good apostle, and makes the *gratis* of his gospel ring on high: *Numquid non habemus potestatem mulierem, sororem circumducendi, sicut et caeteri apostoli et fratres Domini, et Cephas?...si non vobis spiritualia seminavimus, magnum est si nos carnalia vestra metamus.* [5. Have we not the power to take with us a woman who is our sister, as do the other apostles and the brothers of our Lord, and Cephas? 11. So if we have distributed spiritual goods among you, is it a big thing that we take in a little of your *carnal* goods?] And not *temporal* goods, as Sacy has it.

Qui altari deserviunt, cum altari participant. [13. The priest lives from the altar.] In antiquity, ministers of the cult were satisfied with the remains of the victims' flesh; now that sacrifice is no longer bloody, they have substituted honoraria, and have lost nothing thereby.

The beginning of Chapter XI teaches us that an excess of modesty was not Paul's problem: *Imitatores mei estote.* [1. Be my imitators.] What follows is no less odd, about the distinction between men and women. Women will not share the apostle's opinion: *Non est creatus vir propter mulierem, sed mulier propter virum.* [Man was not created for woman, but woman for man.] Women will maintain, and perhaps rightly, that there is reciprocity. The continuation of this chapter is more important. It is generally agreed that this is the origin and establishment of the sacrament of the eucharist: *Alius quidem esurit, alius ebrius est ...* etc. etc. [21. Thus, some have nothing to eat, while others do it to excess...]

Chapter XIII contains a fine praise of charity, though less fine than the passage from Cicero cited below in Saint John's Epistles. But what is charity? An exact and lucid definition was necessary in the first place. Charity is not simply doing good, since the apostle says, in verse 3 of this chapter: *et si distribuo in cibis pauperum omnes facultates meas, charitatem autem non habuero, nihil mihi prodest.* [3. And if I should distribute all my goods to feed the poor, it does nothing for me unless I have charity.] However, we call a man "charitable" who shares what he has with the needy. Despite what Saint Paul says, let people practise doing good, and we can manage without "charity"!

Chapter XIV centers on the gift of prophecy accorded to all the faithful. The chapter opens thus: *Sectamini charitatem, aemulamini spiritualia; magis autem ut prophetetis.* [1. Seek charity with ardor; desire spiritual gifts and above all to prophetize.] and it finishes thus: *Itaque fratres aemulamini prophetare, et loqui linguis nolite prohibere.* [39. So to conclude, my brothers, desire above all the gift of prophecy, and do not prevent the use of the gift of tongues.] The apostle has not specified what was this virtue of prophetizing, which he places above even charity, and which he forbids only to women; though he grants it to them earlier, for he said in Chap. XI: *Omnis mulier prophetans, velato capite,* [5. Any woman who prophetizes without covering her head with a veil, dishonors her head, verse 4.] Is it simply the faculty of preaching? Fortunately, the Catholic Church has not been completely of Saint Paul's opinion. Good God! What a charivari, if women had permission to preach, to catechize, to perform missions of propaganda!

Saint Paul, inspired as he was by the Holy Spirit, could have been a great doctor in the knowledge of salvation; but he was, like his master, greatly ignorant of natural history. What! He gives as proof of resurrection of the body, line 36 of Chapter XV: *Insipiens, tu quod seminas non vivificatur, nisi prius moriatur ... seminatur in corruptione...* [Madman that you are, don't you see that what you sow can't live unless it dies first?] According to Saint Paul, the seed dies in the soil before sprouting. A schoolboy knows more today than Saint Paul; but this is the Church's oracle! But, it will be objected, he spoke to the people; he had to lower himself to their crude intelligence. Perhaps it would have been better had the interpreter of the Holy Spirit elevated the people to his level.

According to the analysis of this Epistle of the most famous of the apostles, what idea can we infer of a religion preached thus? In good faith, is it from this style and with this logic that a person should dare speak to his fellow human beings, on behalf of a God? The missives of Saint Paul are full of locutions similar to this one: *What is madness in God is wiser than any man.*

So there are our oracles! At least one is not ashamed, in the XIXth century, to try to retain human understanding among such hindrances! The Institute of France[50] still dares not touch this blindfold of nations; under its wing, and perhaps in its bosom, priests flout reason with impunity!

---

50 Institute of France, established in 1795 by the government as a grouping of several "academies" or learned societies.

VIII Second Epistle of Paul to the Corinthians

How repulsive Saint Paul's style is, and in such bad taste! Chapter II: *Odorem notitiae suae manifestat per nos in omni loco, quia Christi bonus odor sumus Deo ... Odor mortis in mortem, odor vitae in vitam.* [14. God spreads upon us, everywhere, the odor of knowledge of his name; 15. For we are before God the good odor of Christ. 16. For some an odor of death which makes them die; for others an odor of life which makes them live.] And then, Chapter III: *Epistola nostra vos estis, scripta non atramento, sed spiritu dei vivi; non in tabulis lapideis, sed in tabulis cordis carnalibus.* [You are our letter *of recommendation*, 3. written not in ink but with the spirit of living God; not on stone tablets but on tablets of flesh, which are your hearts.] All this is pitiful! The Holy Spirit was not as eloquent as Demosthenes and Cicero.[51]

In Chapter IX, the apostle occupies himself with minor pecuniary interests. It seems that the Corinthians were not lenders; and Saint Paul also goads them about honor. But grace didn't easily untie their purse strings. According to Chapter X, Saint Paul seems to have been like his successors in that he didn't fear to use little low tricks to reach his goals; besides, the ways of God are extraordinary. He justifies himself the best he can, Chapter XI. His modesty is forced to its last hideout, for he is obliged to praise himself: *Existimo nihil me minus fecisse a magnis apostolis.* [5. I don't think I have been inferior in anything to the greatest among the apostles.] Afterward, he frequently brings up his objectivity. In Chapter XII, we must follow the apostle as he is ravished to the third heaven, etc.

And this is what they call the canonical books of the Church, the rule of faith, the model for behavior! O shame! Poor human species, sometimes one blushes to belong to you.

IX Epistle of Saint Paul to the Galatians

The Galatians received this missive the twenty-third year after the deplorable end of Christ; in this same year, Luke composed his narrative of it. The beginning is remarkable: [Paul, apostle not through men or a man but through Jesus Christ and God his father.] In the rest, missionary commonplaces written in an ordinary style, according to the holy custom of the apostle. We will pause for a

---

51 Respectively, a Greek (fourth century BCE) and a Roman (first-century BCE) politician/orator.

moment at verse 3 of Chapter IV. Isaac Berruyer[52] utters a naiveté in connection with this passage: *God, said he, treated our ancestors like little children.* Preface to his "History of the People of God".

He refers to the Old Testament which, in effect—as we have so often had occasion to demonstrate—is so full of nursery tales that one might call it the Bible of earliest childhood.

X   Epistle of S. Paul to the Ephesians

Moral and mystical commonplaces flatly written. However, it is in his homily on this epistle that Saint Chrysostom, with ridiculous enthusiasm, exclaims: "If someone wanted to give me a place in heaven among the angels, or put me in a dungeon with Saint Paul, I would choose the dungeon". This epistle and the next two were sent thirty years or so after the sad dénouement of the mission of the son of God.

XI   Epistle of S. Paul to the Philippians

More missionary commonplaces. Saint Paul did not always swear *in verba magistri.* Jesus, somewhere in the gospels,[53] forbids his disciples to exchange greetings. The apostle to the gentiles knows better how to live; in one of his epistles, he wishes that they should meet one another with honor.[54]

XII   Epistle of Saint Paul to the Colossians

Saint Paul ought to have profited a bit from the advice he gives *ad Colossenses,* Chap. IV: *Sermo vester semper in gratia sale sit conditus.* [6. Let your conversation, accompanied with sweetness, be seasoned with salt!] But the apostle was a prisoner. Still, there is a bit of unction in this Epistle. One notes that when speaking to the Colossians and the Ephesians, the apostle Paul treats *gospel* and *truth* as synonyms.

---

52   Berruyer (1681–1758): Jesuit historian and Bible scholar.
53   Luke 10:4.
54   Romans 12:10 in Catholic Family Bible; or, "Give pride of place to one another in esteem" (New English Bible).

XIII First Epistle of S. Paul to the Thessalonians

I like to see Saint Paul give the inhabitants of Thessalonica—among the precepts he spouts in the effusion of his heart—this one: *Semper gaudete.* [v.16. Be always joyful.] This advice was more on their level, than saying to them: "One day we shall be exalted to the skies, to go before the Lord, up in the air".

XIV Second Epistle from the Same to the Same

He warns his neophytes against those who, in the future, might be tempted to compete with him or follow in his tracks: as a result, he makes them observe his selflessness. We must admit that, without all these precautions, without all the troubles of the apostle Paul, the Holy Spirit and its grace would have found it difficult to open the human heart. The apostolic letter-writer even goes as far as impudence; he dares to assure the Thessalonians that his word is truly the word of God himself: *A nobis verbum, vere est verbum Dei.* Ch. II. 13. Saint Paul wrote to the Thessalonian citizens nineteen years after the torture of his master.

XV First Epistle of S. Paul to Timothy

I'm not pleased that Saint Paul, the apostle of charity, terminated the first chapter of this letter with this verse: *Quidam repellentes circa fidem naufragaverunt, ex quibus est Himeneus et Alexander QUOS TRADIDIDI SATANAE, ut discant non blasphemare.* [19. Among the number of those who have been shipwrecked in the faith, 20. are Hymenaeus and Alexander, whom I have delivered over to Satan, so that they may learn not to blaspheme.]

If Saint Paul is the apostle for the faith, he isn't the apostle for women; Chapter II proves it once again. But why, in this same chapter, this parenthesis: *Ego praedicator et apostolus (VERITATEM DICO, NON MENTIOR.) Doctor gentium in fide et in veritate.* [7. I am a well-known preacher and apostle; *I tell the truth and I don't lie.* I am the well-known instructor of nations in faith and truth.] It appears that in his own time, these titles were disputed.

It would be good if the great vicars read Chapter III every morning when their bishops arose; it's a very fine and necessary lesson. The clergy ought also to pay attention to this passage: *Unius uxoris virum.* [12. Let them take as deacons those who have married only one wife.] Despite the apostle, the clergy has persisted for a long time in the scandal of celibacy. The next chapter is even more precise on this topic. There, Saint Paul says that there are diabolic spirits: *Spiritus erroris et doctrinis daemoniorum in hypocrisis loquentium mandacium,* PROHIBENTIUM NUBERE *et abstinere a cibis quos Deus creavit ad percipiendum ... Quia omnis creatura Dei bona est, et nihil rejiciendum.* 3. Who will prohibit marriage and consumption of meats which God created to be received; 4. For everything God created is good, and nothing is to be rejected. This text is explicit. It is odd that the Catholic clergy, which has adopted all the fantasies of Saint Paul, should have avoided precisely the only place where he speaks rationally. It will be noted how crude is the version of verse 3 above. An author of less equivocal habits than those of Saint Paul would have avoided this parallel of marriage and the consumption of meat. [55]

Chapter V is admirable from one end to the other, except for this passage, which is rather strong, about a widow: *Si sanctorum pedes lavit.* [10. If she has washed the feet of saints.] This chapter is an affecting portrait of perfect behavior.

Our prelates, successors of Saint Paul, ought also to try to be like their model, who was not embarrassed to confess, Chapter VI: *Habentes alimenta et quibus tegamur, his contenti sumus.* [8. Having what to eat and to cover ourselves with, we must be content.]

XVI Second Epistle of S. Paul to Timothy

This second epistle is from a missionary full of unction, ardent, indefatigable, gifted with intelligence, with a firm character suitable to creating a sect.

N.B. This Timothy was a pupil of the apostle to the gentiles. Named first bishop of Ephesus through his master's grace, he was stoned in this city for having denied to chaste Diana the same incense he burned to honor adulterous Mary.

XVII Epistle of S. Paul to Titus

This too-short missive is full of excellent advice that it would be good to renew today. It is only in these sorts of letters that Saint Paul seems to me to deserve his reputation. We won't address the plagiarism: Paul was Roman, but he was

---

55   The Latin has "cibis" (foods) but SM's (and perhaps Sacy's) French gives, more specifically, "viandes" (meats), which would seem to target Jewish kosher food practises regarding pork.

obsessed with the Jews. Paul's secretary, Titus, became bishop of Crete. The ungrateful islanders had long forgotten the fine laws of Minos[56] when they submitted to those of Jesus.

XVIII   Epistle of S. Paul to Philemon

This letter, which has only one chapter, is quite extraordinary: Philemon, a wealthy benefactor of the newborn church, is robbed by his slave. The scoundrel valet flees to Rome, into the arms of Saint Paul. The apostle baptizes the thief and sends him back to his master; the latter, docile, takes back his slave on the recommendation of Saint Paul.

XIX   Epistle of S. Paul to the Hebrews

The epistle to the Hebrews is completely theological; the apostle disputes with them face to face; he argues against them to bring them under the skirts of the church just being born. I note only this verse, which ends Chapter XII: *Serviamus ... Deo cum metu ... Etenim Deus noster ignis consumens est ...* [28. We serve our God with fear ... 29. For our God is a devouring flame.] One is not moved to love what has to be feared. Chapter XIII is more about behavior and by itself is worth more than all the preceding.

N.B. It is in designating ministers of worship that God, who doesn't approve everything, although he permits everything, has made us say, through the medium of the apostle Paul: *Tradidit mundum disputationibus eorum.* [He has delivered the world to the quarrels of priests.]

XX   Epistle of S. Paul to Seneca the Philosopher[57]

Saint Jerome and Saint Augustine declared the authenticity of this correspondence; but—may it not displease them—the letters from Seneca to the apostle are too barbaric, while those from Paul to the philosopher are not barbaric

---

56 Mythical first king of Crete.
57 Seneca the younger (4 BCE–65 CE), Roman philosopher, politician, dramatist. Although his work was well thought of by early Christians, the correspondence between him and Paul was a fourth-century forgery, as Maréchal would probably have known from his own reading in Biblical studies.

enough, to be authentic. Despite the unlikelihood, Saint Jerome persists in listing Seneca the philosopher among ecclesiastical authors. More certain, though, is that Paul plagiarized Plato, who said: *The sage's entire life is a meditation on death.* The apostle exclaims in one of his Epistles, *I die every day.*

A French bishop, Antoine Godeau,[58] composed a Christian poem in five books, entitled *Saint Paul.* Here is the first hemistich: "I sing great Paul…"

Saint Paul wrote three apocalypses that are lost; we ought not to regret them, if these three works resemble most of his epistles. In one of these apocalypses, Saint Paul reveals all the fine things he was able to see in heaven, when he was carried there! It was a new world he discovered for us. Is it permissible to play this way with human credulity? We have to take Saint Paul at his word when he praises the madness of the cross and of those who embrace this unheard-of belief even before the apostle and his master. Saint Paul had already published an account of his travels, under the title *Acts.* This narrative of the comings and goings of the tireless, restless head of a sect can provide an amusing read.

XXI The Catholic Letter of S. James the Minor and the Just

From the first verses, this apostle shows himself to be more florid, more abundant in images and sentiments than Saint Paul, whom he combats with some advantage. Paul declared himself for the living faith. James declares that one is virtuous only through good works, not through the opinions one professes. Chapter II breathes humaneness. III and IV are full of wisdom. The Vth and last chapter is poetic and worthy of the golden days of prophecy: *Ecce merces operariorum qui messuerunt regiones vestras, quae fraudata est a vobis, clamat, et clamor eorum in aures Domini sabaoth introivit … Ecce judex ante januam assistit … etc.* [4. Know that the payment you withhold from workers who have harvested your fields cries out against you, and those cries mount up to the ears of the god of armies. 9. Here is the judge at the doorway.] What a pity there are only five chapters of Saint James! This is what made Saint Jerome say: *Breves pariter et longas; breves in verbis, longas in sententiis.* Epistle 103. [The Epistles of Saint James are short and long: short in words, long in thoughts.]

James was a close relative of Jesus—*consobrinus* [cousin germane] and a *proto-gospel* is attributed to him, whose loss is regrettable. In it, the apostle

---

58 Godeau (1605–1672), prolific Bible translator and author of many religious studies and biographies.

gave curious details about the illegitimate pregnancy and the labor of the virgin Mary, his aunt. He died bishop and martyr in Jerusalem.

N.B. It's important to distinguish this writer from James the Major, brother of John the Apocalyptic, both of them fishermen. To this James the Major, also a martyr at Jerusalem, is attributed a book entitled *Gospel history.*

One may observe, as a miraculous enough deed, that Jesus, who had the kindness to not write a single line, turned all his apostles into authors of books, though they were chosen from a class of men who hardly knew how to read; this multiplied to infinity the gospels, the apocalypses, the epistles, the liturgies, the acts. Of all religious sects, Christianity is the one that has produced the most writers, and the worst writers.

XXII   The Two Catholic Epistles of Saint Peter

The prince of apostles wrote them a good twenty years after his master's ordeal; they include only missionary commonplaces. Nonetheless, here is a remarkable passage, the judgment of Peter against Paul: "Among the Epistles of our brother Paul, there are things that the least steady twist, as with other holy scriptures, to their own perdition".

Rather than all the epistles of brother Paul, we prefer this simple verse, the 5th of the first chapter of the second letter by the apostle Peter: *Ministrate in virtute scientiam*, which Isaac Sacy rendered badly, in his usual fashion, as [Join knowledge to virtue.] But good Saint Peter meant nothing other than: "Put your knowledge into virtue". This is a precious saying.

We regret the loss of an apocalypse by Saint Peter: this good apostle, less a poet than his comrade John, had a bit more good sense. He might have uttered a few naïve vows, of the kind already reported about him in the New Testament. They also mention a gospel in his style.

A certain Papias,[59] pupil of the first apostles, claims somewhere in the five books of Memoirs he composed, that Mark wrote only what he had heard verbally from Peter. This testimony of Papias confirms the idea we necessarily have of the sacred books; that they are only hearsay. One of the fifty and more gospel books is called: *The Book of the Four Corners of the World.* We might call all of them together: *The Library of Crossroads,* or *The Street Corner Book.*

---

59   SM's note: See the *Ecclesiastical History* by Eusebius. [Eusebius (260–340), Greek bishop, Bible scholar, church historian.—Trans.].

XXIII   The Three Catholic Epistles of Saint John

Written more than sixty years after the execution of the judgment pronounced against Jesus, these offer only theological commonplaces. I do not except this saying, which Jean-François Laharpe treats as sublime: *Major est deus corde nostro.* [God is greater than our heart.] This sublimity requires paraphrasing; and, by paraphrasing, one gives words the significance one wishes to give them.

This other expression of Chapter IV, first epistle, has been much vaunted: *Deus charitas est.* [16. God is love.] Cicero had already said, before the apostle John and the founders of Christianity: *Charitas generis humani.*[60] An evangelist is right to have Saint John say that he is not worthy to wear his master's shoes.

XXIV   Catholic Epistle of S. Jude, Called the Zealous

In truth it is trivial, albeit *full of heaven's grace;* those are Origen's words.

One day Jude uttered—while dining with the son of God, his relative—a naiveté which could have disconcerted anyone other than Christ. Master (said he over dessert) why do you manifest yourself to us and not to the world?— Indeed, since Jesus wanted to make a revolution, it would be simpler to begin by making an impression on the great men of the earth and scholars of the time, rather than addressing himself to a few poor unlettered and impoverished devils. But the son of God didn't mean to expose himself to clear-seeing eyes; it was only by the grace of obscurity that the lights of gospel were to penetrate and spread in the brain of mankind.

To Jude, James's brother, is attributed an authentic and remarkable relation of the life and doctrine, the passion and death of his divine master.

XXV   The Apocalypse of S. John

This revelation was composed about sixty years after the sentence given against Christ. The author decided to write his gospel even later.

The first chapter of the dreams of the apostle John, sleeping in the isle of Patmos, has something imposing to it: *Beatus qui legit et audit verba prophetiae ... tempus enim prope est ... Ecce venit cum nubibus et videbit eum omnis oculus ... Etiam: amen. Ego sum alpha et omega, principium et finis, qui est, qui erat et qui*

---

60   Love for the human race.

venturus est ... Ego sum primus et novissimus et vivus, et fui mortuus et ecce sum vivens in secula seculorum, et habeo claves mortis. [3. Blessed the one who reads and hears the words of this prophecy! For the time is near. 7. Here is the one who arrives on clouds. Every eye will see him; nothing is more true: amen. 8. I am the alpha and omega, the beginning and the end, the one who is, who was and who is to come. 17. I am the first and the last, 18. and the one who lives; for I was dead: but now I am living in the world of worlds, and I have the keys to death.] There is exaltation in all this, a sort of pomp which seems to announce something moderately acceptable.

The next two chapters also have some good features: *Haec dicit sanctus et verus, qui aperit et nemo claudit, claudit et nemo aperit.* [III.7. This is what the true and holy one says, who opens what no one shuts, who shuts what no one opens.] But we need not seek meaning; the intent is with the speaker.

The seven golden vials filled with God's anger, in Chapter XV: *Dedit angelis septem phialas iracundiae Dei viventis,* are a bit bizarre, but one doesn't scrutinize dreams. These seven vials produce some effect in Chapter XVI.

XVIII is full of poetry, and worthy to follow the beautiful Lamentations of Jeremiah. The strangest thing about this Oriental composition isn't really that it was written but that it was ended this way: *Contestor omni audienti verba prophetiae libri hujus: si quis apposuerit ad haec, apponet Deus super illum plagas scriptas in libro isto.* [18. I declare to all who will understand the words of this prophecy that, if someone adds something to it, God will strike him with the afflictions written in this book.] *Et si quis diminuerit de verbis libri prophetiae hujus, auferet Deus partem ejus de libro vitae et de civitate sancta et de his quae scripta sunt in libro isto.* [19. And that, if someone shortens something in the words of the book of this prophecy, God will erase him from the book of life, exclude him from the holy city, and give him no part of anything written in this book ... A curse on whoever dares to add something to this prophecy or take out something!] ... *Risum teneatis, amici.*[61]

As for the rest, let us be careful not to pronounce on Saint John on the basis of his apocalypse; it would be as if we were to judge the genius of Newton[62] based on the commentary this great man deigned to compose on this bad dream. Bossuet[63] also composed a large volume on it, but the bishop of Meaux was only doing his job. There are more than eight hundred commentaries on

---

61 Keep from laughing, friends. An author's curse against textual changes is a long-lived literary topos, extending well into the Middle Ages and beyond.
62 Isaac Newton (1643–1727), English mathematician, physicist, astronomer, Bible commentator; one of Maréchal's intellectual heroes.
63 J.-B. Bossuet (1627–1704), bishop, theologian, orator.

the Apocalypse. There is even an Arab book entitled: *Seven Ways to Read the Koran.* In French one could compose something called *The Hundred Thousand Ways to Read the Bible.*

In *The Origin of Religions,* by the scholar Dupuis,[64] we find a completely new explanation of the logogryph of the evangelist John. Saint Jerome says that the Apocalypse has as many mysteries as words: *Tot habet sacramenta quot verba.*

Apocalyptic John died at nearly a hundred years old. It is said, in the Apocalypse, that God commanded the author to eat a volume: it would have been better to give him his own work to destroy with his tongue. A Christian sect (the Sethians,[65] I think), possessed an apocalypse attributed to Abraham; but in the happy times of that patriarch, no one made books. Abraham was neither priest nor ascetic author; he knew better how to use his life: as a good father of a family, he watched over his herds.

XXVI Prayer of Manasses, King of Judah

We find unction and some grand images in this prayer, which owes much to the spirit of the Bible and oriental books: *Ligasti mare verbo praecepti tui. Conclusisti abyssum et signasti eum terribili nomine tuo ... Nunc flecto genu cordis mei, precam a te bonitatem ... etc. etc. etc.* [You have restrained the sea by the word of your commandment; you have closed the abyss with the redoubtable seal of your name: for you are the benign Lord, who repents having afflicted humanity. I bend the knees of my heart ... etc.] *Protestant translation.*

XXVII Epistles of the Virgin Mary

They tell of several letters written by the Virgin Mary to Saint Ignatius, Bishop of Antioch, and to other individuals in Messina and Florence: we will say nothing about that. It is more probable that Mary, wife of the carpenter Joseph, knew even less than her husband how to read, and did perfectly well without it.

Consult the forty folio volumes on the holy virgin published in 1648 at Madrid by Astorga or Peter d'Arva, Franciscans in Peru. We have not been granted the grace to be able to read them.

---

64 C.-F. Dupuis (1742–1809), professor of rhetoric, lawyer, rationalist scholar and friend of Maréchal; see Mannucci 2012, *passim.*

65 A second and third-century syncretic grouping in some Middle Eastern areas.

XXVIII   Testament of the Holy Virgin

There are forty-one articles: "My dear brothers, in leaving the earth I leave you my purity ... I leave you my charity for one another... I leave you my inner joy... I leave you my obedience to the Holy Spirit... I leave you my holy familiarity with God ... etc". From the 1709 edition, published at Bar-le-Duc.

N.B. Extract from the Catechism of the Curé Meslier

QUESTION: What is the Gospel or New Testament?
ANSWER: It is a divine book, well inferior to the *Offices* of Cicero or the *Manual* of Epictetus ... etc.
This book made good from evil....
In the preface to his *Life of Jesus-Christ,* Saint-Réal[66] lets slip a confession: the academician gives, as a reason why nations of the world have neglected to read gospel, that they would like more order and connection in it. Books of morality, even the weakest, all have some method; books of religion, to the contrary, even the best written, are in the worst disorder as to editing. Gospel and the Koran don't come close to the treaty on wisdom by Charron,[67] for coherency of the whole, clarity of ideas, propriety of expression. Imagination alone rules the first two, good judgment the second.

XXIX   Collection of Ancient Gospels or *Monuments of the 1st Century of Christianity, Taken from Fabricius, Grabius and Other Scholars; by Father B****,* London, 1769, 284 *Pages*

This work—which has remained for a long time only in Latin, and thus removed from most Christians—should be perused by those who wish to know the sources from which the priests chose their four Gospels. The one about the *Childhood of Jesus,* for example, includes quite unusual details. It's a bad trick to have played on the religion, to have brought these shameful details to light.

---

66   César de Saint-Réal (1639–1692), historian, novelist and priest; his biography of Jesus was published in 1678.
67   Pierre Charron (1541–1603), priest and philosopher.

PART 3

Result of Reading the Bible

∴

Result of Reading the Bible

We will terminate our impartial analysis of holy scripture with a few meditations on the ensemble of the canonical books of Old and New Testaments. These reflections are presented quite naturally in closing the sacred volume, and in taking account of the impression that reading it leaves on minds not already made up for or against.

A great thing could have been done at the birth of Christ. Sages, even today, would honor his memory—if, like Moses, or, better than Moses, Christ had inspired in the souls of his degenerate compatriots a spark of liberal virtue, if he had said to them: "What are you waiting for? The impure hand of Tiberius weighs on your head. Are you waiting for the Roman eagle to come and rip up your brood in the nest?[1] In truth, in truth, I tell you: just a little time and the despotic usurpers of all Europe will bring desolation inside the walls of Jerusalem. Run for your weapons, chase out the governor, and take the attitude of people who want to live free henceforth in their homes, without the good will of their prideful conqueror. The yoke of Rome is no more difficult to break than that of Egypt. The mountain lion, chained while he sleeps, shakes his mane, breaks his chains, and makes his pernicious masters tremble. Let the lion of Judah do the same! In the holy anger that transports me, recognize the purest blood of Israel, which flows in my veins. Out with your lying prophets, your greedy pontiffs! Remember your ancestors, those itinerant shepherds who, like Abraham, made themselves respected by neighboring kings. If you have to, set your city Jerusalem on fire, destroy with your own hands this temple of ancient law, which could not preserve you from Babylonian captivity or the protection of Rome; be independent of things and persons; become once again the heads of families, monarchs amidst their children, as were your ancestors; begin a new era … etc".

This is what Christ, born of a virgin, could have said with the authority given by courage and virtue; and one didn't have to be God, or son of a God, to put such a speech into practise. William Tell[2] and various other Swiss mountain hunters knew quite naturally how to deliver their country.

The evangelists tell us what Jesus did for his own. His nation continued to be the victim and still is rejected among peoples. But a new religion resulted from his appearance on earth. We don't accuse Christ. Perhaps he is innocent of all

---

1 SM's note: *Isaiah,* Chap. x.
2 William Tell, late-medieval Swiss folk hero, said to have assassinated a tyrant with bow and arrow.

the evil that has been permitted in his name. But at the same time, this figure is far from having motivated the divine honors he is still rendered today, and the superb testimonials that our most famous authors have put forward on account of him.

It was not a new religion that ought to have been grafted onto the old one. It was much more in the character of a son of God to say to humanity: "Children, leave those baby-rattles of superstition alone; they make you neither happier nor wiser; I come to show you how to do without them. I have come down to earth expressly, not to make it change its sacred or its political idols, but to overturn them all through the power of reason. So, people of Judea, whom I intended to honor with my presence, give an example to the other nations; let every one of you keep to the paternal household! Henceforth, have no other religion than filial piety; this was the only cult in the time of the patriarchs, your ancestors. I wanted to be born in a stable, near the working ox and amid shepherds, to teach a lesson. Benefit from it; take up once again the pastoral and agricultural life. I spent my early years in an artisan's workshop, to return to the useful trades the respect that the parasite arts had usurped from them. When I shall have re-ascended to the eternal source, place no faith in those who would hijack my memory in order to deceive you. They will make me speak much after my death; they will give you my testament[3] to read, which I never thought of; they will boast of my miracles, my dogmas; they will want to make me the founder of a school, or head of a sect; I tell you this in advance. In truth, in truth, all these things will be lies. Do neither more nor less than I did; remain, like me, in peaceful obscurity, and you will be happy in this life".

A sensible and peaceful man could have replied thus to the suggestions which would have been made, that he should place himself at the head of a party of fanatics.

For sure, J.J. Rousseau must have been delirious when he consecrated to the memory of Jesus the three or four fine pages that everyone knows; or when he didn't hesitate to compare to the wise Socrates a charlatan or rather a miserable madman who, interrogated by his judges, replied to them: [I assure you that one day you will see me carried away on clouds, and seated at the right of God's majesty.] *Verumtamen dico vobis, amodo videbitis filium hominis sedentem a dextris virtutis dei, et venientem in nubibus coeli.* Matth. We cite the text faithfully.

If this single item doesn't suffice to appreciate the man—*Ecce homo!*—then reread the narrative of the *Passion!*

---

3   SM's note: The New Testament, or Gospel. [A testament is a legal document, a will, as in "last will and testament".—Trans.].

Jesus had already escaped[4] several times from the hands of escorts. He learns that one of his disciples has sold him out, and will turn him over; he loses his mind; he addresses long lamentations to the other apostles who tremble as much as he does: [Just a little more time and you will see me no more ... O my father! I pray for my disciples and not for the world...] *Ego pro eis rogo, non pro mundo rogo.* There is little charity in these words. Then he meditates on the Mount of Olives to beg God his father to avert from him the bitter potion being prepared for him. Terror overcomes his entire being; he is covered with sweat and falls down in agony: *Coepi evanescere et gravissime angi.* [Jesus gave himself over to fear and appeared cruelly anguished. Mark XIV.33.] *Tristis usque ad mortem.* Luke XXII.41. [My soul, said Jesus to three of his apostles, my soul is overwhelmed with a mortal sadness.] *Abba pater, si velles tranferre calicem.* [My father, if you should wish to spare me from taking the chalice, you can. Mark.] *Factus in agonia ...* Luke.

He wants to save the honor of his sect, but in forcing himself to show some firmness he falls into impertinence. His judge asks: *What have you done?* He answers: *My reign is not of this world.* Pilate says: *So you are king?* Jesus replies astutely: *It is you who say so.* As if to intimidate the tribunal before which he must appear, he had already spoken of a [dozen legions of angels who, at his voice, can descend and save him.] *An putas quia non possum rogare patrem meum, et exhibebit mihi modo plusquam duodecim legions angelorum.* Matth. Are these the methods of an unjustly accused sage? *What a miserable farce!...* forgive the expression!

Seeing that he doesn't impress his judges as much as the multitude, Jesus, who has already spoken too much, decides a bit late to keep silent, and resigns himself to ill treatment and the cruel persiflage inflicted on him because of his earlier retorts. He is whipped, then led to the torture. En route, he tries to move the women to pity him:[5] *Don't weep for me, daughters of Jerusalem; weep instead for yourself and your children.* But the people, far from being moved with pity, watch him go to Calvary, without displaying the least emotion. At last, fixed to the cross and losing all hope, his last words, produced by discouragement, reproach his celestial father, on whose help he seemed to rely: [My God! Why do you abandon me?] *Eloi, eloi, lamma sabacthani.*

It is likely that Jesus hoped, up to the last moment, that his people would arrive to tear him out of the hands of justice; he expected a small insurrection in his favor. If Saul (called Paul) had been converted sooner, things might have gone otherwise. Paul would have managed to rouse the populace and would

---

4   SM's note: Saint-Réal, *Life of Jesus Christ*, p. 211.
5   SM's note: Saint-Réal, same text, p. 228.

have rescued his master. But, betrayed by one of his own, abandoned by cowardly others despite his instructions, indifferent to the people on whose behalf he had never done enough to merit their gratitude, Jesus submitted in a servile way to his death sentence. People think of him only when there is no more time; or rather change their minds a bit late, but usually soon enough to put into practise what Jesus' life could not produce but what his death achieved.

That is the man—*ecce homo*—whom Jean-Jacques confidently contrasts to Socrates, and whom he even wants to place above Socrates. But (it will be repeated with the Genevan orator) Jesus pardons his enemies and prays for his executioners. Had Jean-Jacques forgotten that, long before Jesus, Pythagoras, Socrates and other sages had given the precept and example of this fine devotion,[6] the last effort of virtue?

The hero of gospel succeeded, it is true, in founding a religious sect that still survives; but he did not fulfill the sublime mission that he had announced with so much boldness and emphasis. The human race can add another cult, but has been no more regenerated since Jesus than since Moses. What new virtue did Christ reveal to the world? All were known, written, and practised before him—but perhaps he added to them the seal of perfection! On the contrary, Jesus or his trouble-makers have made morality deteriorate, in rendering it religious, from the naturalness it had before them.

The Bible has obtained only the success it deserved. The appearance of holy books on earth has not made vices disappear, nor crimes, nor the misfortunes that necessarily follow from them. Jesus performed many miracles. Through him the blind were able to see clearly; the dead lived a second time; he himself was resuscitated the third day after his torture. But gospel has made no wonders; it has had no rule over the human spirit to rectify it. What other books have not been able to accomplish, one has the right to expect, even demand, from a divine book. We must apply to the Bible what the Mohammedan sect of Al-Jahedh[7] said of the Koran: "It is a body that can take the form sometimes of a man, sometimes of a beast".

But what are we to think of Christianity and its books, if we turn to the scholar Dupuis? He maintains[8] that Jesus never existed: Christ is only the sun, and the cult of Christians that of worshipers of that star. This is only an erudite conjecture; but the Bible offers a monument that is only too real. From the

---

6 Devotion: The text has "dévouement" (devotion), but this is possibly a misprint for "dénouement" (ending), which makes equal or better sense, considering that Socrates was also put to death for his teachings. Theories attributed to Pythagoras were controversial in his time and later; there are various legends about his death, including that he was killed by an angry mob.
7 Ninth-century Iraqi poet and Koranic scholar.
8 SM's note: In the *Universal Religion*, or *Origin of All Cults*.

thoughtful reading of this book, it is necessary to conclude that it is one of the most dangerous of all books; that, under a government truly the friend of good behavior, it would be a good policy to withdraw this book from commerce, as is done with obscene works. Poets and men of letters, at most, would be able to consult the Bible to complete their studies. This is what the Church fathers and doctors of the Sorbonne themselves thought. Illogical priests blush at their own books.

Of course, we will be opposed by a swarm of witnesses. Thus, Saint Chrysostom exclaims: "The reading of holy books is assuredly a great thing" (*Commentaries on Acts*). For Saint Jerome, every syllable in the Bible emanates from heaven. Saint Augustine, in his book *On the Utility of Believing*, says with a great deal of apostolic confidence: "Believe me, everything in the holy books is great and divine; they contain nothing untrue" (Chap. VI). The same bishop permits himself this further saying, so odd coming from the pen of a Church father: *Incomparabiliter pulchrior est veritas christianorum quam Helena Graecorum.* [The beauty of the Bible is much superior to the beauty of Helen.][9] Saint Ambrose regards the Old and New Testaments as the two breasts of the Church. (*On patriarchal blessing*).

On our side we can cite equally serious authorities. First, the Church lists *biblists* among the heretics, because nothing more disturbing can happen to the authors of the two Testaments than to take them at their word and hold them to their text. "The reading of scripture is a double-edged knife. There have been Church fathers who found it bad that everyone should read holy scripture; and among these fathers of the Church we name Saint Jerome".—Cardinal du Perron. "The translation of the Bible into the vernacular will have consequences fatal to religion".—Cardinal Ximenes. "Without the authority of the church, I would have no greater veneration for the Bible than for Aesop's fables".—*Free thoughts* of a Catholic writer, approved by Cardinal Osius. A tradition, from Saint Irenaeus up to the scholars of recent times, demonstrates that reading the Bible is very dangerous.—The Cardinals de Rohan, Byssi and Noailles. Saint Basil, having heard the kitchen supervisor of Emperor Valens cite holy scripture, was so enraged that, notwithstanding his normal mildness, he couldn't keep from telling the servant: "Get back to your sauces". We owe this little known and curious anecdote to Theodoret;[10] it tends to show that

---

9   A more accurate translation than Sacy's would be: "The truth of Christians is incomparably more beautiful than Helen of the Greeks". Helen is the wife of Menelaus, king of Sparta, whose abduction by the Trojan prince Paris started the Trojan War.

10 Theodoret (393–c. 458), Turkish bishop and theologian.

priests are happy to allow the sun to shine for everyone, but not for the Bible to be read by everyone.

Let us invoke another weighty witness. Mallet, a doctor of the Sorbonne and archdeacon, wrote a book expressly to prove that God's intention was that holy scripture not be read by the people but only by priests, who would give the people whatever knowledge of it they judged suitable—*On Reading Holy Scripture in Vulgar*[11] *Language,* 1620. It is by divine law that the people should not read sacred books. It was never God's intention to abandon his word to the discretion of the people.—*Ibid.* The holy fathers considered it a dangerous innovation, not to be tolerated by the Church, that the liberty of reading holy scripture be permitted to everyone.—*Ibid.* The holy fathers disapproved as an abuse the general permission to read the Bible, in any language whatever.—*Ibid.* It was not the intention of the apostles that common people should learn religious truths by reading holy scripture.—*Ibid.* The prudence of Christians of the first four centuries, and of many others later on, did not judge it useful for the salvation of the people that they should read holy scripture.—*Ibid.* The reading of holy scripture is still today less useful than it was for the Jews; it can, more than ever, bring much damage.—*Ibid.*

The scholars of Church law did not generally permit reading the sacred books, even to the disciples they taught.—Origen. What our Lord did in the synagogue at Nazareth, in closing the book of Isaiah and returning it to the minister after having read it, was to teach us that the book of holy scripture must be closed to the people, because it is not necessary to tell everyone everything.—The venerable Bede.

Through unheard-of illogic, this book which, on the admission of fathers and doctors of the Church, ought not to be put into everyone's hands—this book, whose first lines offer an adulterer as model for Christian women; this book which preaches and advocates the contempt of children for their mother, the desertion of fathers by their children; this book which advises against the last duties to render to the dead; this infernal book which, under the title of good news, declares war, not peace; this dangerous book which includes as many absurdities as immoralities; this book whose best pages are plagiarized and whose originals are bad; this book, monstrous as to form and content— has nonetheless received and continues to receive divine honors; it has altars

---

11   Vulgar: from Latin "vulgus", the ordinary people; hence "Vulgate" for St. Jerome's translation of scripture from Greek and Hebrew into Latin which, at the time, was a vernacular throughout the Roman Empire.

and priests. Every time one wants to read it, one kneels before it;[12] it is kissed, perfumed, placed on one's head; covered with pearls and precious stones. Exposed open in every tribunal, a hand placed above it, it serves as a guarantee of truth and law. The zealous of both sexes hang it on their chest and order that it be enclosed with them in the tomb.[13] People have gone so far as to transcribe the Bible and the gospels in letters of silver and gold. Finally, this book (says the Jesuit Isaac Berruyer) "has had, for many centuries, the admiration of all connoisseurs".

Honorable readers, we ask you: a few centuries from now, will people believe that for more than two thousand years, most of the human population worshiped a cult, burned incense to the Bible and to the gospels, to the Zend-Avesta and to the Koran? Won't they consider the historians of our time to be fabulists? Will they believe that there once were people not completely unenlightened but who daily knelt before the book of gospel and piously pressed their lips to every page of this volume? Will they be able to imagine the decadence of human reason to such a degree of brutalization? Will they believe that to mothers of families, to chaste spouses, to pure virgins was recommended the reading of a book full of obscenities and bad examples?

Nonetheless, at first glance the Bible is a consoling and precious thing! God not only deigned to speak directly to people to enable them to return to the path of virtue, but topped it off with his paternal goodness by taking the trouble to compose a large volume, to write about it with his own finger, on stone (the twelve first paragraphs) and dictate the rest to Moses, to David the just, to the wise Solomon, to the prophets, the apostles, even to holy women. Indeed, so much care can't avoid having the most marvellous consequences. The golden age, at least, must be the necessary result of the Old and New Testaments. Henceforth everyone must be good and happy. The Bible and gospel must make angels on earth.

Alas, not at all: everything carried on quite differently. People continue ever since the Bible and the gospel, to live like demons, just as before the Bible and the gospel. Copyists apparently did not understand the celestial voice that dictated the holy books. This inspired volume is a literary chaos, where good and bad, fine and mediocre, chaste scenes, libidinous pictures, moral severity,

---

12   SM's note: See *Ordo Rom.* SD: The *Ordo Romanus* is one of dozens of documents, some dating from the eighth century, describing in detail various liturgies and rituals of the Roman Catholic Church.
13   SM's note: See *Ancient Monuments,* Jo. Ciampini. [Giovanni G. Ciampini (1633–98), scientist and Church historian.—Trans.].

relapses and even violation of norms, are found pell-mell. *Indigesta moles*[14]... (Ovid, *Metamorphoses*).

Thousands of other volumes have been compiled to explain this one, and have produced exactly the contrary. If the multiplicity of books is a scourge, what book has occasioned more books than the Bible?

And the people, with this code of divine laws in hand, have not felt themselves to be dispensed from composing an infinity of other laws. A god's commandments have become insufficient for humanity. The world, since God himself spoke to it, has not improved. Moreover, all these scriptures dictated by the divine mouth, far from putting an end to the evils and crimes of the poor human race, have heaped them up, throwing amongst them Adam's and Eve's apple of discord.[15]

The Holy Spirit (we are assured) made all the oracles go silent: if the Bible is truly its work, what are we waiting for? Let's be logical; let's throw all other books on the fire; there's nothing more to be done; we only need this one.

The institution of priests and the divinity of their books are two specious ideas which must have impressed the less educated. What a genius was the first one who dared to say to his fellow human beings:

> My friends, I see you in daily discord about the most important things; who will be your arbiter, your judge, your guide, your legislator? It can't be one of you, since you are all equal. For forty days and forty nights I have meditated on this great topic. This morning, on the peak of the nearby mountain, my face raised and turned toward the rising sun, my ears were suddenly struck with the sound of a voice saying: 'Look to your feet, take and read'. I lowered my eyes and found at my feet this volume, written by the very finger of him of whom the sun is only the feeble image. My friends, let us open this book; everything is found in it, and let us render thanks for it to the supreme author.

But, to sustain such high pretensions, it would be necessary to have a perfect book in hand. Only perfection could justify its celestial origin. It would be necessary to produce a book as far above the best books known as these are above

---

14   A disordered mass. From Ovid's description of primordial chaos at the opening of his *Metamorphoses*.

15   In Greek myth, a golden apple inscribed with the words "For the most beautiful" was thrown among guests at the wedding of a goddess and a man, creating competition among the three major goddesses and eventually resulting in the Trojan War. Maréchal refashions the Greek apple of discord into the Christian apple said to have generated original sin.

the mass of others. From the first line to the last of this divine volume, one would not find a single equivocal expression. The style of such a book would have to be as pure as a virgin's heart: the least disproportion would devalue it; a single improper word would suffice to make the fraud known. A book conceived and dictated by God himself would have to be at the very least, *written reason*. The reading of this book would have to rally every spirit, reduce all opinions to one; in a word, take the place of all human institutions civil and religious.

If God had deigned to communicate with humanity through the channel of a book, he would have written neither in Hebrew, Greek, nor Arabic but in an idiom familiar to all people; for, no doubt, the common father of all nations would not have taken the trouble to write for only one of them. Thus, the universal language would be found. So it is clear that the Bible and gospel are not—no more than the *Koran*, the *Shastra*, the *Zend-Avesta*—a divine book or holy scripture. It is equally clear that it is not with these kinds of books that humanity will ever be made happy and good. Thus, it would not be unsuitable to put aside all these volumes that have caused the so much blood to flow and so many brains to founder; and to return to nature by the road of reason.

A great scourge for reason and truth is a book whose basis is bad but whose form bears the imprint of talent. It's even worse when this book, having left the list of other human productions to inhabit the darkness, passes as the work of a divine hand. Its prestige lasts long, even amid enlightenment, above all when a sufficiently numerous class of individuals owes its existence in civil society to this book.

Book of blood and mud! For the two to three thousand years since you fell from heaven, how much evil you have poured out onto the earth! Inexhaustible source of errors and lies, vice and crime! O how much the poor human race has been bastardized through you! Impure emanation of the oldest and most fatal of all prejudices! Monstrous production of a shadowy spirit scattered with a few bright spots! When will you cease outraging taste, reason and manners?

Future generations! Will you be able to conceive the terrible ascendancy of a book over nearly the entire globe? If ever the invention of writing and printing was a benefit, oh, this benefit was costly, since to it we owe the Bible and the gospel! If these two books could be eliminated only in a complete proscription of all others, ah! Let us not hesitate; let all books perish, provided that the Bible and gospel disappear with them!

Old and New Testament, equally guilty! O you, the two most famous of all books! To whom has your reading been beneficial? Or rather, for whom have you not been a subject of scandal? To what type of reader are you suitable? To young virgins? Bible and gospel make them blush from the very first chapters, which are tainted by incest[16] and adultery.[17] To honest wives? The chastity of the first Joseph is an outrage for them. To well-meaning husbands? The second Joseph comes along to trouble household peace. To children obeying their father? Abraham's knife, raised to his son's throat, revolts them. To good mothers of a family? The atrocious word of Christ to his mother: "Woman, what have we in common?"[18] pierces their soul. To the unfortunate? The book of Job puts them into despair. To monarchs? David and Solomon offer the most perfidious examples. To the peoples of the world? The Jewish nation calumniates them all in its history.[19] To peace-lovers? The "make them come in"[20] of gospel has filled the world with persecutors and the excluded.

Fortunately, humanity has its heart and its reason; what need has it for *the religion of the two books*?[21] Does the son of a family wait to be able to read this double volume before he can embrace his mother or honor his father? When will it end, this power of words that overturns things?

Terrible book, whose every line has caused blood and bile to flow! One day, no doubt, your charm will be destroyed, one day our nephews will make an honorable amend for their ancestors' credulity! But before that probably far distant time, alas, and blushing for the human race to which I belong, I want at least to mark the first year of the XIXth century of the common era, with a solemn protest against the religion that has for so long prostituted itself to the most absurd,[22] most useless, most immoral and evil-doing of all books.

And you, whose life was so consistent with the scandal of your birth and the infamy of your death! Ungrateful child, harsh relative, dangerous citizen! Vile egoist, who was never husband or father! Maladroit clown, evil spirit, who

---

16 SM's note: Lot and his daughters in the Old Testament.
17 SM's note. Virgin Mary and the angel Gabriel in the New Testament.
18 SM's note: *Quid mihi et tibi est, mulier?* According to Saint John 11, 4.
19 SM's note: They have been fully repaid for this. One may judge from the following little-known passage, which Plutarch has preserved for us: "Typhon, having lost a battle against Osiris, saved himself on a red donkey, which carried him for seven days and seven nights. On the last night, after having rested together after a long ride, the donkey found herself pregnant by her knight. The fruit of such a strange coupling was two twins, male and female, who served as stock for a little neighboring tribe, envious, despised and ill-considered, that is, the Jewish nation... The Hebrews were, for some time, the helots of Egypt". *Treatise on Isis and Osiris*. [Plutarch (46–120), Greek biographer, politician and priest of Apollo. The anecdote as given is not in Plutarch.—Trans.].
20 SM's note: Luke, XIV, 23.
21 SM's note: Name given to Christianity because of its two foundations, the Old and the New Testament.
22 SM's note: Abbé Millot said, "Every atrocious religion is necessarily absurd". [Claude Millot (1726–85), Jesuit priest and historian.—Trans.].

boasted of having legions of angels[23] at your service! You who, throughout your infernal mission, renounced your mother, troubled families, debauched children of the paternal home, refused burial to the dead, preached intolerance and persecution! Ambitious hypocrite, who wanted to efface Moses who was so superior to you! Adventurer as ignorant as your accomplices, whom you sought at the port and in the taverns! Miserable head of a sect, cowardly and fanatical, who didn't even know how to die and who, as your punishment approached, sweated blood[24] so much did fear act on your organs! I will not sully the memory of Socrates in opposing you to the sublime last moments of this true philosopher! Christ, may your name perish! Or rather may it be doomed to the sage's contempt and the execration of the finally undeceived people!

But be assured, honest and indignant souls: this man-god or god-man, or rather this monster, probably never existed. Obscure charlatans, tormented by the need to torment others in order to be something, will doubtless have imagined this made-up phantom who lent himself to everything, in order to attract the dregs of the nations around their stage. Thus, under the name of Mercury or Hermes Trismegistes, priests of the Nile made inhabitants of Egypt adopt their servile, superstitious doctrine.

And you, good people, who believe someone's word even without visible proof, you herd of docile, routinistic bipeds, throw yourselves under the rod of your priests! Fall to your knees at the foot of the gibbet where the disturber of families and of public order, where the shamed impostor who called himself the son of God and who wasn't even a man, ended his short but long enough career!

Little ladies of the day—the dishonor of your husbands and the female corrupters of your own daughters—hang an ebony and gold cross on your bosom, which the cynicism of our culture no longer lets you keep even half-covered!

And you, literary folk of bad faith or bad mind; you, elegant writers on a party salary, defend with your fragile pens the sacred ark, depository of sacerdotal impostures!

Nineteenth century! Dishonor yourself, like your predecessors, by the same religious turpitudes! While enveloped in their cloaks, the friends of reason, few in number, groan at the lapse of the human race to which they regretfully belong, and for which they will not cease to make vows and consecrate their vigils, even if they are to be repaid with ingratitude and perhaps by persecution!

---

23 SM's note: The gospel according to Saint Matthew, XXVI, 53.
24 SM's note: *Et factus est sudor ejus sicut guttae sanguinis decurrentis in terram.* Gospel according to Luke, XXII.44. ["And so it was that his sweat dropped on the ground like drops of blood". The line doesn't say what Maréchal says it does.—Trans.].

Post-script

We agree that we have been severe in our judgments on the *scriptures* called *sacred*, and on those who exploit them. At the same time, we flatter ourselves to be only the echo of a crowd of sensible persons who believe everything written in this treaty *for and against the Bible*; but these persons care more about their tranquillity than about bearing brilliant witness to the shameless outrages against reason that have lasted so many centuries. We seem to hear most of our readers say in a low voice: "Priests and their books have done and still do much evil; that is certain. It is certain that one can't see a priest pass by, or read a page of the Bible, without shrugging and frowning. The gospel religion offers nonsense, and is in total dissonance with the culture of the human spirit in the xixth century".

Let us end with a simple comparison, which ought to make an impression: Twenty-five years ago, a truly great man published, in both old and new worlds, a booklet of about twenty pages, which has probably already done more good for the human race than all the books composed before or since. The twenty pages of *Goodman Richard's Science*, written by Franklin,[25] include more useful truths and healthy morality than the five Books of Moses, the hundred and fifty Psalms of David, the five Books of Solomon's wisdom, the seventeen Books of the major and minor prophets, the four Gospels of Christ and all the Epistles of his apostles, Brahma's *Shastra*, the *Zend-Avesta* of Zoroaster, Odin's *Edda*, Mahomet's *Koran*, etc.

Yes, one must have the courage to say it (even if it means being the only one, and who will admit it?) yes! Franklin, with his little ten-sheet book, rendered a much greater service to his fellows than Moses, David, Solomon, the prophets, Jesus, Zoroaster, Brahma, Odin, Mahomet with their sublime and holy scriptures. Yes! The human race will be wise, tranquil, and happy only when it will have the strength of mind to close all these fine books, and keep to the twenty pages of Franklin's *The Goodman Richard's Science*.

At the point to which civilization has arrived, people have nearly run through the course of knowledge imparted to them. To avoid a vicious circle, let them return very soon to the good sense whence they came, and let them stay there! Enough raving: they need no more books. It would be a wise measure to withdraw from people's hands all those eloquent and poetic volumes which so far have only inflamed their brains; they require only two or three

---

25   Benjamin Franklin (1706–90). As a printer, experimental scientist, and American ambassador to France (1776–85), Franklin was a popular figure in France.

elementary booklets along the lines of Franklin's *The Goodman Richard's Science*.

Yes! I repeat: without priests and their books, without structures and without expenses, in a little time most people, accustomed to the useful verities and healthy morals included in *The Goodman Richard's Science*, would become similar to the author; and, no doubt, the best of worlds would be one that would have only Benjamin Franklins as inhabitants.

Second P.S. There is a universal tradition, prior to the holy scriptures of every people and that will survive them; it is *proverbs*, so accurately called "the wisdom of nations". Everything necessary for people to learn, to believe and to practise, is found there. A wise choice of all proverbs, ancient and modern, would make the best of books. This book, once edited as it ought to be, would be worthy the support of a government that had at heart the rehabilitation of the degraded human race, to give this volume all the approval and solemnity it deserves and to put it into people's hands in place of the *Bible* and the *gospels*.

In London, there is a Bible Society presided over by the Archbishop of Canterbury: its members, all wealthy, band together with the single intention of furnishing bibles to all Christians who have not the money to buy them; this society has filled both old and new worlds with bibles. Will this example be wasted? In France or elsewhere, will there not be enough honest people with the position and temperament to sacrifice to reason everything that has been sacrificed to religious fanaticism? When will we see an association formed, printing at its own expense and distributing a large number of elementary books in the taste of those we have quoted above? Will truth never have its propaganda? Evil has spread on earth through the channel of bad books; the good can only be done with the help of good books. This war of pens is doubtless preferable to swords of dragonnades and of the Vendée,[26] etc.

To enlighten people is better than killing them to make them better.

END

---

26   In 1681, King Louis XIV ordered Catholic soldiers (dragoons) to occupy Protestant homes, to harass them with a view to conversion or emigration; this policy was the dragonnade. The Vendée was a region in western France, site of a counter-revolutionary uprising (1793–96) that was harshly suppressed.

Bibliography

Bibles and Related Texts Used in This Translation

Alter, Robert. *The Hebrew Bible. A Translation with Commentary*. 3 vols. New York: W.W. Norton, 2019.

Barnstone, Willis, ed. *The Other Bible. Ancient Alternative Scriptures*. New York: HarperCollins, 1984.

Catholic Family Edition of the Holy Bible. New York: Crawley & Co., 1953.

Cruden's Complete Concordance to the Old and New Testaments. By Alexander Cruden; ed. A.D. Adams, C.H. Irwin, S.A. Waters. Philadelphia and Toronto: The John C. Winston Company, 1930.

The New English Bible with Apocrypha. Oxford University Press and Cambridge University Press, 1970.

La Sainte Bible Qui Contient le Vieux et le Nouveau Testament. Revue sur les Textes Hébreux et Grecs. 4 vol. Amsterdam: Pierre Mortier et Pierre Brunet, 1712. https://search.socialhistory.org/Record/ARCH00855, items 60–63.

La Sainte Bible ... trans. Monsieur Le Maistre de Saci. 2 vols. Paris: Guillaume Desprez, 1701.

Tanakh. A New Translation ... Torah, Nevi'im, Kethuvim. Philadelphia: Jewish Publication Society, 1985.

Wills, Lawrence M., ed./trans. *Ancient Jewish Novels. An Anthology*. New York: Oxford University Press, 2002.

Reference List to Works Cited in Introduction, Translator's Note, and Footnotes

Alter, Robert. 2019. *The Art of Biblical Translation*. Princeton, NJ: Princeton University Press.

Alter, Robert. 2010. *Pen of Iron. American Prose and the King James Bible*. Princeton, NJ: Princeton University Press.

Aubert, Françoise. 1975. *Sylvain Maréchal. Passion et Faillite d'un Égalitaire*. Pisa: Goliardica and Paris: Nizet.

Auerbach, Erich. 1953. "Odysseus' Scar". In *Mimesis. The Representation of Reality in Western Literature*, 1–20. Translated by Willard Trask. Princeton, NJ: Princeton University Press; orig. Berne: A. Francke, 1946.

Auerbach, Erich. 1959. "Figura" in *Scenes from the Drama of European Literature*, 11–76. Translated by Ralph Manheim. New York: Meridian.

Barbery, Muriel. 2008. *The Elegance of the Hedgehog*. Translated by Alison Anderson. New York: Europa editions; orig. Paris: Gallimard.

Benot, Yves, ed. 1958. *Le Pour et le Contre. Corréspondance Polémique sur le Respect de la Posterité*. Paris: Editeurs Français Réunis.

Bradley, Arthur and Andrew Tate. 2010. *The New Atheist Novel. Fiction, Philosophy and Polemic after 9/11*. London and New York: Continuum Books.

Brennan, Emily, "The Unbelievers", *New York Times* (November 27, 2011): ST1.

Bouvier, Jeanne. 1931. *Les Femmes Pendant la Révolution*. Paris: Editions E. Figuière.

Brunet, Gustave. 1962. *Imprimeurs Imaginaires et Libraires Supposes. Étude Bibliographique*. Paris, 1866; repr. New York: Burt Franklin.

Chyet, Stanley F. 1958. "The Political Rights of the Jews in the United States: 1776–1840". *American Jewish Archives* (April), 14–75.

Curran, Andrew S. 2019. *Diderot and the Art of Thinking Freely*. New York: Other Press.

Dagenais, Simon. 2016. "L'Almanach de Mathieu Laensbergh: L'Emergence d'une Marque (XVIIe–XIXe Siècles)". Ph.D. diss., University of Quebec at Montreal.

Darnton, Robert. 1995. *The Corpus of Clandestine Literature in France, 1769–1789*. New York: Norton.

Darnton, Robert. 1991. *Édition et Sédition. L'Univers de la Littérature Clandestine au XVIIIe Siècle*. Paris: Gallimard.

Dawkins, Richard. 2006. *The God Delusion*. London: Bantam Press.

Delany, Sheila. 2012. "Bible, Jews, Revolution: Sylvain Maréchal's *Pour et Contre la Bible*". In *Ot Letova. Essays in Honor of Professor Tova Rosen*, edited by Eli Yassif, Haviva Ishay and Uriah Kfir, 95–109. Beer Sheva: Heksherim Institute.

Desroussilles, François Dupigrenet. 1986. "La Production Biblique Catholique en France au XVIIIe Siècle". In *Le Siècle des Lumières et la Bible*, edited by Yvon Belaval and Dominique Bourel, 73–83. Paris: Beauchesne.

Dommanget, Maurice. 1950. *Sylvain Maréchal, l'égalitaire ... (1750–1803)*. Paris: Spartacus.

Dommanget, Maurice. 1970. *Sur Babeuf et la Conjuration des Égaux*. Paris: Maspero.

Eco, Umberto. 2003. *Mouse or Rat? Translation as Negotiation*. London: Weidenfeld and Nicolson.

Fainberg, Sarah. 2014. "French Laïcité: What Does It Stand For?" In *Secularism on the Edge. Rethinking Church-State relations in the United States, France and Israel.* Edited by Jacques Berlinerblau and Sarah Fainberg, 85–94. New York: Palgrave MacMillan.

Febvre, Lucien. 1982. *The Problem of Unbelief in the Sixteenth Century. The Religion of Rabelais*. Translated by Beatrice Gottlieb. Cambridge, Mass.: Harvard University Press; orig. Paris, 1942.

Fleury, Claude. 1682. *Les Moeurs des Israelites*. La Haye.

Herzberg, Arthur. 1970. *The French Enlightenment and the Jews*. New York: Schocken.

Holbach, Paul-Henry Thiry d'. 2008. *Tableau des Saints*. Edited by J.-P. Jackson. Tangier: Coda.
Karmin, Otto. 1911. "Essai d'une Bibliographie de Sylvain Maréchal". *Revue Historique de la Révolution Française* 2, 262–67 and 437–43.
Keane, Mary Beth. 2019. "A Catholic Reckoning". *Vogue* (January) 16–18.
Kors, Alan Charles. 1976. *D'Holbach's Coterie. An Enlightenment in Paris*. Princeton, NJ: Princeton University Press.
Kors, Alan Charles. 1990. *Atheism in France, 1650–1729. The Orthodox Sources of Disbelief*. Princeton, NJ: Princeton University Press.
Latreille, André. 1946. *L'Église Catholique et la Révolution Française*, vol. 1. Paris: Hachette.
Legoupil, Audrey. 2011. "Port-Royal et la Vulgate. Une Entreprise de Traduction Novatrice". www.lurens.ens.fr/travaux/litterature-du-xviie-siecle/article/port-royal-et-la-vulgate.
Lemaître, Henri. 2003. *Dictionnaire Bordas de Littérature Française*. Paris: Bordas.
Luzzato, Sergio. 2001. *L'Automne de la Révolution. Luttes et Cultures Politiques dans la France Thermidorienne*. Paris: Champion.
Mannucci, Erica Joy. 2012. *Finalmente il Popolo Pensa. Sylvain Maréchal nell'Immagine della Rivoluzione Francese*. Naples: Guida.
Maréchal, Sylvain. 1780. *Antiquités d'Herculanum, Gravé par F.A. David*. Paris: David.
Maréchal, Sylvain. 1781. *Ad Majorem Gloriam Virtutis: Fragmens d'un Poème Moral sur Dieu*. Athéopolis [Paris?], n.p.
Maréchal, Sylvain. 1782. *L'Âge d'Or, Receuil de Contes Pastoraux*. Mitylène [Paris]: Guillot.
Maréchal, Sylvain. 1784. *Livre Échappé au Déluge*. Paris: Bibliothèque Mazarine.
Maréchal, Sylvain. [1788]. [Paris.] *Almanach des Honnêtes Gens*. N.d., n.p.
Maréchal, Sylvain. 1790. *Catéchisme du Curé Meslier*. N.p.
Maréchal, Sylvain. [1790]. *La Nouvelle Légende Dorée, ou Dictionnaire des Saintes*. Rome [Brussels?], n.p. Translated by Sheila Delany as *Anti-saints*. Edmonton: University of Alberta Press, 2012.
Maréchal, Sylvain. 1793. *Calendrier des Républicains*. Paris: Gueffier.
Maréchal, Sylvain. [1794]. *La Fable du Christ Dévoilée, ou Lettre du Muphti de Constantinople à Jean Ange Braschy, Muphti de Rome*. Paris: Franklin.
Maréchal, Sylvain. [1796]. "Chanson Nouvelle à l'Usage des Faubourgs". In *Florilège de la Chanson Révolutionnaire de 1789 au Front Populaire*, edited by Robert Brécy, 1978. Milan: Editions hier et demain.
Maréchal, Sylvain. 1798. *Pensées Libres sur les Prêtres*. Rome [Paris]. N.p.
Maréchal, Sylvain. [1800]. *Dictionnaire des Athées Anciens et Modernes*. Paris: Grabit.
Maréchal, Sylvain. 1801. *Projêt. Il ne Faut Pas que les Femmes Sachent Lire*. Paris: Massé.

Maréchal, Sylvain. 1801. *La Femme Abbé*. Paris: Ledoux. Translated by Sheila Delany as *The Woman Priest*. Edmonton: University of Alberta Press, 2016.

Maréchal, Sylvain. 1801. *Pour et Contre la Bible*. Jerusalem [Paris?], n.p.

Marx, Karl. 1964. "Introduction" to *Contribution to the Critique of Hegel's Philosophy of Right*. In *Marx & Engels on Religion*, 41–58. New York: Schocken.

Mathiez, Albert. 1965. *After Robespierre. The Thermidorean Reaction*. Translated by C.A. Phillips. New York: Universal Library.

Menozzi, Daniele. 1986. "La Bible des Révolutionnaires". In *Le Siècle des Lumières et la Bible*, edited by Yvon Belaval and Dominique Bourel, 677–95. Paris: Beauchesne.

Mortier, Roland. 1990 "Voltaire et la Bible" (123–34), "Diderot et les Théologiens: l'Article 'Bible' de l'Encyclopédie" (182–89), "La Remise en Question du Christianisme au XVIIIe Siècle" (336–63). In *Le Coeur et la Raison. Receuil d' Etudes*. Oxford: Voltaire Foundation.

Mortier, Roland. 1995. *Anacharsis Cloots, ou l'Utopie Foudroyée*. Paris: Stock.

Onfray, Michel. 2007. *In Defense of Atheism. The Case Against Christianity, Judaism, and Islam*. Toronto: Viking, Arcade.

Perrot, Michelle, ed. 2007. *Projêt Portant Défense d'Apprendre à Lire aux Femmes*. Paris: Mille et Une Nuits.

Plack, Noelle. 2012. "Liberty, Equality and Taxation: Wine in the French Revolution". *Social History of Alcohol and Drugs* 26, no. 1: 5–22.

Putnam, Robert and David Campbell. 2010. *American Grace. How Religion Divides and Unites Us*. New York: Simon & Schuster.

Rizvi, Ali A. 2016. *The Atheist Muslim. A Journey from Religion to Reason*. New York: St. Martin's Press.

Said, Edward W. 1978. *Orientalism*. New York: Random House.

Sauvy, Anne. 1986. "Lecture et Diffusion de la Bible en France". In *Le Siècle des Lumières et la Bible*, edited by Yvon Belaval and Dominque Bourel, 27–46. Paris: Beauchesne.

Schom, Alan. 1997. *Napoleon Bonaparte*. New York: HarperCollins.

Schwarzbach, Bertram E. 1971. *Voltaire's Old Testament Criticism*. Geneva: Droz.

Serna, Pierre. 1997. *Antonelle. Aristocrate Révolutionnaire, 1747–1817*. Paris: Ed. Du Félin.

Swissinfo.ch. 2018. "500 Years of the Reformation". January 22. https://swissinfo.us12.list-manage.com/track/click?.

Tackett, Timothy. 1986. *Religion, Revolution and Regional Culture in Eighteenth-Century France. The Ecclesiastical Oath of 1791*. Princeton, NJ: Princeton University Press.

Townsend, Mindy. 2012. "1 in 5 Americans Admit to Choosing No Religion". http://www.care2.com/causes/i-in-5-americans-admit-to-choosing... July 24.

Vovelle, Michel. 1991. *The Revolution Against the Church. From Reason to the Supreme Being*. Translated by A. José. Columbus: Ohio State University Press.

Wade, Ira O. 1967. *The Clandestine Organization and Diffusion of Philosophical Ideas in France from 1700 to 1750*. New York: Octagon.

Woloch, Isser. 1970. *Jacobin Legacy. The Democratic Movement under the Directory*. Princeton, NJ: Princeton University Press.

Worth, Robert F., "From Bible-belt Pastor to Atheist Leader", *New York Times Magazine* (August 26, 2012).

Yehoshua, Avraham. 2014. "Everything is Jewish". In *Secularism on the Edge. Rethinking Church-State Relations in the United States, France and Israel*, edited by Jacques Berlinerblau and Sarah Fainberg, 173–87. New York: Palgrave.

Zuckerman, Phil. 2007. "Atheism. Contemporary Numbers and Patterns". In *The Cambridge Companion to Atheism*, edited by Michael Martin, 47–65. New York: Cambridge University Press.

Index

Abelard, Peter   1–2
adultery   14, 27, 71, 110, 123, 125, 137, 149, 153, 154, 168, 188
Antonelle, Pierre-Antoine   3, 4n4
Apocrypha   xiii, 66n64, 69n72
atheism, atheists   3–5, 15–17, 74, 75n82, 156
Augustine, Saint   10, 53, 97, 123, 130, 155, 156, 169, 183

Babeuf, François-Noel   7, 9, 19n10
Brahma, Brahmans   29, 43, 91, 137, 190

Chateaubriand, Auguste   25n7
China, Chinese people   13, 47, 50n24, 138n2, 150
Chrysostom   52, 151, 166, 183
Cloots, Anacharsis   3, 12
Council of Trent   97, 133

Diderot, Denis   2n3, 3, 4, 34n30, 52, 60n51
   See also Encyclopédie

Egypt, Egyptians   28–29, 45, 48, 50n24, 53, 66, 103, 114, 116, 145, 146n20, 189
Encyclopédie   33n29, 52n27, 86
   See also Diderot
Epicurus   46n11, 155
Essene sect   10, 142

Franklin, Benjamin   190–191
Frederick II, king of Prussia   3, 85–86

Greek authors   10, 55, 115, 161, 170
   See also Epicurus, Homer, Plutarch, Pythagoras, Socrates
Greek culture   10, 27, 47n16, 48, 53n35, 54, 58, 84, 93, 98, 99n131, 100, 120, 129, 130, 142, 163, 165, 169, 180, 182, 183, 186

Hebrews, Hebrew spirit   44, 71, 79, 82, 100, 112, 119, 120, 128, 150
   See also Jews, Jewish nation, Jewish culture
Holbach, Baron   3, 4, 9, 12, 156n35
Homer   10, 26, 67n68, 72, 96, 100, 102, 105, 119, 126, 139n6

   See also Greek culture, Greek authors
Horace   75, 92, 144

incest   13, 14, 71, 94, 137, 144, 188

Jerome, Saint   xiii, 15, 44n6, 57, 69, 71, 73, 95, 100, 107, 127, 128, 151, 169, 170, 174, 183, 184n11
Jewish nation, culture, law   30n24, 64, 87, 104, 113, 188
   See also Jews, Hebrews
Jews   9, 10n7, 11, 12–13, 15, 48, 49n21, 51, 54, 56, 69, 70, 80, 100, 104, 107, 116, 127, 131, 150
   See also Hebrews, Jewish nation

Koran (Alkoran, Qur'an)   33, 45n8, 97n127, 174, 175, 182, 185, 187, 190

LaFontaine, Jean   26, 121
Laharpe, Jean-François   74, 75, 78n87, 79, 80, 82, 84, 125, 129, 133
Lalande, Jérôme   3
Louis XIV, king of France   8, 58, 60, 62, 85, 191n26
Louis XVI, king of France   5, 18
Lucretius   4, 92

Marx, Karl   17
Meslier, Jean   3, 34, 129, 133, 175
Molière   3, 76n85
Moses
   as author   43n3, 45, 46, 47, 52, 54, 185, 190
   as leader   9, 11, 44, 46, 48, 49, 51–52, 64, 65, 85, 128, 156, 179, 182, 189

Naigeon, Jacques-André   2n2, 3, 65n62
Napoleon   6, 7, 13, 17, 25nn7 and 8, 53n33
Newton, Isaac   26, 173

Orient, Oriental spirit, style   13, 25, 57, 67, 72, 73, 74, 75, 77, 88, 91, 94, 97, 105, 109, 111, 116, 119, 121n160, 125, 129, 173, 174
Origen   52, 129, 172, 184
Ossian   73, 102, 126
Ovid   161, 186

painting, literal or as metaphor   44, 68, 75, 80, 87, 102, 103, 110, 111, 132
Philo   97
Plutarch   188n19
Pythagoras   90, 120, 154, 157, 161, 182

Racine, Jean   27n16, 55, 61, 71, 77, 105, 107, 133
    See also theatre
reason   5, 23, 27, 30, 31, 33, 34, 35, 36, 51, 60, 78, 84, 122, 130, 138, 143, 145, 148, 150, 155, 160, 164, 180, 185, 187, 188, 189, 190, 191
Révolutions de Paris   4
Robespierre, Maximilian   5
Roman culture, poets, rulers   29, 53n34, 56, 80n93, 91, 116, 141, 165, 169, 172, 179
    See also Horace, Lucretius, Ovid, Virgil
Rousseau, Jean-Jacques   26, 55, 94n120, 142, 152, 180, 182

Sacy, Isaac-Louis leMaistre   xiv, 7–8, 14, 44, 61, 62, 64, 66, 68, 70, 73, 74, 76, 77, 79, 84, 86, 87n106, 88, 102, 106, 107, 113, 114, 118, 119, 141, 147n22, 152n31, 159–160, 171, 183n9

Sade, Marquis   3, 4n4, 6
Shakespeare   60n51, 71, 73n78
Socrates   142, 154, 155, 161, 163, 181, 182, 189
Spinoza, Benedict   3, 4, 52, 158, 160

theatre   27n16, 47n17, 54, 55, 58n48, 60, 67, 69, 122, 133
    See also Shakespeare, Racine, Molière
Thermidor   5–6

unction   9, 59, 77, 81, 82, 119, 154, 174

Virgil   74, 138
Voltaire   4, 10, 34n30, 37n35, 85, 93, 94, 156

William Tell   179
women, woman   xiv, 11, 12, 13–15, 29, 31, 38, 49n22, 64, 69, 71, 86, 88, 99, 101, 130, 149, 163, 164, 189

Zend-Avesta   33, 185, 187, 190

www.ingramcontent.com/pod-product-compliance
Lightning Source LLC
Chambersburg PA
CBHW071342080526
44587CB00017B/2929